Skillstrean the Elementary School Child

REVISED EDITION

New Strategies and Perspectives for Teaching Prosocial Skills

Ellen McGinnis
Arnold P. Goldstein

Research Press • 2612 North Mattis Avenue
Champaign, Illinois 61822
(800) 519-2707 • www.researchpress.com

CONTENTS

FIGURES AND TABLES

FIGURES

TABLES

PREFACE

First introduced in 1976 as one of the first social skills training approaches for adults and adolescents, Skillstreaming is now used in hundreds of schools, agencies, and institutions serving youth throughout the United States and beyond. In the last decade, the Skillstreaming approach has been broadly applied in settings serving elementary and preschool children. The purpose of this revised edition is to share with teachers and other instructors what has been learned about Skillstreaming with elementary-age children during the past decade.

How does this revised edition version differ from the original *Skillstreaming the Elementary School Child* (McGinnis & Goldstein, 1984)? The teaching methods and specific skills, validated by research conducted over many years and with many different populations, remain the same. However, with input from many practitioners, this revision presents the most up-to-date information about implementing the Skillstreaming approach—how it can, for example, best be applied in school settings with diverse groups of elementary-age children.

We begin by introducing Skillstreaming in an educational context (chapter 1), then examine Skillstreaming's history and development, discuss its present use in current educational initiatives, and describe our hopes for its future use (chapter 2). Chapter 3 presents strategies for developing safe school environments and examines how Skillstreaming fits into the goal of school safety. Facilitative arrangements for implementing Skillstreaming groups (chapter 4) and up-to-date teaching procedures (chapter 5) are next presented in a user-friendly manner. Instructional procedures are illustrated by a transcript of an actual Skillstreaming group (chapter 6). Chapter 7 presents the 60 skills for elementary school children, listing each skill's behavioral steps, teacher notes to make instruction more effective, and topics for modeling displays. Real-world use of the skill curriculum, especially in difficult and challenging circumstances, will require students to be able to use skill sequences and combinations. A discussion of skill sequences and combinations is presented in chapter 8, along with other means to improve skill learning and performance. The experience of thousands of Skillstreaming sessions with this age group has yielded a number of interventions to deal with problematic behaviors in the instructional group setting. Chapter 9 describes these motivation-enhancing and resistance-reducing procedures. Chapter 10 addresses the serious challenge of generalization of learned skills and offers a number of means for its enhancement.

Three appendixes respectively present an annotated bibliography of Skillstreaming research, copies of the Skillstreaming checklists and grouping chart, and a description of supplementary Skillstreaming materials at the elementary level, including Skill Cards, a Program Forms book, a Student Manual, and a videotape. A fourth appendix lists Skillstreaming materials for other instructional levels.

Skillstreaming began in isolated classrooms with small groups of students; however, in recent years it has found greater use in general education on a schoolwide and districtwide basis. To reflect this trend, throughout this edition the Skillstreaming trainer or instructor is referred to as the "teacher" or "group leader," and the participants are referred to as "students." If necessary, mental health or other professionals may easily adapt this language for use in their particular setting.

ACKNOWLEDGMENTS

A wide variety of individuals have served as Skillstreaming teachers—regular classroom and special education teachers, mental health professionals, youth service workers, correctional officers, social workers, and others. The experiences, achievements, and questions of many of teachers and trainers—shared in our workshops and training sessions—have been invaluable in our reconceptualization of the program. The students themselves, through their Skillstreaming group interactions and beyond, have provided much additional information. We are grateful to all of these individuals for what they have taught us.

CHAPTER 1
Introduction

Today's elementary schools deal with the same behavioral concerns students experienced decades ago—noncompliance, peer confrontations, failure to participate in academic or social activities, and so forth. Although these concerns continue, classrooms include increasingly violent and aggressive students, as well as students who in their profound social isolation lack a sense of belonging. It is not uncommon to hear teachers comment that, for example, "In all my years of teaching, I've never had a student like Jerry!" or "Students come to school with more problems than ever before." School administrators show their concern in statements like the following: "I spend the majority of my time on discipline. That's not the way it used to be!" Parents and community members are involved as well, most frequently when violent incidents occur, and it is no longer uncommon to read in the newspaper about school violence. Such concerns are illustrated in the following real-life scenarios:

> In one elementary classroom Ann tries to get attention from others by laughing at classmates when they answer a question. She tries to join in the conversations and activities of other girls by making comments that are interpreted by her peers as rude. Ann spends recess time by herself, occasionally trying to join an ongoing activity by making an unrelated, silly remark.

> In a third-grade classroom Joshua has difficulty sitting still and listening to the teacher's instructions. It seems he is always where he isn't supposed to be, wandering about the classroom. He doesn't return to his seat when asked to do so by his teacher. At times Joshua will push and poke other students, and he has been in physical fights in the school hallway and playground. Joshua seems to be bright and capable of academic achievement, but he rarely completes any classwork.

In still another elementary classroom Mario seems to get along okay with most of his classmates. He is very quiet in class, his academic work is average, and he does what the teacher asks him to do. His teacher has noticed that Mario is often alone in social situations and seems to withdraw if a peer challenges him. One day at recess Mario takes a knife from his backpack and threatens a student who apparently has provoked him.

WHAT IS SKILLSTREAMING?

Skillstreaming is a psychoeducational intervention—its roots in both psychology and education. Although used initially by therapists in the mental health field, its processes focus on four direct instruction principles of learning. These learning procedures—modeling, role-playing, feedback, and transfer—have been used to teach a variety of behaviors, from academic competencies to sports, daily living skills, and vocational skills. They are applied in Skillstreaming to teach students desirable prosocial behaviors.

A Skill-Deficit Model

The Skillstreaming model makes the assumption that the learner is weak in or lacks a behavioral skill or skills within his or her skill repertoire. The goal, then, becomes teaching desirable skills. This assumption is made for several very important reasons. First, the belief that most students do not know how to act productively in given situations lessens the frustration experienced by many teachers when a youngster seems continually to react in the same inappropriate way despite efforts to consequate that behavior. This allows teachers to focus on proactive instruction instead of reacting to the youngster's misbehavior as if it were done purposefully to create problems. In addition, the assumption of skill deficit sets the stage for instruction in prosocial skills that the student may actually use and that the teacher can therefore prompt. The assumption furthermore suggests to the student that the teacher and others will be patient and encouraging during the learning of these sometimes very difficult skills.

In workshops we often illustrate or reinforce the skill-deficit model by asking participants to think of a time they agreed to do something asked by a friend, relative, or acquaintance, but which they really did not want to do. Most participants quickly identify situations in which, as adults, they have felt pressured into doing something they didn't want to do, whether it was allowing a neighbor to borrow the lawnmower to taking on extra job responsibilities. In a practice environment, group members are asked to respond to such requests by Saying No (Skill 55). The majority of participants experience difficulty with this skill, even in the practice setting! Yet many times the expectation is that students, even at the elementary level, will be able to resist peer pressure by quickly and emphatically expressing their feelings appropriately.

Planned, Systematic Instruction

Most educators recognize that the days of defining public education's goal as only teaching basic academic competencies are over. During the last decade many educators have realized that students need to be taught desirable behaviors in the same planned and systematic way academic skills are taught. The reasons students do not learn acceptable social skills are many—including lack of knowledge, insufficient practice, insufficient reinforcement, and emotional responses that inhibit skill use (Cox & Gunn, 1980). Incidental learning (discussing alternatives or telling students what to do) is insufficient for students to learn alternative behaviors, just as it is insufficient to tell students how to divide and expect that they will be able to complete division problems. Whatever the reason for skill lack or weakness, schools must establish and implement procedures to teach these skills, just as they would in the case of academic deficits.

A Way to Give Encouragement

Historically, educational interventions dealing with student behavior problems have concentrated on strategies to diminish or extinguish the behavior of concern (e.g., time-out, loss of privileges). Although reinforcement strategies are used to increase positive behaviors, it is necessary to wait until a behavior is displayed before it can be rewarded. Thus, many students with infrequent appropriate behaviors rarely receive positive reinforcement; in most cases, they receive an abundance of negative feedback. Although negative procedures may be a useful part of a comprehensive management plan, emphasis on their use may further discourage children with behavior problems.

Teaching prosocial skills provides the elementary-age child with opportunities to be successful in both hypothetical and real-life situations and lends a sense of balance to behavior management programs. Although inappropriate behaviors will continue to need our intervention, through Skillstreaming, students have the opportunity to build alternative, socially acceptable behaviors. Teachers will also find that prompting students to use a previously learned social skill when problematic situations arise in the classroom or in other school settings will often stop the student's inappropriate actions in midstream and channel his or her energies in a more prosocial direction. Like reminding a student to use a reading strategy to master unknown vocabulary, when given in a helpful and encouraging manner, such prompting fosters a positive classroom and school climate.

A Way to Enhance Self-Esteem

A description of a problematic elementary-age child often includes the phrase "poor self-esteem." Counselors, teachers, and others often struggle to design interventions that improve the child's positive feelings about himself or herself. One way of addressing this issue is to teach the student to be more competent. We have traditionally focused on academic competence, recognizing that such competence contributes to the child's positive feelings about self in relation to achievement. Likewise, increasing competence in a variety of socially related skills will improve a child's self-concept.

While behavior management programs are useful, necessary, and very often effective in reducing problem behaviors, we need to be aware that emphasis on such programs alone may reinforce in students the idea that adults are the dispensers of rewards and punishments. The child may learn to believe that whatever he or she might do or however he or she might act, the positive or negative results of these actions will be determined by someone else in power—a teacher, parent, or other adult. Such a belief, referred to as an *external locus of control,* can foster feelings of helplessness. When students learn, for example, to handle conflict in ways that yield approval from others, they also learn a sense of responsibility and control. They more easily make the connection between their actions (e.g., use of a skill) and positive consequences. When students learn that they have the skills and ability to effect change, their self-esteem is likely to improve.

Remediation and Prevention

The Skillstreaming approach provides remediation for students who are significantly deficient in prosocial skills, whether or not they are receiving special education services. The child with an identified attention deficit, for example, may have a particular need to learn the skills of Following Instructions (Skill 5), Completing Assignments (Skill 6), and Ignoring Distractions (Skill 10). The student with a learning disability may need to learn the skill of Asking for Help (Skill 2), as well as organizational skills such as Bringing Materials to Class (Skill 4). Children with more severe disabilities, those with autism or mental disabilities, can be taught a variety of social skills to enhance their independence and to make their lives more satisfying. Those with emotional or behavioral disorders—whether characterized by withdrawal, aggression, or immaturity—continue to benefit from learning prosocial skills. Although aggression and violence are very visible and perhaps cause more stress to teachers, school administrators, parents, and others, teaching prosocial skills to the withdrawn child or the student who reacts immaturely or inadequately is also important.

Skillstreaming is also intended for the regular education population—students whose behavior is not significantly problematic yet who will increase their personal satisfaction and happiness by learning or improving upon prosocial skills. How many young people do we know who, when they reach adolescence, have significant problems dealing with stress or with interpersonal relationships when none were noticed in elementary school? Many students may need help with skills to form satisfying interpersonal relationships, participate in problem solving, or deal productively with day-to-day stress. Undertaking instruction with students who do not yet experience significant problems offers the hope of preventing future difficulties.

A Strategy to Help Prevent Violence

The literature related to safe school environments, discussed in chapter 3, clearly suggests that schools need to address the increase in school violence by teaching students prosocial ways of resolving conflict, proactive problem solving, and the social skills necessary to enhance self-esteem and engender a sense of belonging. Aggressive children, for example, learn quickly and at an early age that they can get what they want by hitting, pushing, biting, and so forth. Because aggression is a remarkably stable behavior and is unlikely to change without intervention, alternatives to aggression need to be taught early. Skillstreaming is one method of doing just that.

WHAT SKILLSTREAMING IS NOT

Skillstreaming is not an affective education strategy that focuses primarily on discussion of feelings and the individual's strengths as a way to foster positive self-concept. Instead, although discussion is a part, Skillstreaming engages students in active learning through role-playing and practice. This technique will not address all children's needs in every situation at all times. Instead, it is a well-validated instructional procedure that should be included with other techniques, such as behavior management, conflict resolution, and cooperative learning.

Neither is Skillstreaming a procedure for teaching compliance skills, the focus of some skills training programs. Although it will teach students the skills needed to follow school rules better, the program is mainly intended to teach students the skills needed to solve problems that occur in their daily lives, to be assertive in handling situations that cause them stress or unhappiness, and to increase the chance that they will have satisfying relationships with others.

CHAPTER 2
Skillstreaming: Past, Present, Future

This chapter reviews the development of Skillstreaming in an educational context, looks at its present-day use in relationship to what is happening in our schools, and offers some directions for its future revision and growth.

HISTORY AND DEVELOPMENT

The roots of psychological skills training, which began in the early 1970s, lie within both education and psychology. The psychoeducational approach viewed the student or client in educational terms, rather than as an individual in need of therapy, and assumed that individuals were deficient, or at best weak, in the skills necessary for effective and satisfying daily living. The task of the skills trainer, therapist, or teacher was thus the active and deliberate teaching of desirable behaviors. This view was in contrast to the assumptions of prior therapeutic approaches (psychodynamic, nondirective, or behavior modification), which held that the client possessed effective, satisfying, or healthy behaviors but that these behaviors were simply unexpressed.

Psychology's most direct contribution to psychological skills training came from social learning theory—in particular, the work of Albert Bandura. Bandura (1973) described the processes of modeling, behavioral rehearsal, and social reinforcement, and these processes directed the development of the Skillstreaming approach. The Skillstreaming approach differed from the approaches of other behavior theorists, who emphasized operant procedures such as prompting and shaping of behaviors. Although a strictly behavioral approach was found to increase the frequency of a behavior, that behavior must already have been within the child's repertoire of behaviors. If the child did not have a grasp of the needed skill, operant procedures were insufficient to add that skill to the child's repertoire.

The deinstitutionalization movement of the 1970s, which resulted in the discharge of approximately 400,000 persons from mental health and other institutions into local communities, further set the stage for acceptance of an alternative way of providing treatment. The realization was that the more traditional therapeutic interventions, which focused on looking inward to find solutions to one's nonproductive actions (i.e., insight-oriented approaches), were ineffective for many individuals from lower socioeconomic environments, who constituted the majority of individuals discharged from institutions.

In addition to the growing importance of learning methods in applied clinical work and as a preventive focus in community mental health, parallel developments in education clearly encouraged skills training. Specifically, a number of other approaches grew from the personal development context of certain educational movements—for example, progressive education (Dewey, 1938) and character education (Chapman, 1977). The goal of these approaches was to support the teaching of concepts and behaviors relevant to values, morality, and emotional functioning. We refer in particular to Values Clarification (Simon, Howe, & Kirschenbaum, 1972), Moral Education (Kohlberg, 1973), and affective education (Miller, 1976). These three approaches, as well as other personal growth programs, combined to provide a supportive climate and context for skills training. These programs share a concern for personal development, competence, and social effectiveness. Clearly, education had been broadened well beyond basic academic content to include areas traditionally the concern of mental health practitioners.

To summarize, relevant supportive research, the incompleteness of operant approaches, large groups of skill-deficient individuals, and the paucity of useful interventions for a large segment of American society came together in the context of education and psychology to create an alternative intervention. This psychological skills training approach, first termed *Structured Learning* and later renamed *Skillstreaming,* began in the early 1970s. How persons learn most effectively was a major consideration of Skillstreaming, and with this goal in mind, the approach avoided the "one-true-light assumption" that had guided so much intervention work up to that time. Instead, Skillstreaming sought to respond prescriptively to the qualities and needs of the persons whose skill levels we wished to change.

Since its initial development as an intervention prescriptively targeted to low-income, socially skill deficient adults, Skillstreaming has increasingly been used with other populations. These populations have included young children (elementary age and preschool), elderly adults, child-abusing parents, industrial managers, police officers, and others. Over the period of more than 20 years of program use, a considerable amount of evaluation research has been conducted and reported. The results of these several dozen studies support the efficacy of Skillstreaming, as well as suggest guidelines for altering and improving its procedures and materials. A complete, annotated bibliography of Skillstreaming research is presented as Appendix A in this book.

CURRENT INITIATIVES

Where does Skillstreaming fit in the scheme of methods and strategies as our schools are encouraged to move toward "excellence" in the 21st century? Today several initiatives seek to improve our schools by enhancing student learning. Two related initiatives are the current school reform movement (also called school restructuring), which began in the 1980s, and the more recent initiative toward safe schools. These initiatives, drawn from research and "best practice," stress the importance of developing a positive school climate in order to foster student achievement. Some of the principles advocated by these movements include schoolwide management plans; cooperative learning and conflict management to address students' real-life concerns; active, hands-on participation in learning; and the involvement of "stakeholders" in decision making.

As a result of the school reform and safe schools initiatives, the content and delivery of curriculum are receiving much-needed attention. Many schools today continue to teach the same content in the same manner employed decades ago. Though such approaches are not necessarily "wrong," many of today's students need to see greater relevance to their own lives in what they are asked to learn. Glasser (1995), for example, advocates that schools abandon the teaching of "facts," which may not be relevant to the students' future, and instead teach students "what is useful," including verbal and written expression, listening to others, reading, and mathematical problem solving. In their text on school reform, Golarz and Golarz (1995) support a similar philosophy and urge schools to address the question "How can schools provide children with the tools to live personally satisfying and enriching lives?" (p. 11). Wilson and Daviss (1994) further suggest that schools include curricular approaches that teach children "to work together productively and manage controversy and disagreements in positive ways" (p. 186).

According to both the school reform and safe schools initiatives, decisions regarding what curriculum to cover will be largely influenced by a school's culture, including the beliefs of staff, parents, and the community. It is necessary to address curricular issues because of the strong relationship between school failure (specifically, lack of motivation, failure to complete homework, poor academic achievement, and lack of desire to continue some type of education after high school) and antisocial behavior (Benson & Roehlkepartain, 1992). With the participation of a group of school personnel, strategies must be developed to teach social skills, increase student motivation, move toward problem solving rather than rote learning, enhance the relevancy of the curriculum, and make modifications related to student interests and learning styles.

Schools need to create opportunities for students to participate in rule setting and to accept responsibility; students must be taught the skills necessary for prosocial participation in these activities. In addition, positive, nonaggressive behaviors and problem solving must be modeled by school staff and reinforced when demonstrated by students.

Students also must view their school as an inviting and safe place where they feel they belong. Feelings of isolation or alienation from peers need to be addressed not only by creating a safe and welcoming school environment, but also by teaching students the skills needed to form positive relationships with others. Skillstreaming is a process that can help create such safe and relevant schools. When safe and relevant schools exist, all learning, including skill learning, is easier to accomplish.

Another current initiative in schools today provides for increasing inclusion of youngsters with special needs in regular education classrooms. The Education for All Handicapped Children Act of 1975 (Public Law 94–142; now the Individuals with Disabilities Education Act) clearly calls for an increase in educating students with disabilities within the mainstream school environment. It has been accepted in recent years that if academic or social benefit can be attained in the regular classroom setting, then a student with disabilities should receive his or her instruction in this mainstream setting. Yet many experts in the field of special education believe social benefits are unlikely to occur unless planned and systematic instruction in social skills also takes place. Students without disabilities may also need instruction in accepting students with differences. In brief, the trend toward inclusion makes it even more important to teach all students (both with and without disabilities) the social skills they need.

SKILLSTREAMING: FUTURE GOALS

We have discussed the history and development of Skillstreaming and explored ways it can be applied within current school-based initiatives. Since its inception, Skillstreaming has been open to change as practitioners' and research findings warrant it. As an intervention in transition, we turn now to examine some future directions for program revision and growth.

Schoolwide and Districtwide Intervention

Although elementary and preschool students are now taught prosocial skills primarily in individual classrooms, it is our hope based on beginning efforts to do so that Skillstreaming will find its place in the required school curriculum, both at the building and district levels. As one group participant in a recent training workshop remarked, "Wouldn't it be exciting to see what would happen if this process were begun in the early grades and carried throughout a student's school career?" Although it is widely recognized that students must be taught academic skills and that proficiency in these skills requires continued support and instruction, it is sometimes easy to forget that for many students the same is true with prosocial skill behaviors. It *is* exciting to predict what the outcome for our schools would be if these skills were taught and reinforced throughout the school year in every school, then continually reviewed, re-fined, retaught as needed, and reinforced in subsequent years.

We know that the potential for student participation, including generalization and maintenance of learned skills, is greatly enhanced the more the environment is involved in the program. Including entire schools and districts in the skills training process has the potential to increase student motivation and skill awareness. Large-scale program involvement means that many more teachers and other school staff are involved as trainers, thus providing greater opportunity for students to be rewarded for correct skill use and to receive prompting or coaching following incorrect use. In addition, when entire schools or districts are involved, especially at the lower grade levels, added potential exists for Skillstreaming to operate at a preventive level, before youngsters gets into difficulty in school, at home, or with the law.

An Alternative to Exclusion

Out-of-school suspension is the intervention most frequently used in response to school violence (National School Boards Association, 1994). Although out-of-school suspension may quickly reestablish a feeling of safety for the students who remain in school, such an intervention should be only a first step. Walker (1995) refers to suspension and expulsion as a "one-dimensional" approach to student violence and states, "This can protect other students; however it has proven ineffective in preventing children from developing criminal careers" (p. 2). In other words, removing students from school does not teach these students alternative behaviors.

School districts have been mandated to develop "zero tolerance" policies to deal with severe violence, such as threats with weapons. Typically, these policies include the recommendation for expulsion. Although it may be necessary to deal with extreme actions through suspension and/or expulsion, these procedures deal only with the immediate situation of violence. Such district policies are missing a critical element by not addressing a long-term solution to this problem. Sautter (1995) speaks to this issue: "While schools secure their buildings and grounds, it is essential to understand that violent youths who are expelled must be reached in other ways or they will simply wreak havoc somewhere else" (p. K–5). For example, if a student brings a weapon to school because of a real or imagined perception of threat and is subsequently suspended or expelled, there is little opportunity to deal with that student's fear.

It is important that schools not be helpless victims to behavior problems in the school setting, but instead establish proactive interventions to teach alternatives. Johns, Carr, and Hoots (1995), for example, recommend that school discipline be evaluated by asking the following questions:

1. Does the disciplinary process allow students to accept responsibility for their actions?

2. Does the disciplinary process continually place importance on the value of academic participation and achievement?

3. Does the disciplinary action build positive self-image?

4. Does the disciplinary action teach students alternative methods of dealing with problems? (p. 2–2)

In other words, discipline programs in schools today and in the future need to be instructional in nature. Exclusionary practices, those that remove the student from the learning environment, fail to adhere to the four criteria listed above. They fail to foster acceptance of responsibility for action (e.g., the student may stay home and watch television). They do not emphasize the value of academic achievement: The student is excluded from the opportunity to learn. Instead of building positive self-esteem, exclusion tells the student he or she is not wanted at school. And, certainly, exclusion does not teach alternative, prosocial ways of dealing with the behavior problem that resulted in exclusion.

Instructional alternatives may include assigning the student to a social skills class (dealing with specific alternatives to the conflict that resulted in suspension and where more desirable behaviors may be learned), requiring the student to complete community service (where he or she will be more likely to be exposed to appropriate models and receive the attention needed to foster a more positive self-image), and having the student complete an in-school intervention focusing on conflict resolution. We hope in the future such interventions will be implemented on a schoolwide basis, finding a place in ongoing curriculum efforts in our elementary schools.

A More Positive School Climate

It is important to note that creating a welcoming and positive school climate has been frequently cited as a critical element in establishing a safe school environment and is a valued goal in school reform. Creating a better balance of positive to negative consequences is necessary to foster a positive school climate. Some students, in particular those who have well-established patterns of undesirable behavior, are most likely to receive an overabundance of negative consequences. For these students, positive feelings about school and learning itself are unlikely. Such students need more instruction, not less. Skillstreaming can provide this much-needed instruction and, if implemented widely, can help to shift the emphasis from punishment for negative behavior toward natural reward for positive behavior.

Training for Parents and Others

Aggression is a difficult behavior to change. It is primarily a learned behavior, and many children have learned it well. From their early years, they live with family and peers who repeatedly model, reward, and even overtly encourage hurtful actions toward others. In a real sense, aggression becomes for many children a behavior that "works"—both for them and for the significant people in their lives.

In school, agency, and other institutional settings, many chronically aggressive youths participate in interventions like Skillstreaming, designed to teach prosocial alternatives. They learn to maintain self-control or walk away from confrontations, rather than incite, attack, or fight. They then use one of these prosocial alternatives in the presence of a family member or neighborhood peer and, rather than reward the constructive attempt, the other party responds critically. "No son of mine is going to be a punk. You hit him before he hits you!" says the parent. "Are you chicken?" says the peer.

Program evaluations have suggested that children's prosocial responses are more likely to be rewarded, supported, and even reciprocated if significant others also participate in Skillstreaming training programs. Some of these joint efforts have involved teaching empathy skills to adolescents and their parents (Guzzetta, 1974); teaching delinquent youths and their families alternatives to aggression (Goldstein, Glick, Irwin, Pask-McCartney, & Rubama, 1989);

and training adolescents and their peer groups in a variety of social skills (Gibbs, Potter, & Goldstein, 1995; Goldstein, Glick, Carthan, & Blancero, 1994). The success of these programs strongly suggests the effectiveness of instruction for both skill-deficit youths and the significant people in their lives.

As Dryfoos (1994) accurately notes in her book *Full-Service Schools,* the American school has increasingly become a venue in which a wide variety of services for children and adolescents are provided. For students and their families, school is becoming a community resource, offering health-related and social service programming. Such expansion of the purposes of schools is likely to continue. We strongly urge that family Skillstreaming become a regular offering in this context.

Mass Media

There are an average of 6 violent acts per hour on prime-time evening television, and 25 such acts per hour on Saturday morning cartoons. By age 16, the typical child has viewed 200,000 acts of violence, approximately 30,000 of them murders or attempted murders (National Coalition on Television Violence, 1990). Some young viewers of television violence, happily the minority, will actually do what they have seen portrayed. Males do so more than females; younger children more than older. Other youngsters experience increased fearfulness, mistrust, and self-protectiveness. These children come to see the world as more threatening and less safe. A third consequence, and perhaps a more serious one, is that children adapt or adjust to the depicted violence—in other words, they get used to it. Higher and higher levels of violence become tolerable. Still another effect is the continued desire to expose oneself to violent behavior. The more violence is observed via television, the more efforts there are to view yet other violence.

This dismal picture does, however, have a flip side. Television can have positive effects as well. A small amount of research has demonstrated the prosocial, not antisocial, effects television may have. Helpfulness, charity, intervention in crisis situations, empathy, and other positive and antiviolent consequences have been demonstrated as a result of viewing prosocial acts on television. The potential exists to build upon the small number of prosocial programming effects. It is our aspiration that both modeling of prosocial acts (central to Skillstreaming) and Skillstreaming's interpersonal skills curriculum will find a place in future mass media programming.

✧◆✧

Finally, it is our hope that, along with effective consequences provided as soon as possible after aggression, students will receive instruction in prosocial ways to deal with conflict. Such instruction clearly has the potential to prevent further aggressive acts. At the elementary level, implementing such prevention strategies holds special promise to alter the patterns of future aggression.

CHAPTER 3
Skillstreaming and Safe Schools

In the past, schools were safe havens for children and youth, and few people anticipated that violence and weapons would be found in school hallways, playgrounds, and classrooms. Now, however, schools are challenged by the increased violence in our communities. The issue of school safety is not reserved for middle schools and high schools: A U.S. Department of Justice report (1993) noted that the greatest increase in school-related crime occurred at the elementary school level. The majority of elementary school students do not experience violence, either by being a target of a violent act or by observing real-life violence in the school setting. Nonetheless, schools must take steps to counteract the growing trend toward violence and to make school buildings a safe place for teaching and learning.

The issue of school violence is not simple; therefore, there can be no simple solution. However, we can learn much from what experts believe contributes to aggression and violence. Only when we understand these issues will we be able to implement effective and lasting interventions. Just as the growth of violence is a process, so too is the re-creation of safe, productive, and encouraging school environments.

FACTORS ASSOCIATED WITH VIOLENCE

Some of the seeds of increased violence in our communities include frequent exposure to violence through the media, violent role models, health factors such as prenatal substance abuse, poverty, inadequate or abusive parenting, lack of social skills, discrimination, and lack of educational and job opportunities (National Association for the

Education of Young Children, 1993). Aggression is primarily a learned behavior. A predisposition toward violent behavior, however, may exist as a result of hereditary, hormonal, or biological factors (e.g., head injury).

John Reid, clinical psychologist and director of the Oregon Social Learning Center in Eugene, has analyzed numerous studies suggesting that the two strongest predictors of violence and delinquency are (a) ineffective, harsh, abusive, emotional discipline and (b) lack of parental supervision (Bourland, 1995). Patterson, Reid, Jones, and Conger (1975) discuss these actions by describing a cycle of aggression that begins with coercive parenting. In this cycle, the parent frequently reacts to the child in a hostile, threatening, or irritated manner. The parent is inconsistent in his or her discipline, at times providing very tight supervision and at other times providing almost no supervision at all. Discipline is characterized by yelling and corporal punishment. At times the child will comply with the parent's coercion, providing a natural reward for the parent's disciplinary action. At other times, the child will act coercively in return—yelling, threatening, hitting, and so on.

As children so parented grow older, they deal with peer confrontations in a similar manner. If they want a toy, they take it. If they don't like something another child has said, they hit or kick. Other children (or these children's parents) react by not including aggressive youngsters, thus limiting the positive models from whom these children can learn alternative behaviors and leading to social isolation. As these problematic children reach school age, they fulfill their need to have friends by seeking out peers who react similarly. Thus, the main characteristics of children who are the targets of coercive parenting are inadequate social skills and high levels of aggression both in and out of school.

VIOLENCE IN SCHOOLS

A cycle similar to the one described by Patterson et al. (1975) in the home environment can often be seen in school. The child who refuses to follow directions in school may be yelled at by the teacher. The one who verbally threatens to hit a peer may be threatened with punishment by the teacher. Such actions by adults may intensify the student's anger and problematic behavior (Gemelli, 1996).

A power struggle may result in the student's suspension from school, furthering the social isolation.

Benson and Roehlkepartain (1992) state that violence is now an accepted part of our culture and emphasize, "As [children] watch adults resolve conflicts, hear politicians posture, and interact with peers, young people too often see violence as the norm" (p. 3). In addition, as stated by Natale (1994):

> Kids who commit violent acts often do so because they believe their choices are limited. . . . Psychologists say children with that view have learned aggression is a viable tool for resolving conflict—in fact, they've learned it's one of their only tools. (p. 38)

It may be surprising to some that one significant reason for violence is that children may have learned that this is their only way to respond. However, aggression is a remarkably stable behavior. Several longitudinal studies make it quite clear that often the chronically aggressive child will continue to be aggressive in adolescence and adulthood. Aggressive, antisocial behaviors, once learned and working, produce more of the same in the absence of prosocial alternative behaviors.

The availability of guns and other weapons has increased the seriousness of violent acts. As reported by the National School Safety Center, 35 deaths and 92 injuries resulted from the use of guns in the schools in 1994 (Sautter, 1995). One in four students and one in ten teachers are victims of violence on or near schools (Modro, 1995), and 50 percent of all violent crimes against teenagers occur on or near school property (Linquanti & Berliner, 1994). Weapons in schools, as well as violent acts in general, are more visible in larger urban areas, where the number of incidents draws attention from the media ("Violence in the Schools," 1994). Rural areas do not escape such violence. Benson and Roehlkepartain (1992) conducted a survey of 47,000 Midwestern students in sixth through twelfth grades who attended school in communities with a population less than 50,000. This self-report survey revealed that 28 percent of the students said they had been involved in two or more violent acts during the year in question. These authors concluded, "For many youths, aggressiveness is a part of an overall pattern of risky behavior" (e.g., alcohol use, truancy), noting "these findings suggest that violence is becoming increasingly normative within youth culture" (p. 2).

Educators may rationalize that violence in our schools is due to events beyond the school's control. Although it may be true that students today come to school with many more significant concerns than in the past, certain factors related to the school itself have been found to contribute to violence. Some of these relate to the physical environment, such as poor building design with many difficult-to-supervise areas. Other aspects are more subtle and include the school's culture, disciplinary policy and methods, and curriculum.

School Culture

The culture of a school is the prevailing set of values and beliefs held by school staff, parents, and students. These values and beliefs define acceptable behavior and determine the manner in which the school should function. A 1993 report from the American Psychological Association pointed out two aspects of school culture conducive to aggression: large classes in small spaces and an emphasis on conformity and behavioral routines, which may foster resentment and anger (Sautter, 1995).

How does the culture of our schools relate to the increase of violence? As stated by Modro (1995):

> The most important factor that needs to be addressed
> even before policies that will support school safety is the
> atmosphere, or "feeling tone," in which education takes
> place. Does our educational system reflect a genuine belief
> in the essential dignity of each child? Do educators believe
> in the inherent value of the people they serve? The fear
> is that many mirror for our children what some of them
> already see reflected in society. (p. 11)

Thus, to ensure safety schools must address the reasons for increased violence in addition to systematically implementing structural and policy changes. Few would argue that students need to be assertive in their refusal to take drugs or participate in criminal activities, yet in most schools students are expected to accept the school's rules and regulations passively, without question. Some aspects of school culture—including an authoritarian school governance, lack of effective school leadership, and poor interpersonal communication—have been associated with increased school violence ("Violence in the Schools," 1994).

Students need to feel a part of the governance of their school, to believe that they will be listened to and that they can influence policy. They need to believe that their actions can contribute to the safety of their school. Ascher (1994) calls for the development of programs to increase mutual respect among students and school staff. This author further states:

> Although coercive methods may stop violence in the short run, too often they create negative emotions that start their own cycle of undesirable behaviors. An alternate approach, which develops self-respect and self-discipline in students and positive working relationships, is obviously better for both students and adults, and for the climate of the school. (p. 4)

Even with the best of intentions, the typical authoritarian school structure may actually foster student feelings of powerlessness. Lantieri (1995), in describing the Resolving Conflict Creatively Program, states that teachers must learn to deal with conflict in new ways and that "even more difficult, they must adopt a new style of classroom management, one that fundamentally involves a sharing of power with students so that they can learn how to deal with their own disputes" (p. 4).

Prevention

Coben and colleagues (Coben, Weiss, Mulvey, & Dearwater, 1994) have grouped violence prevention programs according to the following strategies, including educational (prevention), environmental/technological (e.g., security guards, metal detectors), regulatory (e.g., zero-tolerance policies), family/community interventions, and combined approaches (strategies from each of the above).

Educational strategies

Educational approaches cited in the literature include conflict management, social skills instruction, mentoring programs, behavioral programs, intensive academic instruction, drug prevention, student advocacy programs, peer helper programs, student assistance (counseling) programs, anti-hate/cultural sensitivity curricula, and community service.

Interventions involving teaching alternative behaviors and conflict resolution strategies need to occur at a very early age and should include many individuals in the child's environment (teachers, peers, and other school staff, such as custodians and paraprofessionals). Furthermore, teachers and other school personnel need professional staff development in the areas of conflict resolution, how to respond to violence, and team building.

Environmental/technological strategies

Supportive environmental/technological strategies include limiting access to and hidden areas of the school building, increasing lighting, reducing class size and overcrowding, increasing the attractiveness of the school, and installing security devices (e.g., metal detectors) or hiring security staff. A security assessment of the school building to determine which measures are most desirable for each building is recommended.

Regulatory strategies

Supportive techniques include establishing policies to prevent weapons in the schools and to deal with the aftermath of violence. Such policies may include zero-tolerance for weapons, locker searches, elimination of lockers, restrictions on book bags, and the development of crisis response procedures.

Family/community interventions

Family/community interventions suggest cooperation between the home, school, and community and include teaching parenting skills, prenatal care, home management, employment support and vocational training, substance abuse counseling, provision of student supervision and recreation programs, and restriction of entertainment violence and access to weapons.

✧◆✧

Each school and school district must decide which strategies will be most effective for their individual setting. For example, the installation of metal detectors, though understandably necessary in some school environments, may inadvertently create more fear, leading others to bring weapons to school to protect themselves.

For other students, such environmental interventions may create a false sense of security and convey the impression that such devices are all that is needed.

IMPLICATIONS FOR PRACTICE

The literature on causes of violence in our society and schools is encouraging in that it shows aggression and violence to be primarily learned behaviors. What better place to provide alternatives and help students learn that nonviolent choices exist than in our schools? Although it may be discouraging to realize that poor parenting skills and supervision appear to play such an important role in the growth of violence, the school can undertake interventions to address these concerns—for example, by increasing parent involvement and working with other agencies to increase positive parenting skills. Furthermore, school personnel can address the areas that can be changed within the school itself, such as working to improve the school culture and move toward a less authoritarian management style.

Schoolwide intervention programs to prevent school violence (e.g., conflict management, social skills training, problem solving) have the potential to make a difference. One goal of such approaches is "to give everyone involved in the school the same skills, language and terminology for handling stress and conflict—to create an environment that is consistently nonviolent and nurturing" (Ascher, 1994, p. 4).

The educational approach to prevention, in which emphasis is placed on teaching students the skills needed to deal with conflict and to get their needs met in prosocial ways, offers the best hope for the future. Such educational strategies have been cited as the most critical and cost-effective element in the fight against violence (Bourland, 1995). Sometimes schools concern themselves with one intervention, such as expulsion, in an effort to provide a "quick fix" to the issue of violence. Unfortunately, the literature is quite clear that such policy efforts alone will neither create nor maintain a safe school environment. Instead, experts advocate a multifaceted or combined program of school safety (Coben et al., 1994), including the development of school policies addressing weapons and crisis response, environmental factors such as school facilities and family and community resources, and prevention through education. For example, curricular interventions, such as peer conflict resolution strategies, are likely to reduce discipline problems, improve the school climate, and increase students' self-esteem and ability to assume responsibility (Walker, 1995).

STAFF ROLES

The role of the building administrator is to lead the school in developing a climate and specific strategies to support a safe school environment. Although it may be easier and more efficient for the principal to simply present his or her policies, the participation of teachers, other school staff, students, parents, and other community members is necessary to achieve a school culture that will support these strategies. It is appropriate in assuming leadership for the principal to guide others in aspects of school safety, as well as in procedures to develop programs and policies to enhance school safety. However, all stakeholders need to feel a part of the governance of the school, to believe that they will be listened to, and that they can, in fact, influence policy.

Administrator Qualities in Low-Aggression Schools

A review of relevant educational literature and our own personal experience in schools consistently reveal several characteristics of school administrators associated with low levels of student aggression.

Visibility and availability to students and teachers

Most elementary schools are small enough or are arranged in such a manner that administrators are able to greet students at the beginning of the day, recognize many students by name, and visit most classrooms on a daily or weekly basis to help create a feeling among students that the school is their school.

Effective intelligence network

A school climate in which school administrators know what is happening or is likely to happen is crucial to maintaining school safety, whether the threat is serious (e.g., weapons or gang fights) or less serious (e.g., bullying). Because they feel the school belongs to them, students, staff, administrators, and even other community members are more open about communicating events that affect school safety.

Fair and consistent rule enforcement

Safe environments are predictable environments. A well-thought-out and fairly and consistently enforced set of school rules or guidelines to live by strongly helps establish such predictability. Consistent enforcement means that all staff are aware of and enforce rules in agreed-upon ways. But the demands of fairness and consistency may contradict each other at times. Consistency requires rule enforcement on all applicable occasions; fairness may require taking special circumstances into account and not enforcing a given rule in some instances. Both aspects are important, but if and when a choice must be made, we believe that in the safe school fairness will prevail.

Fair and consistent response to grievances

When students or staff feel rules have been applied unfairly or protest other decisions, administrators respond by openly considering the complaint. Although a school cannot be a democracy in which all have an equal vote on each management decision, administrators listen respectfully to opinions, consider them on their merits, and act upon them or not in the best interest of the parties involved and the school as a whole.

Support of teachers

In addition to carrying out staff-initiated consequences for student aggression in a fair and consistent manner, administrators in low-aggression schools support staff in a number of other ways. They back up teachers in confrontations with parents, community members—even the school board. Disagreements are resolved fairly and in private. And the best of administrators consistently empower teachers by eliciting their decision-making input, ranging from how the teacher wants an individual behavioral incident to be handled to curricular decisions affecting the entire school.

Openness to intervention

Some administrators fail to take action on the growing concern of school violence, as if they believe violence will not happen in their school. If an act of violence occurs, they view it as an isolated incident, thus denying the problem. Somehow, they conclude, weapons or violence in their schools reflects badly upon them, and they fail to take appropriate precautions. Competent administrators, in contrast, recognize problems such as growing aggression early in their development and are open to taking decisive steps to intervene.

Culturally appropriate and appreciative interventions

Classrooms in this country are increasingly characterized by different languages, cultures, and learning styles. To reach all students, skilled administrators (and teachers) will to the degree possible employ materials that are consistent with diverse backgrounds and learning styles (i.e., "appropriate") and that have been selected in active and continuing consultation with persons representing the cultural groups concerned (i.e., "appreciative"). Appropriate and appreciative programming also applies to interventions designed to reduce student aggression.

Ongoing assessment of interventions

It has been estimated that over 200 different approaches to the management of student aggression are currently in practice in America's schools (Goldstein, Apter, & Harootunian, 1984). Yet program effectiveness in reducing violence or increasing positive, alternative behaviors is largely unmeasured and unknown. Most programs are initiated because they "sound good" and continue on the strength of anecdote or impression. Effective administrators do more. Before the intervention begins, they carefully track the frequency of the target behaviors they hope to change (e.g., office referrals, fights, calls to parents). This systematic tracking of effectiveness continues during the intervention. If frequency comparisons reveal that the intervention is in fact changing student behavior for the better, the intervention is continued or expanded. If not, the program is dropped and a new approach tried.

Safety-oriented policies and procedures

Schools and school systems have a number of ways to formalize safe school policies and procedures, many of which have already been discussed in this chapter. The wise administrator involves school staff, parents, and others in choosing among these options, selecting those that best fit the school. Rather than rely on punitive techniques or elaborate technology, this administrator seeks to create an efficient governance structure that is subject to change as changing circumstances warrant.

Learning from administrators in high-aggression schools

Finally, it may help in identifying administrative qualities in low-aggression schools if we enumerate governance methods research has suggested are characteristic in high-aggression schools. Both vandalism (aggression toward property) and violence (aggression toward persons) are more frequent in schools whose administration is (a) either autocratic (too strict) or laissez-faire (too lax), rather than "firm but fair"; (b) impersonal, unresponsive, nonparticipatory, overregulated, oppressive, arbitrary, or inconsistent; (c) characterized by overuse of punitive control methods; or (d) weak or inconsistent in its support of faculty. Each of these negative qualities implies its opposite as a way to promote low-aggression schools and classrooms.

✧◆✧

Other effective leadership activities in the move toward developing safe schools include the following:

1. Listening to others, including students, teachers, parents, and community members

2. Involving parents and teachers in solving problems and developing interventions

3. Being receptive to and guiding school personnel and parents in evaluating the culture of the school

4. Prompting and guiding staff to think about how the curriculum is being taught and how it can be made more relevant to the lives of students

5. Involving teachers in planning a schoolwide discipline program that emphasizes having students learn strategies to deal with their problematic behavior

6. Providing time for professional staff development activities

7. Providing time and opportunities for staff to work together and plan curricular strategies

Teacher Qualities in Low-Aggression Schools

Classroom teachers typically assume a role even more prominent than that of administrators in shaping the school environment. A number of teacher qualities and characteristics have been shown to be associated with low levels of student aggression.

Planning for success

Most educators understand well the importance of advance preparation for the school year. However, preparation in low-aggression schools takes into account not only academic goals and optimal instructional methods, but also more subtle aspects of the learning context—specifically, the school's formal and informal rules—and the needs of the students in each class. Teachers in low-aggression classrooms make a major effort to avoid the types of self-fulfilling prophecies that often follow when one learns that students who have been in trouble in the past are in one's class.

Community building

It is common in low-aggression schools for the teacher to spend time at the beginning of the school year creating a sense of community among his or her students. In this effort, the teacher instills a climate of cooperation and collaboration, rather than competition or indifference. Curriculum is certainly not ignored during this process; instead, it is used as a vehicle to achieve the goal of community building. Students are encouraged to share information to learn more about one another—likes, strengths, similarities, and so forth. Activities involve the entire class, focus on cooperative games and simulations, and often include structured cooperative learning.

Relevant curricula

Students often complain that school is boring. Curriculum content students perceive as irrelevant has been linked to aggression by a number of researchers. Csikszentmihalyi and Larsen (1978), for example, in proposing their "enjoyment theory" of vandalism, note that a large percentage of students find their school experiences to be especially boring and irrelevant to their life goals. These youth often respond with vandalistic acts directed toward the institution they perceive as its source. At the elementary school level, time devoted to learning facts (e.g., state capitals) could be better spent in activities that teach students *how* to learn (e.g., problem solving).

Classroom management

What do teachers actually *do* in low-aggression classrooms? Kounin's (1970) observations, as well as our own (Goldstein, Palumbo, Striepling, & Voutsinas, 1995) suggest some particularly important teacher behaviors. First, the teacher knows what is going on. Such *with-it-ness* is communicated to the class in a number of ways, including swift and consistent recognition and, when necessary, consequating of low-level behaviors likely to grow into disruptiveness or more serious aggression. Closely connected to such attentiveness is *overlapping,* the ability to manage simultaneously two or more classroom events, whether instructional or disciplinary. *Smoothness,* the ability to transition from one activity to another without "downtime," is a third facilitative teacher behavior. Downtime is a time for students to become bored and act out; avoiding or minimizing downtime significantly deters such behaviors.

Another way to minimize boredom is by instructing with *momentum,* maintaining a steady progress or movement throughout a particular lesson, class, or school day. A *group focus,* the ability to keep the entire class involved in a given instructional activity, also diminishes the likelihood of student aggression. Finally, an especially significant contributor to a low-aggression classroom is the teacher's communication of *optimistic expectations.* Students live up to (and, unfortunately, also down to) what important people in their lives expect of them. The teacher who expects a child to be a "slow learner" or a "behavior problem" because of his or her past record, a sibling's past poor performance in the same school, or the neighborhood he or she came from will likely be rewarded with low performance or behavior problems. By contrast, the teacher who lets the student know he or she can achieve and will have the teacher's help along the way is likely to motivate the student to be more academically successful and less behaviorally disruptive. The message is, Expect the best of your students—you may well get it!

Rules and procedures

Rules are guidelines governing appropriate and inappropriate student behaviors; procedures are what students need to know and follow to meet their own personal needs and perform routine instructional and classroom housekeeping activities. Teachers with low-aggression classrooms teach rules and procedures as explicitly as they teach academic content. Effective teachers integrate their rules and procedures—as well as consequences for not following them—into their classroom routines.

A number of effective "rules for the use of rules" have emerged in the behavior management literature (Greenwood, Hops, Delquadri, & Guild, 1974; Sarason, Glaser, & Fargo, 1972; Walker, 1979), including the following:

1. Define and communicate rules for student behavior in clear, specific, and, especially, behavioral terms. As Walker (1979) notes, it is better (more concrete and behavioral) to say, "Raise your hand before asking a question" than "Be considerate of others." A statement such as "Be kind or considerate to others" is a good goal, but too abstract. Instead, student behaviors should be clearly defined and phrased in a manner that students will understand, such as "Wait until another person has finished talking before you begin" and "Leave toys and other objects at your desk."

2. It is more effective to tell students what to do, rather than what not to do. For example, if it is necessary to address aggression, instead of "No pushing or shoving" the rule should be phrased as "Keep hands and feet to yourself." Other positive examples include "Talk over disagreements" instead of "No fighting" or "Work quietly" instead of "Don't talk out."

3. Rules should be communicated in a manner that will help students memorize them. Depending upon the age group and rule difficulty, memorization aids may include keeping rules short and few in number (four or five rules is a workable number to use in most elementary classes), repeating your presentation of the rules several times, and posting the rules in written form in the classroom, as well as sending them home to parents. Rules should be reviewed at the beginning of each session until they are remembered by all. Periodic review of rules may also be needed.

4. Following the rules is more likely when students have had a role in their development, modification, and implementation. However, often school and classroom rules are established by a committee of adults without student participation. Allowing the group to participate encourages students' commitment to abide by the rules. Students can be asked to think of behaviors they feel are needed to work together. It has been our experience, and that of many other practitioners, that students will state many rules that group leaders themselves would have identified. At times, more specific guidance may be needed, ideally in the form of leading questions, such as "Would everyone have a chance to be heard if everyone talked at once?" or "How might you let the leader know that you have something you want to say?"

5. In addition to the preceding ideas, further effective rules for rules are (a) that they be developed before group instruction begins; (b) that they be fair, reasonable, and within students' capacity to follow; (c) that all members of the group understand them; and (d) that they be applied consistently and fairly to all group members.

As is the case for rules, classroom procedures need to be explicitly taught; one cannot assume that students will know them without such instruction. Unlike rules, which need to be taught "up front," procedures (e.g., for obtaining help, leaving the room, using bathroom passes, sharpening pencils, handing in class work) usually can be explained as the need arises. However, procedures also will need to be clearly stated, closely monitored, consistently followed, retaught when necessary, and consequated when not followed.

Consistent application of rules and procedures provides clear expectations for student behavior and establishes that the teacher is in charge of the classroom. Yet such consistency is difficult to maintain over time. Teachers become tired, overworked, distracted. When this occurs, students are quick to get the message that perhaps "just this once" can become more than once. Then the boundary between what is and is not acceptable is no longer clear. Students begin to test the limits in order to reestablish where the boundary is, and as this happens, the foundation for a safe, low-aggression classroom begins to erode.

Home-school collaboration

Schools have long sought home-school contact, but many times such contact has meant the school's (the experts) telling the parents (the nonexperts) what to do. Traditionally, parent contact has taken the form of PTA meetings, parent-teacher conferences, or, as far too often has been the case with youngsters prone to behave aggressively or disruptively, the "bad news call." Teachers able to create and maintain low levels of aggression in their classrooms often view and deal with parents quite differently. They recognize and appreciate parents as the child's first (and continuing) teacher. They seek contact early and frequently, seeing this as an opportunity to collaborate in a supportive, mutually reinforcing way. Displaying such an attitude helps create the opportunity for the parents, teacher, and student to become a problem-solving team. The opportunities for the student to be successful in school are increased, and, because those experiencing success are less likely to be disruptive, aggression in the classroom is diminished.

Learning from teachers in high-aggression schools

Just as it is useful to consider administrative qualities in high-aggression schools, examining the behavior of teachers in such settings sheds light on the situation. Remboldt's (1994) exploration of the ways in which teachers may actually promote, encourage, or enable student aggression is helpful for this purpose. Student aggression will be reduced, and a safe, skill-promoting environment will be enhanced, to the degree that teachers avoid the following aggression-enabling behaviors:

1. Ignoring student complaints of being threatened

2. Avoiding high-violence school locations

3. Ignoring low-level violence (e.g., put-downs, bullying, harassment)

4. Ignoring student threats of planned violence

5. Ignoring rumors about students who may have weapons

6. Failing to intervene or report witnessed student violence

7. Excusing violent behavior of "good kids" as necessary for self-defense

✧◆✧

Aggression is an unpleasant act to confront. Nonetheless, it is the duty of responsible adults in the school to do so. School safety also relies on students' reporting aggression and their confidence that the school administration will make appropriate responses to curb it.

Just as the cause of violence is complex, so is the solution. When a youngster in a school or other setting behaves aggressively, adults typically respond as though the source of the aggression lies solely within the child. In their punitive, administrative, counseling, or other interventions, teachers and administrators often assume that the problem can best be dealt with by removing the perpetrator. However, as discussed in this chapter, many of the factors contributing to school violence lie outside the child and are within our control to change. If we are willing to make these changes, students will be more likely to acquire, perform, and generalize the nonaggressive, prosocial behaviors they learn.

CHAPTER 4
Skillstreaming Arrangements

The preceding chapters have focused on the goals of Skillstreaming, the program's history and development, and general characteristics of the environment that will make implementation more successful. This chapter describes specific arrangements to maximize the effectiveness of the Skillstreaming instructional environment. In particular, we consider group leader selection and preparation; student selection, grouping, and preparation; the role of support staff and parents; and specific instructional concerns such as skill selection and negotiation, setting, materials, and instructional variations.

GROUP LEADER SELECTION AND PREPARATION

Leader Selection

Since Skillstreaming began, hundreds of persons with a wide variety of backgrounds and positions have been effective group leaders. Teachers, counselors, and psychologists in the schools; youth care workers in treatment facilities and delinquency centers; and social workers in mental health and other community agencies are primary examples of such personnel.

In the school setting or in any instructional group focusing on skill building, several qualities of effective group leadership are apparent. First, the competent leader demonstrates good group-process skills. For example, rather than presenting a lecture, the leader listens to what the students are saying, gives feedback to let students know their viewpoints have been heard, and then adjusts instruction according to the needs of participants. Much of the Skillstreaming group can be directed by the students themselves (e.g., selection of topics, skill sequences, role-plays) with the group leader's acting as facilitator.

A second quality of effective group leadership, also a component of group processing, is the ability to manage the diverse concerns or behavior problems that may arise throughout instruction. One child may persist in a lengthy discussion that bores the rest of the group, another student may have difficulty paying attention, and still another may refuse to participate at all. The skilled leader is able to respond to such events in a firm, helpful, and unobtrusive manner and to maintain the flow of instruction. Chapter 9 presents a number of techniques for preventing and reducing the frequency or intensity of problematic behaviors. Effective leaders use these strategies while keeping in mind the goal of providing an encouraging environment for learning. The child's behavior, rather than the child himself or herself, is always the target.

In a Skillstreaming group, as in any learning environment, effective teaching skills are necessary. The teaching agenda, as described in chapter 5, is delivered in a clear and organized fashion. Techniques that contribute to low aggression in the classroom (discussed in chapter 3) are used in the group. Specifically, transitions from one activity to another are smooth, the lesson moves at an energetic pace, students are actively engaged, and the relevance of skills to students' real-life needs is emphasized. Finally, the effective group leader believes in what he or she is teaching and demonstrates enthusiasm, thus conveying an excitement in learning.

Though a great many Skillstreaming groups have been productively led by one teacher alone, we strongly recommend that, whenever possible, two staff members work together. Skill-deficient children are often quite proficient in generating the behavior management problems that make successful training difficult. To arrange and conduct a role-play between two children while at the same time overseeing the attention of other, easily distractible group members is daunting for anyone. A much better arrangement involves two teachers (or one teacher and another adult, such as a paraprofessional, volunteer, or school support staff member). One stands at the front of the group and leads the role-play while the second sits in the group, preferably next to the youth or youths most likely to have attention problems or act disruptively.

Leader Preparation

Teachers and other group leaders may prepare for the Skillstreaming group in a variety of ways, depending upon their own learning styles. Some may read and study this Skillstreaming program text and the Student Manual that accompanies it, then be ready to begin. Others may read and study the Skillstreaming materials, then choose to attend a workshop or training session, finding that listening to others who have implemented the techniques successfully augments what they have read. Still others may rely on the demonstration of real-life groups in operation presented in *The Skillstreaming Video* (Goldstein & McGinnis, 1988). (For a list of all supplementary Skillstreaming components, see Appendix C.)

An incremental training sequence

Although there is no right or wrong way to prepare for group instruction, we have found that many adult learners respond most effectively to what might be called an apprenticeship training sequence. Reading this book, viewing *The Skillstreaming Video,* and/or attending a workshop are first steps in this sequence. A good next step in leader preparation is the opportunity to participate first in a mock Skillstreaming group led by experienced trainers and made up of leaders-to-be pretending to be students. After one or more such role-play opportunities, the potential group leader can observe an experienced leader conduct an actual group, then co-lead such a group with the experienced leader, and, finally, lead the group while being observed by the experienced leader. This incremental training sequence, each of its steps adjustable in duration, has proven to be most satisfactory in training Skillstreaming group leaders.

In a school setting, for example, school social workers, psychologists, or counselors often carry out Skillstreaming groups, pulling individual children from various classrooms. A group of classroom teachers might request staff development training, which would first include participation in a mock Skillstreaming group. During planning time, individual teachers could observe, then participate as co-leader, in an ongoing skills group. Support staff could then assist teachers in beginning groups in their own regular or special classroom settings. Some support staff and teachers together have decided to continue this team arrangement, with the teacher running the group alone only when the other leader must be absent.

Cultural understanding

Which specific behaviors ideally define a given Skillstreaming skill? Which skills are optimal for use in any given setting? Which teaching and learning processes will best be used to acquire a skill? The answers will vary from culture to culture. Whether culture is defined by geography, ethnicity, nationality, social class, gender, sexual orientation, age, or some combination thereof, for Skillstreaming to be meaningful it must be viewed and practiced within a multicultural context. Cartledge and Milburn (1996) state this idea well:

> To be effective, social skill trainers need to understand
> learners' motivations and social goals, the ways in which
> the learners have been socialized in other environments
> such as the family or the community, and the interference
> of this alternative socialization with the trainers' goals
> and the culture of the school and the mainstream society.
> Equally important, social skill trainers must differentiate
> between social skill deficits that need to be changed and
> cultural differences that either need to be respected in their
> current form or simply need to be switched according to
> specific social conditions. (p. 1)

When the teacher and student are members of or are only minimally familiar with different cultural groups, definitions and prescriptions may conflict. Learning goals may not be met. For example, youngsters may engage in verbal bantering that appears to observers from a different cultural orientation to be aggressive, yet these behaviors may be common and acceptable in their culture. In such an instance, the behaviors themselves do not need to be changed; instead, instructional emphasis may need to be placed on when and where such verbal exchanges are appropriate within the school context. In contrasting Asian American culture with predominantly Western culture, Cartledge and Feng (1996) encourage teachers to "validate cultural background, making sure learners understand that certain situations will call for different responses, not that their ways of doing things are inferior" (p. 112).

In discussing social skills interventions and what educators can do to interact with a culturally diverse student population, Cartledge and Johnson (1997) state:

> Social skill interventions are not to be viewed as a means for controlling students for the comfort of teachers or for homogenizing students so they conform to some middle-class prototype designated by the majority group in this society. Inherent in the concept of culturally-relevant social skill instruction is a reciprocal process where the educator: (a) learns to respect the learner's cultural background, (b) encourages the learner to appreciate the richness of this culture, (c) when needed, helps the learner to acquire additional or alternative behaviors as demanded by the social situation, and (d) similarly employs and practices the taught behaviors.

Skillstreaming will be most effective when it is delivered in a manner appreciative of and responsive to such notions as skill strengths and differences versus skill deficits, differential teaching strategies and instructional methods, student channels of accessibility and communication styles, stereotyping of and by culturally different student populations, and culturally associated characteristics of the target students. Teacher knowledge, skill, and sensitivity are required.

Motivation

Teachers and other professionals working with children who have problems are often overworked, underpaid, and subject to pressures to implement or teach a variety of other interventions and curricular approaches. External rewards in the form of salary, awards, or compensatory time are uncommon. In the final analysis, the decision to learn and teach this particular approach is typically motivated by the potential group leader's desire to enhance his or her own teaching or intervention skill to better serve children. Teachers who implement Skillstreaming in their classrooms often hear positive comments from other school staff regarding their students' behavior. For example, one principal queried a special education teacher, "I rarely see any of your students in the office for discipline anymore. What is it you are doing in your classroom?" These types of rewards are immeasurable.

STUDENT SELECTION, GROUPING, AND PREPARATION

Student Selection

Skillstreaming is a method for teaching an extended curriculum of interpersonal, aggression management, and related skills to children who are weak or lacking in these competencies. The assessment task, therefore, is twofold: first, to identify those youngsters who can benefit from direct instruction in skill building and, second, to determine the level of proficiency or deficiency in necessary skills. For a culturally diverse group, the assessment process will need to take into account "differences versus deficits" (Cartledge & Milburn, 1996). These authors state:

> A child socialized in culturally specific ways may be socially competent in the home environment but may evidence differences when measured against the behavioral standards and norms of another culture. Depending on the nature of the child's behaviors, the differences may be overlooked, the child may need to learn to switch behaviors according to cultural and situational demands, or—if the behavior is dysfunctional or self-destructive—the child may need instruction in replacing inappropriate actions with more productive, self-enhancing ones. (p. 50)

The selection process for elementary school children may involve a number of assessment strategies, including sociometrics, analogue role-play observations, behavior rating scales, naturalistic observations, and skill checklists. The two latter strategies are the most user-friendly and are the ones that lead most directly from assessment to instruction. It is important to remember, however, that assessment results are most useful when more than one type of evaluation procedure is implemented (i.e., multimodal) and when the youngster's strengths and deficits are assessed in a variety of situations and settings and by a variety of individuals—for example, peers, adults, parents (i.e., multisource). In most Skillstreaming programs, such assessment has typically involved each child's teacher and parent, as well as the child. It is common, however, for discrepancies between adult and child ratings to occur. Whether such a discrepancy reflects overconfidence, denial, blaming others, lack of ability to assess one's own skills, or some other process in the child's perception, it is important to get the perspective of each child on his or her own skill strengths and weaknesses. As our later discussion of motivation shows (see chapter 9), teaching the skills the student believes necessary has proven to be a major motivational tactic.

Direct observation

Direct, or naturalistic, observation involves observing what the child does at particular times or in particular situations. Such observations, easily implemented by a classroom teacher, might involve taking frequency counts (e.g., how often a child deals with being teased or reacts to frustration in a particular manner), recording duration (e.g., how long it takes for a student to decide on something to do or the length of a crying episode), or making anecdotal records (e.g., what specific behaviors are of concern and their antecedents and consequences). Direct observation is especially valuable if the person or persons (teachers, youth care workers, etc.) who are planning to serve as group leaders are the same persons who are with the youngster all day and routinely see the child in interactions with others. In such circumstances, the behavioral observations can be frequent, take place in the youngster's natural environment, and reflect skill competence across diverse settings and situations.

Skill checklists

Skill checklists are designed to assess various individuals' perceptions of a student's skill proficiency. Checklists for teachers and other school staff, parents, and students are included in Appendix B. The Teacher/Staff Skillstreaming Checklist is completed by a teacher or another person in the school environment who is familiar with the student's behaviors in a variety of situations. The rater is asked to gauge the frequency of a particular student's use of each of the 60 Skillstreaming skills. The checklist also provides an opportunity for the rater to identify situations in which skill use is particularly problematic, information that will be useful for later modeling scenarios. The numerical value assigned to each skill targets the most problematic skills, leading to effective grouping of students for instruction and prioritizing of skills for instruction.

The Parent Skillstreaming Checklist is completed by the student's parent in an attempt to assess the parent's perceptions of the child's skill levels in the home and neighborhood. As for the Teacher/Staff Skillstreaming Checklist, parents are asked to respond to descriptions of the 60 prosocial skills in terms of frequency of skill use. Even though information relative to the student's skill use outside of the school setting may be useful to the teacher in identifying specific skills, in planning modeling displays, and in encouraging role-play scenarios, some discretion in requesting a parent to complete this checklist is in order. As an alternative to requesting that a parent complete the entire checklist, specific questions on the checklist may be selected to assess the child's strengths and weaknesses in skill areas that are of concern in the school setting. Parents can also be asked to respond to portions of the checklist during an interview.

The Student Skillstreaming Checklist is designed to assess students' perceptions. Requesting students to complete this self-rating may enhance their awareness of the skills they need to learn. Their willingness to participate actively in the group will likely be increased if students see the relevance of the skills to their daily lives (e.g., as a way of having more satisfactory peer relationships). The checklist is written at a third-grade reading level and is suggested for independent administration at this level or higher. It may, however, be simplified and read individually or in small-group settings to younger students or students less proficient in reading. Because of its length, the teacher may decide to give only a part of the checklist at one time. It may take two or more sessions spaced a day or so apart to complete the entire checklist.

Student Grouping

Once selected for participation, how are youngsters grouped? We have relied most heavily on two grouping criteria. The first criterion is shared skill deficiency. It is useful to group students who share similar skill deficiencies or patterns of deficits. By doing so, instruction will more intensely provide skill remediation in the areas of need for selected students. The Skillstreaming Grouping Chart (Appendix B) is designed to summarize the scores on all 60 skills for entire classes, units, or other large sets of youngsters; it can readily be used to identify shared skill deficiencies.

The second grouping criterion concerns the generalization-enhancing principle of identical elements. This principle is discussed at greater length in chapter 10, on generalization. The heart of this notion, however, is that the greater the similarity between qualities of the teaching session and the real-world setting, the greater the likelihood that the student will use the skill outside the group. Cross-setting similarity is operationalized by constructing Skillstreaming groups of children from the same class, living unit, neighborhood, and the like.

Student Preparation

After student selection and grouping, the next task is preparing students for Skillstreaming group participation. Preparation is conducted first on an individual basis to provide information about the group routine and to motivate the student to participate by relating the process to his or her real-life needs. This introduction to Skillstreaming should cover the following topics. This same information is reiterated as appropriate in the initial Skillstreaming group session.

Purposes

A description of the purposes of the group as related to the youngster's specific skill deficits comes first. For example, the teacher might say something like this:

> Remember on Tuesday when you threw the rock at Sam
> when you were angry and then lost the privilege of being
> on the playground with your class? In this group you'll
> learn skills to help you stay out of that kind of trouble so
> that you can have your recess with the others.

A statement such as this can serve both preparatory and motivational purposes.

Procedures

Next is a general description of the procedures involved in Skillstreaming. This might include something like the following:

> In order to handle difficult situations in ways that will
> keep you out of trouble yet will still help you get what you
> need, we'll first show you some good examples of the
> skills needed. Then you and the others in your group will

take turns trying the skill in the group. We'll all talk about
how well we did, and then you'll try out the skill on your
own, in a situation where you need to use it.

This brief description of modeling, role-play, feedback, and generalization procedures will be illustrated more completely once students
have actually participated in a Skillstreaming session or two.

Incentives

After the description of procedures comes an explanation of any
incentive plans or systems in place in the class, school, agency, or
institution. These include strategies such as token rewards, points,
privilege/level systems, or other reinforcement plans. Although the
relevance of skills to real life motivates most youngsters, in the initial
stages of this type of group work with elementary-age children it is
often helpful to plan and implement a reinforcement system to help
manage group members' problem behaviors and to encourage participation. Whether in the form of tokens, points, and/or verbal praise,
frequent positive reinforcement is important in the initial stages of
learning any new skill (Bornstein & Quevillon, 1976).

Rules

Rules to guide student behavior have long been used in elementary classrooms. In chapter 3, we presented a series of useful "rules
for the use of rules" as they might be applied in the Skillstreaming
group, among these that rules be few in number, negotiated with
the students, stated behaviorally, stated positively, posted in the
classroom, and sent home to parents. All of these recommendations
apply to the use of rules in the Skillstreaming group.

To develop rules for the group, the teacher might say something
like the following:

In this group, we want to encourage and help one another.
There are some things we can all do that will be helpful.
Let's come up with a number of helpful things we can do,
and I'll list them on the board. Who can think of a helpful
rule for the group?

Clearly defining rules in the early stages of group work may prevent many student behavior problems. In addition, providing positive

reinforcement for obeying the rules (e.g., "Thank you for waiting your turn to talk") will increase the likelihood that rules will be followed.

SUPPORT STAFF AND PARENT ROLES

Support Staff Preparation

The effort to teach prosocial behavior should not go forward in isolation; teachers and their students are a part of a school, a residential facility, or another institution. We have already suggested ways to prepare staff members who will serve as Skillstreaming group leaders. What about the rest of the staff? They also have a meaningful role to play in this effort, even though they will not be serving as group leaders.

The goal of changing the behaviors of aggressive, withdrawn, or immature students often succeeds only at a certain time and in a certain place. That is, the program works, but only at or shortly after the instruction and only in the same place. Thus, a program may make a child behave in more desirable ways during and immediately following the weeks of teaching, in the classroom where it took place. But a few weeks later, or in the school hallway, outside on the playground, on a field trip, at home, or elsewhere outside the classroom, the child's behavior may be as problematic as ever. This temporary success followed by a relapse to old, negative ways of behaving is a failure of generalization. Generalization failures are much more the rule than the exception with many youth. During Skillstreaming instruction, students receive a great deal of support, encouragement, and reward for their efforts. However, between group sessions or after instruction ends many students receive little support or other positive response.

The common failure of generalization is not surprising. However, this outcome can be minimized. Newly learned and thus fragile skills need not fade away after a Skillstreaming unit has ended. If attempts to use such skills in the real world are met with success (i.e., support, enthusiasm, encouragement, reward), children will be much more likely to continue using the skills. Teachers, school staff, community workers, parents, friends, counselors, peers, school administrators, and others who work directly with students are in an ideal position to promote continued skill use. All of these individuals can be powerful "transfer coaches," helping to make sure the Skillstreaming curriculum turns into long-term or even permanent gain. Following are some specific ways these individuals can assist.

Prompting

Under the pressure of real-life situations, both in and out of school, children may forget all or part of skills learned earlier. If their anxiety is not too great or their forgetting too complete, all they may need to perform the skill correctly is prompting. Prompting is reminding the person what to do (the skill), how to do it (the steps), when to do it (now or at another "good time"), where to do it (and where not to), and/or why to use the skill (the positive outcomes expected). For example, the lunchroom supervisor may prompt a student to ignore distractions, in the school hallway the principal may suggest that a student avoid trouble or use self-control, and in the library the librarian may prompt a student to ask a question or offer help to a classmate. The school playground offers many opportunities for students to practice friendship-making skills and alternatives to aggression; playground supervisors need to take an active role in prompting skill use in such environments.

Encouraging

Offering encouragement to students assumes they know a skill well enough but are reluctant to use it. Encouragement may be necessary, therefore, when the problem is lack of motivation rather than lack of knowledge or skill. Encouragement can often best be given by gently urging students to try using what they know, by showing enthusiasm for the skill being used, and by communicating optimism about the likely positive outcome of skill use.

Reassuring

For particularly anxious students, skill generalization attempts will be more likely to occur if the threat of failure is reduced. Reassurance is an effective threat-reduction technique. "You can do it" and "I'll be there to help if you need it" are examples of the kinds of reassuring statements the transfer coach can provide.

Rewarding

The most important contribution by far that the transfer coach can make for skill generalization is to provide (or help someone else provide) rewards for correct skill use. Rewards may take the form of approval, praise, or compliments, or they may consist of special privileges, points, tokens, recognition, or other reinforcers built into a school's management system. For example, one school successfully enhanced skill generalization by having all staff in the school distribute "Gotcha Cards" whenever they observed a student using a prosocial skill. All such rewards will increase the likelihood of continued skill use in new settings and at later times.

The most powerful reward that can be offered, however, is the success of the skill itself. For example, if a youth practices Dealing with an Accusation (Skill 43), then a real-life interaction goes very well, that reward (the successful interaction) will help the skill transfer and endure more than any external reward can. The same conclusion, that success increases generalization, applies to all of the Skillstreaming skills. It is important for all adults and peers to react with behaviors that signal awareness of effective skill use. If transfer and maintenance become schoolwide goals—supported by staff, administrators, students, and parents—and all make a concerted effort toward this end, fragile skills will become lasting skills, and Skillstreaming will have been successful.

PROGRAM COORDINATOR ROLE

Even if teachers, students, and support staff are prepared and motivated to begin a Skillstreaming program, the participation of one more professional helps ensure a successful outcome. Many effective programs involve the appointment of a program coordinator or master teacher. It is unfortunately common for Skillstreaming programs to begin with appropriate organization, good intentions, and adequate enthusiasm, only to wind up being discarded a few months later because of a lack of oversight. The barrage of other responsibilities often placed on teachers and other front-line staff makes intervention programs more likely to fail in the absence of such guidance.

The program coordinator or master teacher should be well versed in both Skillstreaming and program management. Her or his Skillstreaming responsibilities may include providing staff development, observing sessions, monitoring schoolwide progress, setting up specific generalization-increasing efforts, motivating staff, facilitating the gathering and distribution of materials, and handling the many other details upon which program success depends.

Parent Preparation

Parent involvement can and should be an integral part of the Skillstreaming program. Initially, informing parents of program goals will help them better understand and support program efforts. Role-plays and homework assignments may depict problems that occur at home, and students are likely to discuss with parents the new ways they are learning to handle such problems. Unless parents understand the purpose of the program, they may question why the school is involved with home-related issues. Potential misunderstandings can be averted if parents are kept informed.

One way to encourage parent involvement is to hold an orientation meeting to describe Skillstreaming objectives and ways parents might help their child use the prosocial skills at home. An alternative to an orientation meeting is to send a letter home explaining the skill-enhancement goals of instruction and the activities in which their child will be participating (i.e., watching leaders act out a skill, trying out the skill steps in the group, giving and receiving feedback about skill performance, and completing skill homework assignments).

Other ways to promote parent involvement include the following:

1. Have parents assess their child's skill strengths and weaknesses by completing all or part of the Parent Skillstreaming Checklist (presented in Appendix B) and by talking with them about skills they value in the home.

2. Frequently inform parents of their child's progress in given skill areas, focusing on positive reports.

3. Videotape the child in a role-play situation and share this videotape with the parents during conferences to encourage further understanding.

4. Invite parents to observe a Skillstreaming group in progress and to participate as co-actors in the group.

5. Instruct parents in ways to encourage the child's skill use at home.

Approaching skill instruction as a cooperative effort between parents and teachers will likely enhance communication and improve the relationship between home and school. In addition, cooperation permits parents to encourage and reinforce the child's attempts to practice newly learned behaviors.

SPECIFIC INSTRUCTIONAL CONCERNS

Program planners and group leaders will need to consider the following factors, essentially the mechanics of the Skillstreaming group.

Skill Selection and Negotiation

Many children for whom Skillstreaming is appropriate ascribe their negative and undesirable behavior to others. From this externalized perspective, rarely is anything their fault! Experience suggests that one of the most effective methods of student motivation is "negotiating the skill curriculum," or selecting skills the students themselves say they need and want to learn. Students can identify which skills they feel they need by filling out all or part of the Student Skillstreaming Checklist (see Appendix B).

Teaching skills that provide students with positive alternatives for dealing with their immediate needs will increase their feelings of social competence and their desire to learn other skills. When students perceive a need to learn a new behavior, then have the opportunity to use that newly acquired behavior in situations that will benefit them, learning is likely to be far more effective and enduring. Teaching skills important to others (e.g., teachers and parents) is a program goal but is of secondary importance in determining the skill agenda.

Placement in the School Curriculum

In schools, Skillstreaming has found a place at various times—from homeroom at the beginning of the day to after-school detention at its end. Frequent placements include the resource room and in-school suspension. Sometimes Skillstreaming has been included in a school's regular curriculum—specifically, in subject areas that deal with personal or interpersonal development such as social studies (e.g., family and community relationships), language arts (e.g., communication and problem-solving skills), and health (e.g., stress management, peer relationships). At the elementary level social skills training and other relationship-based initiatives have more recently been recognized as deserving a place of their own. Including Skillstreaming as part of the regular curriculum increases the likelihood that students will use and retain the skills taught, thus enhancing the program's effectiveness as both intervention and prevention.

Instructional Setting

Whenever possible, the setting for Skillstreaming should be the classroom or other location where the students spend the majority of their time. Research provides two reasons in support of this recommendation. First, because the target child's peers in this setting will also have received the instruction, they will be more likely to help the skill-deficient child perform the skill by providing encouragement and feedback as the child practices the newly learned behavior. Second, because generalization from the teaching setting to the application setting does not occur automatically, carrying out the instruction in the setting in which the child will most often need the prosocial skill (i.e., the natural environment) will help the learning to generalize. Alternative and typically less structured school areas— such as hallways, playgrounds, the school cafeteria, and the school bus—are good places to carry out instruction and practice sessions. When a given skill applies in an easily accessible school environment, modeling and role-playing should occur in that environment.

Occasionally, it may be necessary to provide skill instruction in another, more artificial environment, such as a counselor's office or a special education resource room. This can and should be done in cases in which the student needs additional guidance or practice to learn the skill, but such settings are not recommended either for ongoing instruction or as the only teaching environment.

A special group space should be provided in the classroom for the majority of group instruction. Ideally, chairs will be positioned in a semicircle in an area that allows all students to easily view modeling displays and role-play vignettes. In some large-group settings, this may not be possible. In such cases, alternatives may include having students sit on the floor or at their desks, arranged in a semicircle.

Time Factors

Frequency and length of sessions

Skillstreaming sessions are best held three to five times per week. They should be frequent enough for a series of skills to be taught and far enough apart for the students to have opportunities to complete assigned homework between sessions. Specific Skillstreaming procedures should be followed for at least three sessions per week; the other two sessions might consist of work on specific skill steps, such as relaxation training, asking on-topic questions, or using a game-type format to review a group of previously learned skills.

Throughout the school day in both structured and unstructured settings, teachers may prompt, encourage, reassure, and reward students' use of prosocial skills. When a situation suggesting instruction in Skillstreaming arises, teachers may choose to provide additional group or individual sessions. From this viewpoint, Skillstreaming is an ongoing effort, the initial instruction occurring at the time set for the group, with additional learning and transfer-enhancing procedures taking place throughout the school day.

Sessions of approximately 25 to 40 minutes each are suggested, with the shorter time period for students in the lower elementary grades and increased time for older students, as their behavior, interest, and attention span permit. The upper time limit of the group is clear when several children become restless and inattentive. It is important to maintain the students' interest for subsequent Skillstreaming sessions, and sessions should therefore be planned in the future to end slightly before students become restless. As with any lesson, teachers will need to adjust the session's length to respond to a variety of factors, some of which include student behavioral needs.

To facilitate the continued use of newly learned skills, an additional 5 to 10 minutes at the end of the school day can be allotted for students to chart the skills they have practiced throughout the day. This and other suggested generalization- enhancing procedures are discussed in chapter 10.

Program duration

Skillstreaming programs have been as brief as 2 days, as long as 3 years, and just about all lengths in between. The 2-day programs take place in in-school detention rooms, in which detained students are taught a single skill. Three-year and other lengthy programs are open Skillstreaming groups, adding new members one at a time as older members "graduate" or otherwise leave. A more typical program lasts the school year, although students may participate over consecutive school years.

Another way of defining duration of program, beyond days or months of meetings, concerns the number of skills taught. The goal of Skillstreaming is teaching prosocial skills so they are not only learned (acquired), but also used (performed) effectively in a variety of settings and for an enduring period of time. As such, the program takes time. Although the full curriculum includes 60 skills, not all will be taught to any given Skillstreaming group. Because the goal is to teach those skills in which students are weak or deficient and those that will be most helpful in their daily lives, a full curriculum for some groups may be only a few skills—for other groups, several skills. In a few cases in which Skillstreaming is used on a schoolwide basis, with the entire school working on a given skill at the same time, students may be exposed to a greater number of skills, though not all 60.

Whether a few skills or several are included, teachers should not move on to a second skill until the first is both well learned (as evidenced by successful role-play within the group) and regularly performed (as evidenced by successful homework outside the group). This teaching goal usually requires that the same skill be taught during more than two sessions. In fact, even at the price of student boredom, skills should be taught until they are nearly automatic, or "overlearned," as described in chapter 10, on generalization.

Materials

Other than the substantial cost of staff time, Skillstreaming is not an expensive program to implement. A chalkboard or easel pad, Skill Cards listing the skill steps, and skill step posters to hang in the classroom and school are the core materials needed. Skill Cards may be of the preprinted variety available with the program (see the example in Figure 1); group leaders (or students) may also make these cards themselves.

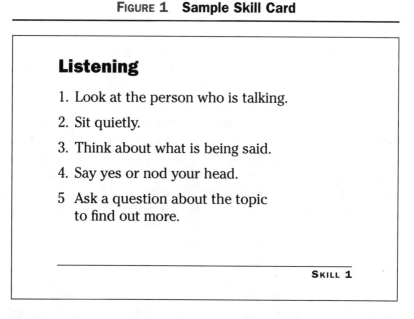

FIGURE 1 Sample Skill Card

Listening

1. Look at the person who is talking.

2. Sit quietly.

3. Think about what is being said.

4. Say yes or nod your head.

5 Ask a question about the topic
to find out more.

SKILL 1

In addition to these materials, two booklets augment the basic Skillstreaming procedures and enhance their effectiveness. The first is the Skillstreaming Student Manual. This manual orients participants to Skillstreaming. In language appropriate for typical group members, it is designed to supplement and reaffirm group leaders' verbal structuring of the Skillstreaming group's purpose and goals. Specifically, the manual introduces students to the Skillstreaming procedures of modeling, role-playing, performance feedback, and transfer training (homework). The Program Forms booklet compiles essential program forms, checklists, and charts in a reproducible 8½ × 11–inch format. These resources and other supplementary Skillstreaming components are fully described in Appendix C.

Instructional Variations

In general, applications of Skillstreaming have been directed toward children and adolescents selected from a larger classroom group. There are advantages to doing so, as well as other gains to be achieved from providing instruction to the whole class. Therefore, instruction may be carried out in large or small groups and occasionally, in special circumstances, with individual students.

Large-group instruction

General instruction and modeling displays can be successfully carried out in view of a group of 20 or more students. Role-plays, however, are better carried out in two or more smaller groups, preferably with an adult leader assigned to each group. With fewer children in a role-play group, more opportunity exists for each child to assume the role of the main actor and to receive constructive suggestions, encouragement, and reinforcement. The more practice a student has with a particular skill, the more likely he or she will be to apply that skill over time and in other environments. Thus, the whole group would meet first to generate skill-relevant situations, present the skill steps, and discuss the skill and its modeling. It is important not to stop instruction at this point. Skillstreaming is an experiential activity; the rehearsal component (role-playing) is vital for learning. The role-plays, feedback, and homework are therefore done in smaller groups.

When working with large groups, teachers have elicited assistance from other adults in the school (e.g., volunteers, school administrators, even custodians). Others have found success by using several students as co-actors in role-plays; by asking students who are not role-playing at the moment to watch for and provide feedback on particular skill steps; and/or by assigning other helper roles (e.g., pointing to skill steps on the chalkboard as the role-play unfolds, helping arrange props to make the role-play more realistic).

Still others choose to teach Skillstreaming within the classroom, in a fashion similar to traditional classroom reading groups. In this variation, the group leader introduces the skill and presents the modeling display to the whole group but conducts role-plays, feedback sessions, and assignment of homework in small groups. Thus, the group leader is able to spend time with students who need extra practice role-playing to learn the skill.

Small-group instruction

Under certain circumstances, elementary students may be assigned to smaller groups according to common skill needs. This will likely mean that participating students will not be from the same classroom or even from the same age group. Because role-playing is more effective when the teaching setting closely resembles the real-life environment, it is useful to include children whose social environments (e.g., peer groups) are similar. Selecting participants from a common peer group will not only make the role-play more realistic, but also will increase the likelihood that students will attempt the skill with peers in the classroom or neighborhood.

The ideal small group consists of eight students, depending upon student needs. If students exhibit particularly problematic behaviors, a more appropriate group size may be three or four students, or even fewer. If a smaller number is necessary due to members' aggression or out-of-control behavior, additional students may be added (perhaps at the rate of one new member per week) once the smaller group is operating successfully.

Individual instruction

Although Skillstreaming is primarily designed to be carried out in a group setting, in special cases modifications can be made to include one-to-one instruction. The child who needs additional help in learning a specific skill, who withdraws from group involvement, or who is behaviorally out of control would benefit from this type of instruction. When carried out individually, the Skillstreaming procedures remain the same, but the adult—or the child's peer if this is feasible—serves as the co-actor in each role-play, providing the feedback except for that elicited from the child. Although individual instruction is a useful way of providing skill instruction to some youngsters, the main objective should be to include all youngsters in a Skillstreaming group as soon as possible.

CHAPTER 5
Skillstreaming Teaching Procedures

In order to carry out the core teaching procedures that constitute the Skillstreaming method—modeling, role-playing, performance feedback, and transfer—teachers lead the group through the nine steps listed in Table 1. This chapter describes these steps and illustrates the Skillstreaming procedure in operation.

STEP 1: DEFINE THE SKILL

In this brief activity, the teacher leads a discussion of the skill to be taught. Whether the skill has been selected by the teacher or as a result of the recommended periodic skill negotiation between teacher and group members, this activity is a necessary beginning. The goal

---

Table 1   Skillstreaming Teaching Steps

1. Define the skill
2. Model the skill
3. Establish student skill need
4. Select role-player
5. Set up the role-play
6. Conduct the role-play
7. Provide performance feedback
8. Assign skill homework
9. Select next role-player

---

is to help students understand the skill to be taught in the session. This goal can typically be achieved in a few minutes of discussion; a long lecture is not required. The following dialogue shows a teacher briefly defining Skill 43, Dealing with an Accusation:

Teacher: Thank you for getting ready for the group so quickly. Today's skill is quite an important one, one that lots of people have trouble doing well—or even at all. It's called Dealing with an Accusation. Can anyone tell me what an accusation is? Margie? Yes, what do you think?

Margie: When somebody says you did something, like hitting somebody.

Teacher: That's one good way to explain it. Thank you. Anyone else? Devin, you had your hand up.

Devin: You do something that gets you in trouble, and somebody finds out. Then you get in trouble for it.

Teacher: That's a good part of it, Devin. Can someone make an accusation if you didn't really do something wrong, like hitting someone? Yes, Jeff?

Jeff: Somebody can say you did something, but you really didn't. Like my little brother told my mom I messed up his room, but I didn't.

Teacher: Thank you, Jeff. That's another good way of explaining what an accusation is. Someone may believe that you did something and may accuse you. You may have done it, or you may not have. Most times, it is upsetting to be accused of doing something, whether or not you actually did it. So the skill we are going to learn today is how to handle these types of situations—how to deal with an accusation. Russ [second teacher], would you please hand out the Skill Cards?

(To the group) You may look for the steps on the Skill Card or on the chalkboard, where they are written.

STEP 2: MODEL THE SKILL

Modeling is defined as learning by imitation. Imitation has been examined in a great deal of research that has consistently shown it to be effective and reliable for both learning new behaviors and strengthening or weakening previously learned behaviors. Three types of learning by modeling have been identified.

Observational learning refers to the learning of behaviors the person has never performed before. Children and adolescents are great imitators. Even very young children learn new behaviors by observing others (mostly peers), whether these are styles of dressing, ways of talking, or other positive or negative behaviors.

Inhibitory and *disinhibitory effects* involve the strengthening or weakening of behaviors previously performed only rarely by the person due to a history of punishment or other negative reactions. Modeling offered by peers is, again, a major source of inhibitory and disinhibitory effects, and it frequently results in children's succumbing to peer pressure. Youngsters who know how to be altruistic and caring and the like may inhibit such behaviors in the presence of models who are behaving more egocentrically and being rewarded for their egocentric behavior. Aggressive models may have a disinhibitory effect: If a child sees another go unpunished for aggression, the observing youngster may engage in aggressive behavior as well.

Behavioral facilitation refers to the performance of previously learned behaviors that are neither new nor a source of potential negative reactions from others. One person buys something he or she seems to enjoy, so a friend buys one, too. A child deals with a confrontational peer in an effective manner, then a classmate approaches a similar problem the same way. These are examples of behavioral facilitation effects.

Research has demonstrated that a wide array of behaviors can be learned, strengthened, weakened, or facilitated through modeling. These include acting aggressively, helping others, behaving independently, planning a career, becoming emotionally aroused, interacting socially, displaying dependency, exhibiting certain speech patterns, behaving empathically, self-disclosing, and more. It is clear from such research that modeling can be an effective way to teach people new behaviors.

Yet it is also true that most people observe dozens and perhaps hundreds of behaviors that they do not then engage in themselves. Television, radio, magazines, and newspapers expose people to very polished, professional modeling displays of someone's buying one product or another, but observers do not later buy the product. People observe expensively produced instructional videos, but they may not learn the skills depicted. Children may see many behaviors enacted by peers in a given school day, but copy only a few, or none.

Modeling Enhancers

Research on modeling has successfully identified what we have called "modeling enhancers," or conditions that increase the effectiveness of modeling. These modeling enhancers are characteristics of the model, the modeling display, or the observer (the student). A coping model also makes learning more likely.

Model characteristics. More effective modeling will occur when the model (the person to be imitated) (a) seems to be highly skilled or expert; (b) is of high status; (c) controls rewards desired by the observer; (d) is of the same sex, approximate age, and social status as the observer; (e) is friendly and helpful; and, of particular importance, (f) is rewarded for the behavior. That is, we are all more likely to imitate expert or powerful yet pleasant people who receive rewards for what they are doing, especially when the particular rewards involved are things we too desire.

Modeling display characteristics. More effective modeling will occur when the modeling display shows the behaviors to be imitated (a) in a clear and detailed manner; (b) in the order from least to most difficult behaviors; (c) with enough repetition to make overlearning likely; (d) with as little irrelevant detail as possible; and (e) performed by several different models, rather than a single one.

Observer (student) characteristics. More effective modeling will occur when the person observing the model is (a) told to imitate the model; (b) similar to the model in background or attitude toward the skill; (c) friendly toward or likes the model; and, most important, (d) rewarded for performing the modeled behaviors.

Coping model. Modeling is more effective when a coping model, or one who struggles a little to achieve the goal of competent skill performance, is presented (Bandura, 1977). When demonstrating Dealing with Your Anger (Skill 31) or Saying No (Skill 55), it is important to show some emotion and to struggle a little with modeling. This struggling model must be demonstrated in a low-key manner, and in an acceptable way, so that the struggle does not detract from the modeling display. However, if students perceive that the skill is "easy" and can be performed without any feeling, they may be less likely to try the skill when caught up in the emotion of a real-life event. Depicting coping models will further enhance students' ability to identify with the model and will likely give them more courage to try the skill themselves.

Stages of Modeling

The effects of these modeling enhancers, as well as of modeling itself, can be better understood by examining the three stages of learning by modeling.

Attention. Clearly, students cannot learn from watching a model unless they pay attention to the modeling display and, in particular, to the specific behaviors being modeled. Students are better able to attend to the modeling by eliminating irrelevant detail in the display, minimizing the complexity of the modeled material, making the display vivid, and implementing the modeling enhancers previously described.

Retention. In order to later reproduce the behaviors the student has observed, he or she must remember or retain them. Because the behaviors of the modeling display itself are no longer present, retention must occur by memory. Memory is aided if the behaviors displayed are classified by the observer. Another name for such classification is *covert rehearsal* (i.e., reviewing in one's mind the performance of the behaviors modeled). Research has shown, however, that an even more important aid to retention is *overt rehearsal* (i.e., behavioral rehearsal). Such practice of the specific behavioral steps is critical for learning and, indeed, is the second major procedure of Skillstreaming. This is role-playing, a procedure to be examined in more depth later in this chapter. It should be noted at this point, however, that the likelihood of retention by either covert or overt rehearsal is greatly aided by rewards provided to both the model and/or the student observer.

Reproduction. Researchers in the area of learning have distinguished between learning (acquiring or gaining knowledge) and performance. If a person has paid attention to the modeling display and has remembered the behaviors shown, it may be said that the person has learned. However, the main interest is not so much that the person *can* produce the behaviors observed, but in whether he or she *does* produce them. As with retention, the likelihood that a person will actually perform a learned behavior depends greatly on the expectation of a reward for doing so.

Modeling Guidelines

In planning live modeling displays, teachers should incorporate the following guidelines:

1. Use at least two examples for each skill demonstration. If a skill is used in more than one group session, develop two new modeling displays.

2. Select situations relevant to students' real-life circumstances.

3. The model (i.e., the person enacting the behavioral steps of the skill) should be portrayed as a youngster reasonably similar in age, socioeconomic background, verbal ability, and other characteristics salient to the youngsters in the Skillstreaming group.

4. Modeling displays should depict positive outcomes. In addition, the model who is using the skill well should always be reinforced.

5. Modeling displays should depict all the behavioral steps of the skill in the correct sequence.

6. Modeling displays should depict only one skill at a time, with no extraneous content.

In order to encourage students to attend to the skill portrayals, Skill Cards, which list the name of the skill being taught and its behavioral steps, are distributed prior to the modeling displays (see Figure 1, p. 53). Students are asked to watch and listen closely as the modeling unfolds. Particular care should be given to helping students identify the behavioral steps as they are being modeled. Teachers can do this by pointing to the steps, which have been written on the chalkboard or easel pad, or by having the model state aloud the behavioral steps in the course of the modeling. Students should be reminded that models will often "think aloud" statements that would normally be thoughts to oneself in order to depict some of these behavioral steps and thus facilitate learning.

STEP 3: ESTABLISH STUDENT SKILL NEED

Behavioral rehearsal is the purpose of the role-play. Before group members begin role-playing, it is important to identify each student's current and future need for the skill. Reenactment of a past problem or circumstances is less relevant, unless the student predicts that such circumstances are likely to reoccur in the future. Such current student needs will likely have been established earlier as part of the selection and grouping process. Nonetheless, an open discussion within the group is needed to establish relevant and realistic role-plays. Each student is in turn asked to describe briefly where, when, and with whom he or she would find it useful to use the skill just modeled. To make effective use of such information, it is often valuable to list the names of the group members on the chalkboard or easel pad at the front of the room and to record next to each name the theme of the role-play and the name (or role) of the person with whom the skill will be used.

STEP 4: SELECT ROLE-PLAYER

Because all members of the Skillstreaming group will be expected to role-play each skill taught, in most instances it is not of great concern who does so first. Typically, teachers may ask for volunteers to begin the role-play series. If for any reason there are group members who appear to be reluctant to role-play a particular skill on a particular day, it may be helpful not to ask them to role-play first or second. Observing other students do so first can be reassuring and may help ease their way into the activity. For a few students, reluctance may turn into resistance and refusal. Refusal occurs infrequently with elementary-age students. However, because it does occur at times and is a significant roadblock to that student's learning, strategies for dealing with such problems are described at length in chapter 9. In general, students should be encouraged, reassured, and reminded to use the skill to meet their own needs, rather than penalized, threatened, or otherwise coerced into participation.

STEP 5: SET UP THE ROLE-PLAY

Once a student has described a situation in which skill use may be useful, that student is designated as the main actor. The main actor chooses a second person (the co-actor) to play the role of the other person (e.g., teacher, peer, parent) with whom he or she will use the skill in real life. The main actor should be encouraged to select as the co-actor someone who resembles the significant other in as many ways as possible—in other words, someone who reminds the main actor most of the actual person. The group leader then elicits from the main actor any additional information needed to set the stage for the role-play. In order to make role-playing as realistic as possible, the leader should obtain a description of the physical setting, the events immediately preceding the situation, and the mood or manner the co-actor should portray, along with any other information that would enhance realism.

STEP 6: CONDUCT THE ROLE-PLAY

At this point the group leader should remind group members of their roles and responsibilities: The main actor is told to follow the behavioral steps and to "think aloud" what would normally be thought silently; the co-actor, to stay in the role of the other person; and the other students, to watch carefully for the enactment of the behavioral steps. We find it useful to assign separate behavioral steps to the observers, have them watch for the display of these steps, and then report on step use during the subsequent feedback session. For the first several role-plays, observers can be coached as to what kinds of cues to observe (e.g., posture, words chosen, tone of voice, facial expression). Then the role-players are instructed to begin. At this point it is the group leader's responsibility to provide the main actor with any help or coaching needed in order to keep the role-play going according to the behavioral steps. Students who "break role" to offer other information should be urged to get back into the role and explain later. If the role-play is clearly going astray from the behavioral steps, the scene can be stopped, needed instruction provided, and the role-play resumed. One group leader should be positioned near the chalkboard or easel pad and point to each of the behavioral steps as they are enacted. This will help the main actor, as well as the observers and co-actor, follow each of the steps in order.

Role-playing should be continued until all group members have had an opportunity to participate in the role of the main actor. Sometimes this will require two or three sessions for a given skill. We suggest that each session begin with two modeling vignettes for the selected skill, even if the skill is not new to the group. It is important to note that, although the framework (behavioral steps) of each role-play remains the same, the content can and should change from role-play to role-play. When the role-plays have been completed, each student will be better equipped to act appropriately in a real-life situation requiring skill use.

Other strategies may be used to increase the effectiveness of role-plays. For example, role reversal is often a useful procedure. If a student has a difficult time perceiving his co-actor's point of view (and vice versa), having the two exchange roles and resume the role-play can be most helpful. On occasion the group leader can also assume the co-actor role in an effort to give students the opportunity to handle types of reactions not otherwise role-played during the session. It may be critical to have a difficult adult role realistically portrayed, for instance. The leader as a co-actor may also be particularly helpful when dealing with less verbal or more hesitant students.

STEP 7: PROVIDE PERFORMANCE FEEDBACK

A brief period of feedback follows each role-play. Such feedback lets the main actor find out how well he or she followed or departed from the behavioral steps, evaluates the impact of the enactment on the co-actor, and gives the main actor encouragement to try out the behavior in real life.

The co-actor is asked to react first. Next, the observers comment on whether or not the skill steps they were assigned to watch for were followed and on other relevant aspects of the role-play. Then the group leaders comment in particular on how well the behavioral steps were followed and provide social reinforcement (praise, approval, encouragement) for close following of the skill steps. To be most effective in providing reinforcement, leaders should follow these guidelines:

1. Provide reinforcement only after role-plays that follow the behavioral steps.

2. Provide reinforcement at the earliest appropriate opportunity after role-plays that follow the behavioral steps.

3. Provide reinforcement to the co-actor for being helpful, cooperative, and so forth.

4. Vary the specific content of the reinforcement offered (e.g., praise particular aspects of the performance, such as tone of voice, posture, phrasing).

5. Provide enough role-playing activity for each group member to have sufficient opportunity to be reinforced.

6. Provide reinforcement in an amount consistent with the quality of the given role-play.

7. Provide no reinforcement when the role-play departs significantly from the behavioral steps (except for "trying"). Instead, reteach.

8. Provide reinforcement for an individual student's improvement over previous performances.

After listening to the feedback from the co-actor, observers, and group leaders, the main actor is asked to make comments regarding the role-play and, if appropriate, to respond to the comments of others. In this way the main actor can learn to evaluate the effectiveness of his or her skill performance in light of others' viewpoints.

In all aspects of feedback, group leaders must maintain the behavioral focus of Skillstreaming. Leader comments must point to the presence or absence of specific, concrete behaviors and not take the form of general evaluative comments or generalizations. Feedback, of course, may be positive or negative in content. Positive feedback should always be given first; otherwise the student may be concentrating on the negative comment and not hear other feedback. Negative feedback should be constructive in nature, offering suggestions for what might improve skill enactment. Group leaders will very likely need to model constructive comments before allowing students to give this type of feedback to a peer. Whenever possible, youngsters failing to follow the behavioral steps in the role-play should be given the opportunity to repeat the same behavioral steps after receiving corrective, constructive criticism. At times, as a further feedback procedure, we have audiotaped or videotaped entire role-plays. Giving students the opportunity to observe themselves on tape can be an effective aid, enabling them to reflect on their own verbal and nonverbal behavior.

Because a primary goal of Skillstreaming is skill flexibility, role-play enactment that departs somewhat from the behavioral steps may not be "wrong." That is, a different approach to the skill may actually work in some situations. Group leaders should stress that they are trying to teach effective alternatives and that learning the behavioral steps as presented will increase the number of behavioral choices group members have.

STEP 8: ASSIGN SKILL HOMEWORK

Following each successful role-play, students are instructed to try in their own real-life settings the behaviors practiced during the session. It is useful to begin with relatively simple homework assignments (e.g., situations that occur in the school environment, situations without a high level of stress) and, as mastery is achieved, work up to more complex and demanding assignments. This provides the teacher with an opportunity to reinforce each approximation toward proficiency. The student should not be expected to perform the skill perfectly when first using it in real-life contexts. Reinforcement should be given as the student's performance becomes closer to the ideal. Successful experiences when beginning to use the skill in the real world (homework assignments) and rewards received for doing so are critical in encouraging the student to attempt further skill use.

Homework assignments begin with the teacher and student together deciding when, how, and with whom the student will use the skill and progress to the stage where the student independently records the skills he or she has used. One of three stages of homework can be assigned, depending upon the student's level of skill mastery. It is best to begin with Homework Level 1 for each skill and gradually progress to a more independent level.

Homework Level 1

When using Homework Report 1 (Figure 2), the student thinks of a situation (either at home, at school, or with peers) in which he or she feels the need to practice the skill. It is especially useful if the student selects the same situation he or she has role-played; having prior practice will likely increase the student's comfort level in trying the skill in real-life. On the homework report, the student or the teacher lists the student's name and the date the assignment is made, along with the skill name and its behavioral steps. Together, teacher and student decide on and enter the name of the person with whom the skill will be tried and the time the student will make the attempt (e.g., during science class, on the playground, at home after school). After using the skill, the student writes down what happened, then evaluates his or her skill use by circling one of the faces on the report (☺ = I did great! ☺ = I did okay, but could have done better; or ☹ = I had trouble following the steps) and gives a reason for this self-evaluation (e.g., I used all of the steps, or I forgot a step). It is important to convey to students that this evaluation pertains to how well they performed the skill steps, rather than how well the skill actually worked.

Homework Level 2

The student who has nearly achieved mastery of a particular skill (i.e., who knows the steps well and shows success with the assignments on Homework Report 1) is ready to attempt self-recording or monitoring skill use independently. Following a Skillstreaming session, the student is given Homework Report 2 (see Figure 3). Then, throughout the course of the day or week, the student lists the times of skill practice and completes the self-evaluation portion of the homework report according to the same criteria used in earlier homework assignments. He or she hands in the completed report periodically, at the group leader's request. After writing comments, giving verbal praise, or providing other reinforcement, the group leader returns the form to the student.

Homework Level 3

In this final stage of structured homework, more than one skill is listed on a 3 × 5–inch index card. The student then tallies each

Figure 2 Homework Report 1

Name: _____ Date: _____

SKILL: _____

STEPS:

With whom will I try this? _____

When?_____

What happened? _____

_____

_____

How did I do?

Why did I circle this?_____

_____

Figure 3   Homework Report 2

Name: _____ Date: _____

SKILL: _____

STEPS:

When did I practice?   How did I do?

skill practice throughout the school or week in school, home, or with peers. This method of self-recording gives the older student an inconspicuous way to chart skills used outside the group.

Using the Homework Reports

The first part of each Skillstreaming session is devoted to presenting and discussing the homework reports. When students have made an effort to complete their homework reports, teachers should provide social reinforcement. Failure to do homework should be met with the teachers' disappointment and followed by reteaching. It cannot be stressed too strongly that without these or similar attempts to maximize generalization, the value of the entire teaching session is in jeopardy.

The majority of elementary school children will be able to progress through all stages of homework. If, however, particular students (those in the lower elementary grades or students with disabilities, for example) are unsuccessful with the more independent levels of homework (Levels 2 and 3), these may be simplified or eliminated. For example, instead of requesting that a second grader complete a Level 3 self-recording assignment, the child may be asked to inform the teacher immediately after he or she has used a skill in the school setting. The teacher may then place a sticker or a star on a chart to record the student's skill performance.

Group Self-Report Chart

Group self-recording is a valuable additional component of the homework process, used successfully by some schools. In this method, the teacher uses the Group Self-Report Chart (see Figure 4) and asks each child to make a tally mark (or place a sticker or a star) next to each skill he or she practiced that day. Initially, time should be allowed for this reporting, most often the last 10 minutes or so of the school day. As time permits, several students might be asked to describe the specific situations in which they used a skill or skills. Again, teachers should praise these self-reports. As class members become used to this self-reporting method, students may be allowed to record their skill use on the chart independently. If students do record their own skill use, it is important for the teacher to comment on the self-reporting, thus providing reinforcement. Although the

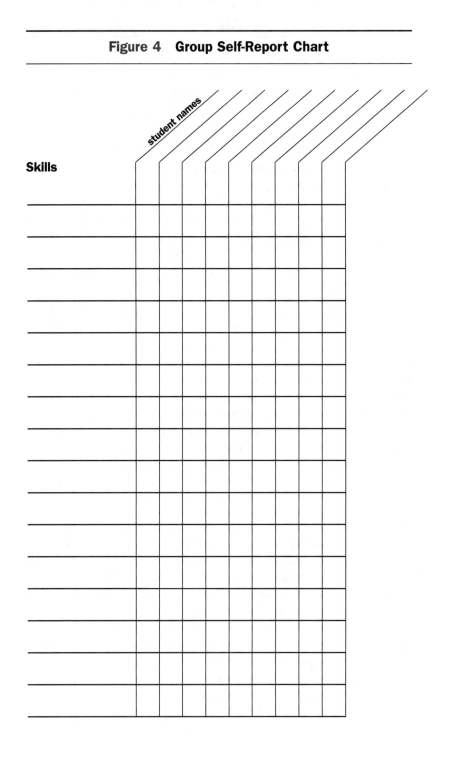

Figure 4 Group Self-Report Chart

Skills

primary purpose of this chart is to encourage the continued use of skills taught in earlier Skillstreaming sessions, the chart also provides a record of the skills students are continuing to practice. If students do not report using specific skills, teachers will know which areas need review or reteaching.

Skill Contracts, Self-Recording Forms, and Awards

Skill Contracts like the one shown in Figure 5 can help students follow through with skill practice, as can Self-Recording Forms (see Figure 6). Skill Awards like the example given in Figure 7 can likewise motivate continued skill use. The Program Forms book supplements this text by including a variety of different skill contracts, self-recording forms, and awards (see Appendix C for a complete description). Suggestions for using such materials to enhance skill generalization are given in chapter 10.

STEP 9: SELECT NEXT ROLE-PLAYER

The next student is selected to serve as main actor, and the sequence just described is repeated until all members of the Skillstreaming group are reliably demonstrating in-group and out-of-group proficiency in using the skill.

Figure 5 Sample Skill Contract

I will practice _Staying Out of Fights_

Lakeesha
Student

If I do, then _I'll earn an extra recess_

for the class

Mr. Grant
Teacher

Date _April 3_

To be reevaluated
on or before

April 10
Date

Figure 6   Sample Self-Recording Form

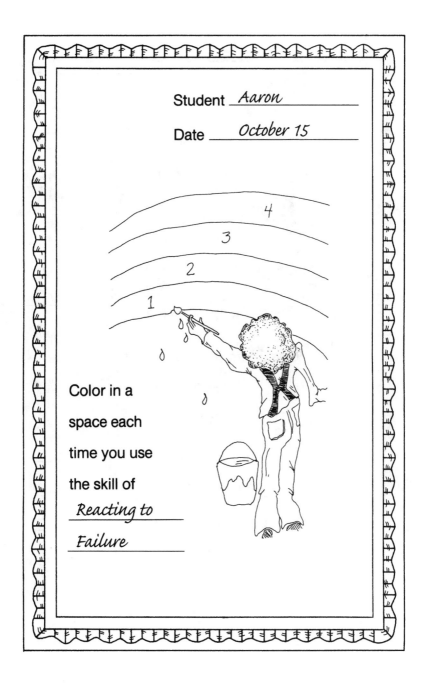

Student _Aaron_

Date _October 15_

4

3

2

1

Color in a
space each
time you use
the skill of
Reacting to
Failure

Figure 7 Sample Skill Award

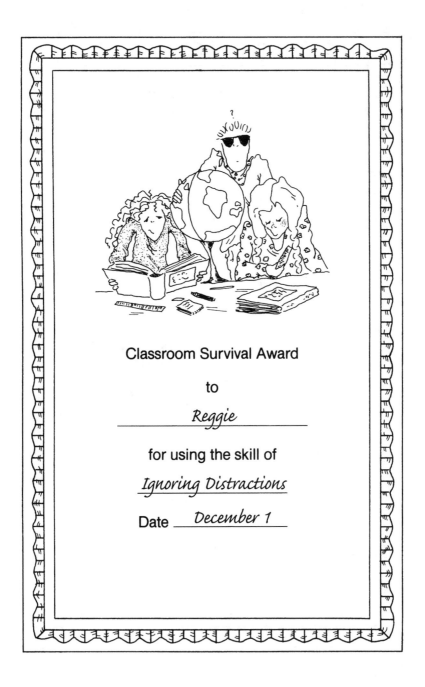

Classroom Survival Award

to

Reggie

for using the skill of

Ignoring Distractions

Date *December 1*

CHAPTER 6
A Sample Skillstreaming Session

This chapter presents an edited transcript of a Skillstreaming group session with students in a fourth-grade regular education classroom. The group consists of two leaders and 10 students. This transcript depicts the leaders introducing students to what will happen in the group (as explained in chapter 4) and follows the Skillstreaming teaching procedures discussed in chapter 5. The skill used for instruction is Responding to Teasing (Skill 38).

Teacher: I want to welcome you to the Skillstreaming group. I've talked with each of you individually, so I know you have some idea of what we will be learning in this group. Let's review what the goal of this group is. All of us, at certain times, have difficulty getting along with others. So we will be learning "people skills," ways we can get along better with others—our friends, parents, and teachers, too. In this group, you'll need to let me know the skills you think you need and want to learn. First, let's talk about skills. What are examples of skills that people learn?

Mario: Riding a bike.

Lakeesha: Playing basketball.

Hannah: Roller-blading.

Darwin: Keeping your temper.

Joel: Playing the guitar.

Teacher: Those are all very good examples of skills. Darwin's skill is also a good example of a people skill. There are many others, like how to make a complaint if something happens that you don't think is fair, how to handle being teased by someone, or how to handle being left out of an activity with your friends. But whether it's people skills, or sports skills, or music skills, all skills are learned the same way. Let's take Lakeesha's example of basketball. Let's say that Mr. Staton here has never played basketball, but he would like to learn. What's the first thing that has to happen? Let's say he wanted to learn the skill of shooting a lay-up.

Amanda: He would need to watch somebody shooting a lay-up.

Tanner: He would need a coach to tell him what to do.

Teacher: You're both right. The coach is the expert, and Mr. Staton needs to watch someone doing a good job shooting the ball. So the coach would need to show him how. After the coach shows him, what would he need to do next?

Brenda: Well, then he would do it.

Teacher: Exactly. After the coach shows Mr. Staton how to shoot a lay-up, he needs to try it. But what if he has trouble and can't get the ball in the basket? What does the coach do then?

Joel: Mr. Staton needs help . . . to know how to do better.

Teacher: Yes, Joel. The coach needs to tell Mr. Staton what he did that was right and what he needs to do better. When an expert or coach tells someone what's good about his or her skill and what needs work, that's called *feedback*. So the coach gives Mr. Staton feedback on how well he did the lay-up. Now, is Mr. Staton ready to go out and play with the team?

Joel: He'd better shoot a lot more first!

Teacher: I agree. He would need to practice the skill first. So, that's how you learn the skill of shooting a lay-up. First, someone who knows how to do the skill well, like a coach, *shows* you. Then you *try* it. You get *feedback* on how you did, and then you *practice* what you've learned. These steps—show, try, feedback, practice. It's how you learn any skill. Shooting a lay-up, playing the guitar, riding a bike, roller-blading, or controlling your temper.

Step 1: Define the Skill

Teacher: Today we're going to learn a really important people skill. It's one that most of you told me that you would like to learn. It's called Responding to Teasing. What do you think that means?

Amanda: When somebody calls you a name and you get mad at them.

Hannah: Like when my brother tells me my mom grounded me, but he lied.

Mario: This kid across the street calls me stupid all the time when I walk by his house.

Teacher: Those are all good examples of teasing. And as Amanda said, it's hard not to get mad when you are teased. But if you get mad and fight with the person who is teasing you, then you are the one who ends up getting in trouble. Is that right?

Tanner: Yeah. I get in trouble a lot for fighting.

Teacher: Okay, then. Let's talk about how you can respond to teasing without getting into a fight and getting in trouble. Here are the steps that make up the skill of Responding to Teasing. Joel, will you give everyone one of these cards, please.

(Joel hands out the Skill Cards while the teacher shows the steps on the easel pad in front of the group.)

Thank you, Joel. I'd like to read you the steps to the skill of Responding to Teasing:

1. Stop and count to five.

2. Think about your choices:

      a. Ignore the teasing.

      b. Say how you feel.

      c. Give a reason for the person to stop.

3. Act out your best choice.

Step 2: Model the Skill

Teacher: These three steps, in this order, make up a good way to respond to teasing. Mr. Staton and I are going to model the skill for you— we're going to show you how to follow these steps. Just like the basketball coach, we'll show you the skill being done well. Try to pick out the steps as we model the skill. Later, you'll all have a chance to go through these same steps. Here's the situation. There's a student in my class who keeps saying mean things to me when we're outside at recess. I'll just be talking with my friends, and he'll come up to me and say things like my mother is ugly and make faces. What should I do first? What's the first step *(pointing to the step)*.

Darwin: You stop and count to five.

Teacher: Good. Now the second thing I do?

Brenda: Think about your choices.

Teacher: Yes. And I could ignore the teasing. I could say how I feel in a friendly way. Or I could give a reason to stop. And the third step?

Mario: You act out your best choice.

Teacher: Thank you. Now, I'm out here at recess, standing here talking with my friends. The kid who usually teases me is walking up to me—he's probably going to tap me on the shoulder to get my attention.

Mr. Staton: Hey, you, did you know that your mother is one ugly dude?

Teacher: Okay, I need to calm down, so I'll stop and count to five. 1 . . . 2 . . . 3 . . . 4 . . . 5. Now I need to think of my choices. I could ignore him, but I've ignored him before. I could say how I feel. Or I could give him a reason to stop. I need to act out my best choice. I think it's best to keep ignoring him. Eventually he'll stop when he knows he can't get me mad.

(Turns away and acts as if she's listening to friends talk.)

Did I follow all of the skill steps? Did I follow the first step? Did I stop and count to five? *(Students respond.)* Did I think of my choices? *(Students respond.)* And what choice did I make?

Joel: You ignored him and kept talking with your friends.

Teacher: Yes, that's the choice I made. And how do you think I did on this skill?

(Students respond with positive comments.)

Yes, I think I did a good job, too.

Step 3: Establish Student Skill Need

Teacher: That's our modeling of the skill. Let's think of some times in your real lives when you are teased and it's difficult for you to deal with this teasing. I'll write your names on the easel pad and your situation beside it so that we can remember the situations. Who can think of a time when you're being teased and it bothers you?

Lakeesha: When I go roller-blading, my brother always laughs at me. He says I'm really bad at it.

Mario: That kid across the street, he's always sayin' somethin'.

Hannah: There's this guy who keeps calling me. My mom calls me to the phone, and then the guy hangs up!

(The list continues as each student identifies a situation for skill use.)

Step 4: Select Role-Player

Teacher: You all came up with really good examples of situations when you are teased that are difficult for you. Who would like to try the skill first? Who would like to role-play? Okay, Mario. That kid across the street seems to really be bothering you.

Step 5: Set Up the Role-Play

Teacher: All right, Mario. Could you tell us a little more about the situation so that we can help you feel that you are in that situation?

Mario: Well, I go that way to get to Josie's house. I walk by after school. He's there, kinda by this big tree, in his yard, you know. I go by. I don't see him, but then he kinda comes out and starts talkin' to me.

Teacher: What kinds of things does he say, Mario?

Mario: He says he's got proof that I'm into bad stuff and he's gonna tell. I know there's nothin' he's got to tell anybody.

Teacher: All right. I think that gives us a pretty good idea of the situation. Is there anything else?

Mario: *(Shakes his head no.)*

Teacher: Mario, who in the group reminds you most of the boy who is teasing you?

Mario: I guess Tanner.

Teacher: Tanner, would you be willing to help us out with this? Will you be the co-actor in the role-play? We'll help you with what to say to Mario. Will you come on up in front? Tanner will be the kid across the street, and when Mario walks by, Tanner will step out and say that he knows Mario is into bad stuff and he's going to tell. Is that right, Mario?

Mario: Yeah. He says he'll tell the cops.

Teacher: Okay, then. Before we get started with the actual role-play, I'm going to ask each of you to watch the role-play carefully. I want you each to watch for a certain step. Darwin and Brenda, will you watch to see if Mario does the first step, see if he stops and counts to five? Lakeesha and Amanda, will you watch to see if he thinks of his choices? And Hannah and Joel, will you watch to see if he acts out his choice? When the role-play is over, I need you to tell Mario and the rest of us just what he did and how well you think he did. Mario, you will need to talk aloud what you are thinking so that we know you are following the steps. Are you all ready?

Step 6: Conduct the Role-Play

Tanner: Hey, you. I'm talkin' to you. I tell you, I'm gonna tell on you, man. I'm gonna tell the cops you're into some pretty bad stuff.

Teacher: Good, Tanner. Now Mario, look at the skill steps. Go ahead and talk out loud what you are thinking. What's the first thing you need to do?

Mario: Stop and count to five.

Teacher: Okay. Go ahead.

Mario: 1...2...3...4...5.

(The teacher points to the second skill step on the easel pad.)

Mario: I think of my choices.

Teacher: You could ignore. Say how you feel or give a reason to stop.

Mario: I'll ignore. It doesn't matter anyway, 'cause there's nothin' he's gonna tell.

(Mario walks away.)

Teacher: Okay, Mario!

Step 7: Provide Performance Feedback

Teacher: Let's get some feedback for Mario. Tanner, if you were the real kid across the street, how do you think you'd react to what Mario did?

Tanner: I'd feel pretty stupid. I couldn't get him goin'. Maybe I'd do it to somebody different.

Teacher: So you felt Mario did a good job ignoring, that you wouldn't keep teasing him?

Tanner: Yeah. He did a good job.

Teacher: Thank you, Tanner. Thanks for helping out, too. Who watched to see if Mario followed the first step? Did he stop and count to five?

Observers: Yeah.

Teacher: For the second step, did Mario think of his choices?

Observers: Yeah.

Teacher: How do you know that he was thinking of his choices?

Amanda: He talked it out loud. I heard him say it.

Teacher: Good watching, Amanda. What choice did he decide on?

Lakeesha: To ignore.

Teacher: Did he follow the third step? Did he act out his best choice?

Observers: Yeah. He ignored.

Teacher: How did he ignore?

Hannah: He walked away from the kid.

Teacher: Nice job, everyone! Mario, how did it feel? Was it easy to do?

Mario: It wasn't easy. But okay, it was okay.

Teacher: Was there something you would like to have done better?

Mario: No. But sometimes it gets to me.

Step 8: Assign Skill Homework

Teacher: You certainly did a nice job in this role-play. Are you saying that in real life, when the kid across the street really says those things to you, that you might have some trouble?

Mario: Maybe. I can try it.

Teacher: Good for you, Mario. Let's plan out your homework assignment together when the group is finished.

Step 9: Select Next Role-Player

Teacher: Who would like to role-play the skill next?

CHAPTER 7
Skills for Elementary Students

Thus far, we have discussed how Skillstreaming groups are planned, organized, and conducted. This chapter presents the Skillstreaming curriculum—the specific skills designed to enhance the prosocial skill development of the elementary school child. The 60 skills, divided into five skill groups, are presented here along with their behavioral steps, notes for discussion, suggested situations for modeling displays, and comments to enhance the effectiveness of instruction. Table 2 shows the skills and their groupings.

This skill curriculum is not all-inclusive. As students express concerns and difficulties, and as teachers observe problems, new skills can and should be developed. Consider the situation, for example, in which a group of students are continually disruptive when moving into the group setting. The perceptive teacher, recognizing that transitions are difficult for this particular group of students, develops a new skill, entitled "Coming to Group." Skill steps might include the following:

1. Put materials away.

2. Look up to show the teacher you are ready.

3. Wait quietly until your name is called.

In a different situation, a student may have difficulty when not picked to be first for a game. Steps for a new skill, entitled "Dealing with Not Being First" might be as follows:

1. Take a deep breath.

2. Say, "Everybody can't be first. Maybe I'll be first next time."

Table 2
The Skillstreaming Curriculum for Elementary Students

Group I: Classroom Survival Skills

1. Listening
2. Asking for Help
3. Saying Thank You
4. Bringing Materials to Class
5. Following Instructions
6. Completing Assignments
7. Contributing to Discussions
8. Offering Help to an Adult
9. Asking a Question
10. Ignoring Distractions
11. Making Corrections
12. Deciding on Something to Do
13. Setting a Goal

Group II: Friendship-Making Skills

14. Introducing Yourself
15. Beginning a Conversation
16. Ending a Conversation
17. Joining In
18. Playing a Game
19. Asking a Favor
20. Offering Help to a Classmate
21. Giving a Compliment
22. Accepting a Compliment
23. Suggesting an Activity
24. Sharing
25. Apologizing

Group III: Skills for Dealing with Feelings

26. Knowing Your Feelings
27. Expressing Your Feelings
28. Recognizing Another's Feelings

29. Showing Understanding of Another's Feelings
30. Expressing Concern for Another
31. Dealing with Your Anger
32. Dealing with Another's Anger
33. Expressing Affection
34. Dealing with Fear
35. Rewarding Yourself

Group IV: Skill Alternatives to Aggression
36. Using Self-Control
37. Asking Permission
38. Responding to Teasing
39. Avoiding Trouble
40. Staying Out of Fights
41. Problem Solving
42. Accepting Consequences
43. Dealing with an Accusation
44. Negotiating

Group V: Skills for Dealing with Stress
45. Dealing with Boredom
46. Deciding What Caused a Problem
47. Making a Complaint
48. Answering a Complaint
49. Dealing with Losing
50. Being a Good Sport
51. Dealing with Being Left Out
52. Dealing with Embarrassment
53. Reacting to Failure
54. Accepting No
55. Saying No
56. Relaxing
57. Dealing with Group Pressure
58. Dealing with Wanting Something That Isn't Yours
59. Making a Decision
60. Being Honest

In some circumstances it may be appropriate to retain a given skill but alter one or more of its behavioral steps. Steps may be simplified as the skills and needs of the students suggest. For example, a child who repeatedly becomes out of control when losing may learn only two of the behavioral steps constituting Skill 49, Dealing with Losing:

1. Say, "Everybody can't win."

2. Say, "Maybe I'll win next time."

Group leaders should use their experience and judgment in adjusting the content of these skills.

Skill 1: Listening

STEPS

NOTES FOR DISCUSSION

1. Look at the person who is talking.

Point out to students that sometimes others may think someone isn't listening, even though he/she has heard what was said.

2. Sit quietly.

These steps are to show someone that you really are listening.

3. Think about what is being said.

Tell students to sit (or stand) facing the person and remember not to laugh, fidget, play with something, and so on.

4. Say yes or nod your head.

Discuss with students that both verbal and nonverbal messages are important to show that a person is listening.

5. Ask a question about the topic to find out more.

Discuss relevant questions (i.e., ones that do not change the topic).

SUGGESTED SITUATIONS

School: Your teacher explains an assignment.

Home: Your parents are talking with you about how to do a chore.

Peer group: Another student tells about a story he/she read or what he/she did over the weekend.

COMMENTS

This is an excellent skill with which to begin your Skillstreaming group. Once students learn the skill of Listening, it can be incorporated into group or classroom rules. You can emphasize the behaviors that show someone is listening by modeling listening behaviors yourself.

Skill 2: Asking for Help

STEPS	NOTES FOR DISCUSSION
1. Ask yourself, "Can I do this alone?"	Students should be sure to read directions and try the task on their own (at least one problem or question) before going on to the next skill step.
2. If not, raise your hand.	Discuss that this is appropriate in class, not at home or with friends.
3. Wait. Say to yourself, "I know I can wait without talking."	Instruct the students to say this to themselves until the desired help is given.
4. Ask for help in a friendly way.	Discuss what constitutes a friendly manner (tone of voice, facial expression, content).

SUGGESTED SITUATIONS

School: You want help with an assignment, or you don't understand what you are supposed to do.

Home: You can't find your skates and ask your mom to help look for them.

Peer group: You want your friend to teach you a new dance that everyone is doing.

COMMENTS

It is very important to discuss body language throughout Skillstreaming. When first introducing terminology such as "in a friendly way," discussing and modeling friendly behaviors and nonverbal communicators are essential. Nonverbal behaviors include voice tone and volume, body posture, gestures, and facial expression.

Skill 3: Saying Thank You

STEPS	**NOTES FOR DISCUSSION**
1. Decide if you want to thank someone.	Discuss the purpose of saying thank you (i.e., it is a way of telling someone that you appreciate what he/she did). Emphasize sincerity. You thank someone when you want to or feel it is deserved—for example, for a favor, help given, or a compliment.
2. Choose a good time and place.	Discuss how to choose a good time (when the person is not busy with something or someone else).
3. Thank the person in a friendly way.	Let students know that it is okay to tell why you are thanking the person (that they really needed the help or that something the person did made them feel good).

SUGGESTED SITUATIONS

School: Someone helps you with your schoolwork.

Home: Your parents help you with your chores or homework, or they let you do something you have asked to do.

Peer group: Someone lends you a pencil or compliments you.

COMMENTS

Students may begin to use this skill frequently, and somewhat mechanically, following initial instruction. This is natural and should not be interpreted as insincere use of the skill. It may be useful to discuss and practice different ways of saying thank you (e.g., "It made me feel good when you . . ." or doing something nice for the person).

Skill 4: Bringing Materials to Class

STEPS

1. Ask yourself, "What materials do I need for this class?"

2. Gather the materials together.

3. Ask yourself, "Do I have everything I need?"

4. Recheck your materials and pack them up.

NOTES FOR DISCUSSION

Students may have to make a list of needed items, such as pencil, crayons, paper, or notebook.

Students should remember not to take things that aren't needed— for example, toys.

SUGGESTED SITUATIONS

School: You are going to a special area class (art, music, physical education) or attending a class in another classroom.

Home: You are going to attend an outside club event or activity, or you are getting your backpack ready for school in the morning.

Peer group: You will be staying overnight at a friend's house.

COMMENTS

This skill helps students become more organized. For some students, at first you may need to provide a written list of what is needed. Also, providing a notebook or folder where the materials can be kept may help students perform this skill.

Posting a list of skill steps near the classroom door may help students remember to check for the materials they will need before they leave the classroom.

Skill 5: Following Instructions

STEPS	**NOTES FOR DISCUSSION**
1. Listen carefully to the instructions.	Remind students that they should think about what is being said.
2. Ask questions about anything you don't understand.	Teach students Asking for Help (Skill 2) or Asking a Question (Skill 9).
3. Repeat the instructions to the person (or to yourself).	This step is necessary to be sure students clearly understand the directions.
4. Follow the instructions.	

SUGGESTED SITUATIONS

School: A teacher explains an assignment.

Home: Your mom or dad gives you instructions on how to cook or how to do a chore.

Peer group: A friend gives you directions for getting to his/her house.

COMMENTS

For students to perform this skill successfully, they must be able to complete the task required of them independently. The skill will only frustrate them if they follow the steps and then find that the task is too difficult.

Skill 6: Completing Assignments

STEPS	**NOTES FOR DISCUSSION**
1. Ask yourself, "Is my work finished?"	Have students practice reviewing each item to be certain that all questions are answered.
2. Look over each question to be sure.	Remind students to fill in the missing answers if items aren't complete.
3. When you are sure your work is finished, hand it in.	Specific classroom rules for handing in completed work can be included in this step.
4. Say to yourself, "Good for me! I finished it!"	Discuss ways of rewarding yourself.

SUGGESTED SITUATIONS

School: Complete academic assignments given by the teacher or activities at a learning center.

Home: Finish a project or activity you started at home (making a model car from a kit or cleaning your room).

Peer group: Complete a project or a chore you promised to do for a friend.

COMMENTS

This skill facilitates organizational ability and is particularly useful for the student with a learning disability or others who have specific difficulties in task completion. Ideally, this skill should be practiced in the setting where the skill is needed. For example, if practice in seatwork completion is needed, the student should practice this skill at his or her desk. Again, it is important for students to be able to complete the task independently.

Rewarding Yourself (Skill 35) is a part of this skill (Step 4). Self-reinforcement may be necessary until the skill can be reinforced by teachers or parents.

Skill 7: Contributing to Discussions

STEPS

1. Decide if you have something you want to say.

2. Ask yourself, "Is this related to the discussion?"

3. Decide exactly what you want to say.

4. Raise your hand.

5. When you are called on, say what you want to say.

NOTES FOR DISCUSSION

Discuss that the comments must be relevant to the discussion. Give examples of relevant comments.

Students may need the additional step of deciding how to say it.

Steps 4 and 5 should be in accordance with your classroom rules. Explain that students should eliminate these steps at home or with friends.

SUGGESTED SITUATIONS

School: Say something in a class discussion when you have something you want to say.

Home: Say something in a family meeting or during dinner.

Peer group: Say something in a discussion with friends after school.

COMMENTS

Discussion should include times this skill is appropriate to use. Students must learn which teacher cues indicate when contributions are and are not welcome. Students will also need to discriminate among the persons with whom the skill is used. For example, contributing to a discussion among friends would be very different from contributing to a discussion in class.

When providing the opportunities for students to practice this skill, choose familiar and interesting topics for discussion.

Skill 8: Offering Help to an Adult

STEPS	**NOTES FOR DISCUSSION**
1. Decide if the adult needs your help.	Discuss how the adult might act if he or she needed help. Discuss different ways of asking—for example, "May I help you do that?"
2. Decide how to ask if you can help.	
3. Ask yourself, "Is this a good time to offer help?"	Remind students to be sure that their work is completed and there isn't something else they are supposed to do. If this is not a good time, they should wait until it is a good time.
4. Ask the adult if you may help.	Discuss the importance of following through with help.

SUGGESTED SITUATIONS

School: The teacher is making a bulletin board or rearranging the classroom.

Home: Your mom or dad is fixing dinner.

COMMENTS

With some students, it is especially important to emphasize Step 1, deciding if the teacher or parent needs the help. A student who frequently requests to help may be attempting to gain attention or avoid academic tasks. In such cases this skill can be useful to teach the student when offering assistance is appropriate.

Skill 9: Asking a Question

STEPS	NOTES FOR DISCUSSION
1. Decide what you need to ask.	Discuss how students can decide whether they really need to ask this question.
2. Decide whom you will ask.	Discuss how to decide whether to ask the teacher, an aide, a classmate, or someone else.
3. Decide what to say.	Stress asking in a friendly way— it is not only what you say but how you say it.
4. Choose a good time.	Discuss how to choose a good time (when the other person isn't busy or talking with someone else).
5. Ask your question.	Teach students Saying Thank You (Skill 3) and encourage them to use it when they receive the answer to their question.

SUGGESTED SITUATIONS

School: Ask the teacher about something you don't understand.

Home: Ask your mom and dad about their work or hobbies.

Peer group: Ask another student how to play a game.

COMMENTS

Discuss the times when it is necessary to ask a question. Encourage students to use this skill only when they have a legitimate question. Discussion should include other ways of finding needed information—for example, consulting a dictionary, encyclopedia, or computer program.

Skill 10: Ignoring Distractions

STEPS	NOTES FOR DISCUSSION
1. Count to five.	Discuss that counting to five will give the student the time to calm down if frustrated and to recall the rest of the skill steps.
2. Say to yourself, "I won't look. I'll keep on working."	Statements should be spoken aloud during modeling and role-playing.
3. Continue to work.	
4. Say to yourself, "Good for me. I did it!"	Discuss ways of rewarding yourself.

SUGGESTED SITUATIONS

School: Another teacher comes into the room to talk with your teacher.

Home: Your brother or sister tries to distract you from your chores or homework.

Peer group: A classmate tries to get your attention in class or to distract you from a game at recess.

COMMENTS

Each time students ignore a distraction, they may make a check mark on an index card or color a space on one of the Self-Recording Forms from the Program Forms book (see the example in Figure 6, p. 75). Self-recording efforts can then be reinforced if needed.

Rewarding Yourself (Skill 35) is a part of this skill (Step 4). Self-reinforcement may be necessary until the skill can be reinforced by teachers or parents.

Skill 11: Making Corrections

STEPS

1. Look at the first correction.

2. Try to answer the question (or do the task) again.

3. If you don't understand the question, ask someone.

4. Write in your new answer.

5. Say to yourself, "Good. That one is done."

6. Go on to the next correction.

NOTES FOR DISCUSSION

Discuss dealing with one correction at a time, rather than looking at them all. This will help lessen frustration and make the task seem less overwhelming.

Teach students Asking for Help (Skill 2).

SUGGESTED SITUATIONS

School: Your teacher gives your math assignment back for you to correct.

Home: You must do a chore over again.

Peer group: You made something for a friend, but it didn't turn out right.

COMMENTS

Redoing tasks or academic assignments can be extremely frustrating for children. Discuss the normal feeling of frustration when tasks must be done again.

If many errors are made on any assignment, it is important to analyze these errors and reteach the necessary skills. This skill is most useful following such a reteaching effort or for assignments that are completed carelessly, not for assignments beyond the student's abilities.

Skill 12: Deciding on Something to Do

STEPS	NOTES FOR DISCUSSION
1. Check to be sure you have finished all of your work.	An assignment sheet to check off work as it is completed will help many students with this first step.
2. Think of the activities you would like to do.	Guide students to generate a list of acceptable activities.
3. Choose one.	Students should be sure the activity chosen will not disrupt classmates who have not yet completed their schoolwork (or brothers or sisters, if the students are at home).
4. Start the activity.	

SUGGESTED SITUATIONS

School: Decide on an activity during free time in the classroom or when you have a few minutes after finishing your work.

Home: Choose something to do after you have finished your homework and chores.

COMMENTS

Encourage students to list both quiet activities (those in which they could engage when other students are still working on their academic assignments) and less quiet activities (those in which they can participate during a free activity period for the entire class). This list, along with the behavioral steps for this skill, can then be displayed in the classroom for easy student reference. Dealing with Boredom (Skill 45) is a similar skill geared for use outside of the academic setting.

Skill 13: Setting a Goal

STEPS	NOTES FOR DISCUSSION
1. Decide on a goal you want to reach.	Discuss choosing a realistic goal (considering content, time frame).
2. Decide on the steps you will need to take to get there.	It may be helpful to list these steps on a bulletin board, include them in a student folder, or write them on a card taped to students' desks.
3. Take the first step.	
4. Take all other steps, one at a time.	Encourage students to mark off each step as it is achieved. (This also gives students practice in organization.)
5. Reward yourself when your goal is reached.	Discuss ways of rewarding yourself.

SUGGESTED SITUATIONS

School: Set and reach an academic, behavioral, or social skills goal.

Home: Clean your room or the garage.

Peer group: Make a new friend.

COMMENTS

Many elementary-age students enjoy setting academic goals (e.g., learning addition facts, reading a given number of books). Setting small goals that can be easily achieved in a relatively short period of time (e.g., reading one book) is more beneficial than setting less attainable goals. Goal setting is also useful for nonacademic areas, such as prosocial skills development. Examples include practicing a given skill a certain number of times or using it at home or with peers.

Rewarding Yourself (Skill 35) is a part of this skill (Step 5). Self-reinforcement may be necessary until the skill can be reinforced by teachers or parents.

Skill 14: Introducing Yourself

STEPS	NOTES FOR DISCUSSION
1. Decide if you want to meet the person.	Discuss why students might want to meet a person: The person looks friendly, is new to the school, and so forth.
2. Decide if it is a good time.	Discuss how to choose a good time: The person is not busy with something or someone else.
3. Walk up to the person.	Watch for appropriate distance.
4. Introduce yourself.	Discuss ways to introduce yourself (say, "Hi, my name is _____").
5. Wait for the person to tell you his/her name. (If he/she doesn't tell you, ask.)	Discuss appropriate ways to ask a person's name.

SUGGESTED SITUATIONS

School: There is a new student in your classroom.

Home: A friend of your parents is visiting your home.

Peer group: A new boy or girl moves into your neighborhood.

COMMENTS

Practicing this skill also helps students know what to do when someone else introduces himself or herself.

A logical next skill to teach is Beginning a Conversation (Skill 15). Students may then practice putting the two skills together in one role-play.

Skill 15: Beginning a Conversation

STEPS	NOTES FOR DISCUSSION
1. Choose the person with whom you want to talk.	Remind students to consider whether their talking is going to bother someone else—for example, someone who is trying to work.
2. Decide what you want to say.	Suggest topics like something students did during the weekend, a hobby, or a favorite sport.
3. Choose a good time and place.	Discuss how to choose a good time: when the other person isn't busy or when the student isn't supposed to be doing something else.
4. Start talking in a friendly way.	Discuss the body language and nonverbal communicators that show a friendly attitude and suggest watching the person to see if he or she seems interested. Stress not talking too long without giving the other person a chance to talk.

SUGGESTED SITUATIONS

School: Tell a classmate about an art project you did.

Home: Tell your parents what happened at school.

Peer group: Tell a friend what you did during the weekend.

COMMENTS

Students should role-play this skill with both adults and peers to determine language and nonverbal signals appropriate for persons in different roles—for example, teachers, parents, friends.

This skill can be taught directly following Skill 14 (Introducing Yourself). Skill 16 (Ending a Conversation) may follow this skill as needed.

Skill 16: Ending a Conversation

STEPS	NOTES FOR DISCUSSION
1. Decide if you need to end the conversation.	Students should decide why they need to end the conversation.
2. Decide what to say.	Tell students to ask themselves, What is the reason? Give examples: "I have to go now, but I'll talk with you later"; "I have to do my work."
3. Wait until the other person stops talking.	Discuss the importance of not interrupting and of thinking whether or not this is a good time to end the conversation.
4. Say it in a friendly way.	Remind students of the body language and nonverbal communicators that show a friendly attitude.

SUGGESTED SITUATIONS

School: Recess or free time in the classroom is over.

Home: You are talking with your parents, and a friend is waiting for you.

Peer group: Your mother tells you to come inside or to stop talking on the telephone.

COMMENTS

Learning how to end a conversation may help students stay out of trouble—for example, be on time to class, be home on time, not disrupt the class. Discussing such situations helps students understand the purpose of this skill.

After practicing Skills 14, 15, and 16 separately, give students practice in using these skills successively.

Skill 17: Joining In

STEPS

1. Decide if you want to join in.

2. Decide what to say.

3. Choose a good time.

4. Say it in a friendly way.

NOTES FOR DISCUSSION

Students should decide whether they really want to participate.

Suggest possible things to say: "Can one more person play?"; "Can I play, too?"

Discuss how to choose a good time: during a break in the activity or before the activity has begun.

Discuss the body language and nonverbal communicators that show a friendly attitude.

SUGGESTED SITUATIONS

School: Ask to join in a group game at recess.

Home: Ask to join a game with parents or brothers and sisters.

Peer group: Ask to join an activity in the neighborhood.

COMMENTS

This skill is very useful for students who have difficulty deciding what to do in social play situations. The skill gives them the opportunity to join peers in an ongoing activity.

Encourage students to try out this skill first with peers or adults they feel will accept their overtures.

Skill 18: Playing a Game

STEPS	NOTES FOR DISCUSSION
1. Be sure you know the rules.	Discuss what to do if students don't know the rules (ask someone to explain them).
2. Decide who starts the game.	Discuss methods of deciding who begins the game—for example, roll the dice or offer to let the other person go first.
3. Remember to wait your turn.	Suggest that students repeat silently to themselves, "I can wait until it's my turn."
4. When the game is over, say something nice to the other person.	Discuss and practice appropriate ways of handling winning (tell the person he/she played a good game) and losing (congratulate the other person).

SUGGESTED SITUATIONS

School: Play a board game with a classmate or a group game at recess.

Home: Play a game with your parents, brother, or sister.

Peer group: Play a group game with friends in the neighborhood.

COMMENTS

It may be helpful to coach students in how to play a variety of board games and group games played at recess or in the neighborhood so they will feel confident playing. Posting lists of familiar classroom and recess games may also encourage them to play acceptable games.

Good skills to teach following this one are Dealing with Losing (Skill 49) and Being a Good Sport (Skill 50).

Skill 19: Asking a Favor

STEPS

NOTES FOR DISCUSSION

1. Decide if you want or need to ask a favor.

Discuss how to evaluate whether or not the skill is necessary. If it isn't necessary, the student should stop at this step.

2. Plan what you want to say.

Suggest things to say: "Could you help me with this?"; "I can't see if I sit over there. Would you mind making room for me?"; "I'm having trouble getting my work done. Would you please not talk?" Giving reasons may increase the chance that the person will help.

3. Ask the favor in a friendly way.

Discuss the body language and nonverbal communicators that show a friendly attitude.

4. Remember to thank the person.

Teach the skill Saying Thank You (Skill 3).

SUGGESTED SITUATIONS

School: You would like to join a group and someone must move over to make room for you, or someone is making a noise that interferes with your work.

Home: The television is too loud for you to do your homework.

Peer group: A friend is going to a movie and you'd like to go along, or you would like to borrow something of a friend's.

COMMENTS

The definition of a "favor," as used in this skill, is anything a student needs help with, varying from problems with other people to school and other informational problems. Students may need guidance in deciding on the individual they should ask in different situations.

Teach students to use Accepting No (Skill 54) if the person they ask can't help.

Skill 20: Offering Help to a Classmate

STEPS	NOTES FOR DISCUSSION
1. Decide if the person needs or wants help.	Discuss how to determine if another student needs help: How does he look? What is she doing or saying?
2. Think of how you can help.	Observing the person can help the student decide whether to offer physical help or verbal guidance.
3. Decide what to say.	Discuss a variety of ways to offer help.
4. Choose a good time.	Remind students to be sure that they are not supposed to be doing something else.
5. Ask in a friendly way.	Discuss the body language and nonverbal communicators that show a friendly attitude.

SUGGESTED SITUATIONS

School: A classmate drops his/her books or is having difficulty with an assignment or a project.

Peer group: A friend is having difficulty completing a chore or project.

COMMENTS

Discuss how people feel when helping someone or being helped. Emphasize not feeling hurt or offended if the person says no or asks someone else for help. If the person wants help, the student should follow through.

Skill 21: Giving a Compliment

STEPS

NOTES FOR DISCUSSION

1. Decide what you want to tell the other person.

Discuss the types of things students may want to compliment someone on: appearance, behavior, an achievement.

2. Decide what to say.

Give examples of compliments.

3. Choose a good time and place.

Discuss how to choose: when the student and the other person aren't busy and perhaps when a lot of other people aren't around.

4. Give the compliment in a friendly way.

Emphasize giving the compliment in a sincere manner. Discuss the body language and facial expressions associated with sincerity.

SUGGESTED SITUATIONS

School: A classmate has done really well on an assignment or has worked very hard on a project.

Home: Your mom or dad makes a good dinner.

Peer group: You like what someone is wearing.

COMMENTS

When students first begin using this skill, it may appear mechanical and insincere. Once they have had sufficient practice, their skill use will be more natural.

Discuss the way both the giver and recipient of the compliment might feel (e.g., embarrassed, pleased).

Skill 22: Accepting a Compliment

STEPS	NOTES FOR DISCUSSION
1. Decide if someone has given you a compliment.	Discuss ways students can tell whether someone has given them a compliment—for instance, how the person looked and sounded when making the comment.
2. Say thank you.	If necessary, teach students Saying Thank You (Skill 3).
3. Say something else if you want to.	Give an example: "Yes, I tried hard." Encourage students to give credit to someone else who may have helped also: "Joey helped, too."

SUGGESTED SITUATIONS

School: The teacher compliments you on work well done.

Home: Your parents compliment you on how well you did your chores.

Peer group: A friend compliments you on the way you look.

COMMENTS

This skill is important because children are frequently embarrassed when given a compliment. Children with low self-esteem may also interpret compliments as negative and become defensive, as if they don't believe what the person is saying. When receiving a compliment is presented as a skill to be learned, such children are frequently more accepting.

Skill 23: Suggesting an Activity

STEPS	NOTES FOR DISCUSSION
1. Decide on an activity you want to suggest.	Discuss a variety of appropriate activities in various settings (playground, during free time in the classroom, etc.).
2. Decide what to say.	Give an example: "Would you like to _____?"
3. Choose a good time.	Discuss how to choose a good time: when others aren't involved with another activity.
4. Say it in a friendly way.	Discuss the body language and nonverbal communicators that show a friendly attitude.

SUGGESTED SITUATIONS

School: Suggest a group game to be played at recess.

Home: Suggest an evening out with your parents—for example, going to a movie.

Peer group: Suggest a game or an activity to a friend.

COMMENTS

It may be helpful to coach students in how to play a variety of games. The activity must be appropriate to the setting (e.g., the classroom versus the playground or neighborhood) and to the number of students involved (group versus individual) so certain individuals are not left out.

Discuss what to say if someone says no to a suggested activity: Students could ask, "What would you like to do?" or invite someone else.

Skill 24: Sharing

STEPS

1. Decide if you want to share something.

2. Decide on the person with whom you want to share.

3. Choose a good time and place.

4. Offer to share in a friendly and sincere way.

NOTES FOR DISCUSSION

Talk about how the other person might feel if the student does or doesn't share.

If the student can share only with one person, point out that others around may feel left out.

Discuss how to choose a good time: when another person needs or would enjoy using something of the student's.

Discuss appropriate body language, voice tone, and facial expression.

SUGGESTED SITUATIONS

School: Offer to share your materials (crayons, pencils, paper) with a classmate.

Home: Offer to share a treat with a friend, brother, or sister.

Peer group: Offer to share a game or toys with a friend.

COMMENTS

Teachers should create opportunities in the classroom for students to share work materials, information, and other items. Doing so will not only increase the chances that students will master this skill but also enhance a sense of community within the instructional setting.

Skill 25: Apologizing

STEPS	NOTES FOR DISCUSSION
1. Decide if you need to apologize.	Discuss how we sometimes do things for which we are later sorry. Apologizing is something we can do to let other people know we are sorry. It also often makes us feel better.
2. Think about your choices: a. Say it out loud to the person. b. Write the person a note.	Discuss when it is best to use verbal or written ways to apologize.
3. Choose a good time and place.	Discuss how to choose a good time (i.e., soon after the problem). The student may want to be alone with the person for a verbal apology.
4. Carry out your best choice in a sincere way.	Discuss the body language, voice tone, and facial expressions associated with sincerity.

SUGGESTED SITUATIONS

School: You are late for a class.

Home: You accidentally break something.

Peer group: You said something cruel because you were angry, or you had planned to do something with a friend but you had to go somewhere with your parents instead.

COMMENTS

It may be beneficial to discuss how difficult it might be to apologize. Discussion of how a person might feel before apologizing (e.g., anxious, afraid) as well as how a person might feel receiving the apology (e.g., relieved, less upset, less angry) may make students more willing to use this skill.

Skill 26: Knowing Your Feelings

STEPS

1. Think of how your body feels.

2. Decide what you could call the feeling.

3. Say to yourself, "I feel _____."

NOTES FOR DISCUSSION

Discuss the cues students' bodies may give—for example, blushing, tight muscles, or queasy stomach.

Discuss feelings such as frustration, fear, and embarrassment and their associated physical reactions.

SUGGESTED SITUATIONS

School: You are frustrated with a difficult assignment, or you are embarrassed about a grade.

Home: You are disappointed because your parents forgot to do something they had promised.

Peer group: You are disappointed because a friend promised to go to a movie with you but now can't go.

COMMENTS

Additional activities specific to identifying and labeling feelings will likely be needed. Such activities might include generating a list of feeling words to be displayed in the classroom, finding pictures in magazines of persons expressing those feelings, and discussing different situations and how people might feel in them.

Skill 27: Expressing Your Feelings

STEPS

NOTES FOR DISCUSSION

1. Stop and think of how your body feels.

   Discuss how students can identify feelings by paying attention to body cues.

2. Decide what to call the feeling.

   Display a list of feeling words. Discuss what events may have contributed to the feeling.

3. Think about your choices:

   a. Say to the person, "I feel _____."

   Consider when and where the student may be able to talk about the feeling.

   b. Walk away for now.

   Suggest this alternative as a way to calm down.

   c. Get involved in an activity.

   Discuss alternative activities.

4. Act out your best choice.

   If the student is still having an intense feeling—such as anger—after following these steps, he or she should wait until the feeling isn't so intense before acting on the best choice. If one choice doesn't work, the student should try another one.

SUGGESTED SITUATIONS

School: You want to answer in class, but you are afraid your answer will be wrong.

Home: Your parents won't allow you to watch a movie on TV that many of your friends are going to watch.

Peer group: Someone calls you a name or ignores you.

COMMENTS

You can model this skill throughout the year by expressing your own feelings to the class in an appropriate manner.

Skill 28: Recognizing Another's Feelings

STEPS	NOTES FOR DISCUSSION
1. Watch the person.	Discuss paying attention to the way the person looks (posture, facial expression), what the person does and says, and how the person says it.
2. Name what you think the person is feeling.	Display a list of feeling words for reference.
3. Decide whether or not to ask the person if he/she is feeling that way.	If the person seems very angry or upset, it may be best to wait until the person has calmed down.
4. Ask in a concerned way.	Discuss desirable ways to ask: facial expression, voice tone, and so on that show concern.

SUGGESTED SITUATIONS

School: After assignments are handed back, a student puts his head on the desk.

Home: Your dad or mom is slamming doors and muttering to himself/herself.

Peer group: A friend wasn't chosen for a game, or a classmate is watching a game instead of asking to join in.

COMMENTS

Include role-plays targeted toward both adults and peers. This skill should precede Showing Understanding of Another's Feelings (Skill 29).

118

Skill 29: Showing Understanding of Another's Feelings

STEPS

1. Name what you think the person is feeling.

2. Think about your choices:

   a. Ask the person if he/she feels this way.

   b. Ask the person if you can help.

   c. Leave the person alone.

3. Act out your best choice.

NOTES FOR DISCUSSION

Discuss how the student might feel if he or she were in that situation.

Discuss how the student should base the choice on how well he or she knows the other person and on the cues the person is giving.

If the person seems very upset or angry, it may be best to leave the person alone and then make another choice when the person is less upset.

If one choice doesn't work, the student should try another one.

SUGGESTED SITUATIONS

School: A classmate is crying because someone teased her.

Home: Your brother or sister won't talk to anyone after having a talk with a parent.

Peer group: A friend throws a board game after losing.

COMMENTS

Teach Recognizing Another's Feelings (Skill 28) prior to this skill. It will then be beneficial to have students practice using the two skills together.

Skill 30: Expressing Concern for Another

STEPS	NOTES FOR DISCUSSION
1. Decide if someone is having a problem.	Discuss ways to determine if someone is having a problem: What is the person doing? How does he or she look? Discuss the meaning of empathy and its importance in using this skill.
2. Think about your choices:	
a. Say, "Can I help you?"	Emphasize sincerity.
b. Do something nice for the person.	Suggest sharing something with the person or asking the person to join an activity.
3. Act out your best choice.	If one choice doesn't work, the student should try another one.

SUGGESTED SITUATIONS

School: A classmate is struggling with a difficult assignment.

Home: A parent is having difficulty with a chore.

Peer group: A friend has hurt himself/herself.

COMMENTS

Students may need instruction in the skill of Recognizing Another's Feelings (Skill 28) before using this one.

Skill 31: Dealing with Your Anger

STEPS	**NOTES FOR DISCUSSION**
1. Stop and count to 10.	Discuss the importance of allowing yourself time to cool off and think.
2. Think about your choices:	
a. Tell the person in words why you are angry.	Discuss how to tell the person in a way that won't get that person angry, too.
b. Walk away for now.	Students may need to ask the teacher if they can leave the classroom and run an errand or take a break.
c. Do a relaxation exercise.	Teach students Relaxing (Skill 56).
3. Act out your best choice.	If one choice doesn't work, the student should try another one.

SUGGESTED SITUATIONS

School: You don't think the teacher has been fair to you, you are angry at yourself for forgetting your homework, or you are having a day where everything seems to go wrong.

Home: Your parents won't let you have a friend over or won't let you leave the house.

Peer group: A friend talks about you behind your back.

COMMENTS

For a child who directs anger inward, additional choices may be necessary. Such choices might include "Write about how you feel" or "Decide what you can change to keep this from happening again." Skills such as Problem Solving (Skill 41) may also help children who direct anger toward themselves.

Skill 32: Dealing with Another's Anger

STEPS	**NOTES FOR DISCUSSION**
1. Listen to what the person has to say.	Discuss the importance of not interrupting or becoming defensive. If needed, students may say to themselves, "I can stay calm."
2. Think about your choices:	Discuss the possible consequences of each choice.
a. Keep listening.	
b. Ask why the person is angry.	
c. Give the person an idea to fix the problem.	
d. Walk away for now.	If the student begins to feel angry, too, he/she should walk away until feeling calmer. This action will not fix the problem, but will keep the student out of trouble. Later, the student can make a different choice.
3. Act out your best choice.	

SUGGESTED SITUATIONS

School: The teacher is angry at you for not doing well on a test.

Home: Your parents are angry because you didn't clean your room.

Peer group: Another student is angry at you because you didn't choose him to play a game.

COMMENTS

Students need to know that it may be okay to delay discussing the situation when a peer is angry. If an adult is angry, delaying may only create more problems for the student. Stress the importance of adjusting one's behavior according to the role of the person with whom the problem exists.

Skill 33: Expressing Affection

STEPS	**NOTES FOR DISCUSSION**
1. Decide if you have good feelings about the other person.	Discuss these feelings.
2. Decide if you think the other person would like to know you feel this way.	Discuss possible consequences of telling the person—for example, the person may become embarrassed or feel good.
3. Decide what to say.	
4. Choose a good time and place.	Discuss how to choose a good time: Being alone may make it easier to express affection.
5. Tell the person in a friendly way.	Discuss the body language and nonverbal communicators that show a friendly attitude.

SUGGESTED SITUATIONS

School: Thank a teacher for something he/she has done.

Home: Tell your parents that you love them.

Peer group: Tell friends that you like them and want to continue being friends.

COMMENTS

This skill is difficult for many adults to carry out, and therefore students may have had the skill modeled for them quite infrequently. It is important for teachers to provide this type of modeling.

Students may need to discuss how to express affection to persons in different roles: teachers, adult friends, peers. The way in which students display this affection will differ from one person to another.

Skill 34: Dealing with Fear

STEPS	NOTES FOR DISCUSSION
1. Decide if you are feeling afraid.	Discuss bodily cues of fear (e.g., sweaty hands, nausea, pounding heart).
2. Decide what you are afraid of.	Discuss real versus imagined threats. The student may need to check this out with another person.
3. Think about your choices:	
a. Talk to someone about it.	Discuss choosing someone reassuring (teacher or parent).
b. Do a relaxation exercise.	Teach students Relaxing (Skill 56).
c. Try what you are afraid of doing anyway.	Discuss the feelings of accomplishment that can come from doing something difficult.
4. Act out your best choice.	Discuss possible consequences of each choice. If one choice doesn't work, the student should try another one.

SUGGESTED SITUATIONS

School: You are afraid to take a test, or you are afraid to go out to recess because someone said he/she would beat you up.

Home: You are home alone at night.

Peer group: Someone in the neighborhood challenges you to do something dangerous, or a peer threatens to say you did something that will get you into trouble.

COMMENTS

Encourage students to evaluate realistic versus unrealistic fears. When fears are realistic, talking to someone about them would be the best choice. Students may also need to problem solve ways to deal with realistic fears (see Skill 41: Problem Solving).

Skill 35: Rewarding Yourself

STEPS	**NOTES FOR DISCUSSION**
1. Decide if you did a good job.	Discuss ways to evaluate your own performance.
2. Say to yourself, "I did a good job."	
3. Decide how else you will reward yourself.	Give examples of other self-rewards—take a break, do something you enjoy. Discuss.
4. Do it.	Point out that students should reward themselves as soon after their performance as possible.

SUGGESTED SITUATIONS

School: You completed all of your assignments.

Home: You cleaned your room, you finished a difficult homework assignment, or you helped a neighbor who needed your help.

Peer group: You helped a friend do his/her chores.

COMMENTS

Emphasize that people don't always have to depend on others to reward their actions.

Skill 36: Using Self-Control

STEPS	NOTES FOR DISCUSSION
1. Stop and count to 10.	Discuss the importance of allowing yourself time to cool off and think.
2. Think of how your body feels.	Discuss how bodily cues may signal losing control (e.g., your hands become sweaty, you feel hot or weak).
3. Think about your choices:	
a. Walk away for now.	Students should ask to leave the area for a few minutes, if necessary, until they regain control.
b. Do a relaxation exercise.	Teach students Relaxing (Skill 56).
c. Write about how you feel.	
d. Talk to someone about it.	Discuss choosing someone who would be likely to understand.
4. Act out your best choice.	If one choice doesn't work, the student should try another one.

SUGGESTED SITUATIONS

School: You are behind in your schoolwork and must stay after school to finish.

Home: Your parents won't let you go to a friend's house.

Peer group: A friend borrows something of yours and breaks it.

COMMENTS

Students should use this skill when they are too angry or upset to identify what they are feeling and need to gain control before dealing with the problem. Tell students that sometimes when people are very angry or upset, it is okay to delay dealing with the problem.

Skill 37: Asking Permission

STEPS	**NOTES FOR DISCUSSION**
1. Decide what you want to do.	Remind students to be sure this activity won't be harmful to themselves or another person.
2. Decide whom to ask.	This will usually be a parent or teacher.
3. Plan what to say.	
4. Choose the right time and place.	Discuss how to choose a good time: when the person isn't involved with another activity. The student may want to ask privately.
5. Ask in a friendly way.	Discuss the body language and nonverbal communicators that show a friendly attitude.

SUGGESTED SITUATIONS

School: Ask the teacher for a special privilege.

Home: Ask your parents if you may go to a friend's house or if you may participate in a school activity.

Peer group: Ask a friend if you may borrow something.

COMMENTS

We hope students' skill use will be successful most of the time. With this skill, however, many times permission may not be granted (e.g., parents can't afford it, the friend's house is too far away, or it's too late at night). It is therefore important to teach Rewarding Yourself (Skill 35) and/or Accepting No (Skill 54) immediately after this skill.

Skill 38: Responding to Teasing

STEPS	NOTES FOR DISCUSSION
1. Stop and count to five.	Discuss how using this skill can prevent students from losing control.
2. Think about your choices:	
a. Ignore the teasing.	Point out that ignoring for a short time doesn't always work; the student may need to ignore for a long time. Discuss ways to ignore (e.g., walk away).
b. Say how you feel.	Give an example of an "I feel" statement: "I feel _____ when _____."
c. Give a reason for the person to stop.	Suggest possible reasons: The student will talk to an adult about the problem or knows the teaser just wants to get someone upset. Emphasize giving the reason in a friendly tone of voice.
3. Act out your best choice.	If one choice doesn't work, the student should try another one.

SUGGESTED SITUATIONS

School: Someone is poking you or making faces at you in class.

Home: Your brother or sister laughs at you.

Peer group: Someone calls you a name or teases you about the way you look or the clothes you wear.

COMMENTS

Students may need practice in making appropriate, nonthreatening "I feel" statements.

Skill 39: Avoiding Trouble

STEPS

NOTES FOR DISCUSSION

1. Stop and think about what the consequences of an action might be.

With students, create a list of the possible consequences of particular actions.

2. Decide if you want to stay out of trouble.

Discuss how to decide if it is important to avoid these consequences.

3. Decide what to tell the other person.

4. Tell the person.

Discuss how to say no in a friendly but firm way.

SUGGESTED SITUATIONS

School: Another student wants you to help him/her cheat on a test.

Home: Your brother or sister wants you to take money from your parents.

Peer group: A friend wants you to tease another friend.

COMMENTS

It is important to teach students to anticipate the consequences of their actions. They may still choose to accept the consequences.

Skill 40: Staying Out of Fights

STEPS	NOTES FOR DISCUSSION
1. Stop and count to 10.	Discuss how this can help the student to calm down.
2. Decide what the problem is.	Discuss the consequences of fighting and whether fighting can solve a problem.
3. Think about your choices:	
a. Walk away for now.	Students should ask to leave the area for a few minutes, if needed.
b. Talk to the person in a friendly way.	Discuss how to "read" the behavior of the other person (i.e., is he/she calm enough to talk with) and evaluate one's own degree of calmness and readiness to talk about the problem. Discuss ways to state the problem inoffensively.
c. Ask someone for help in solving the problem.	Discuss who can be the most help: teacher, parent, or friend.
4. Act out your best choice.	If one choice doesn't work, the student should try another one.

SUGGESTED SITUATIONS

School: Someone says that you did poorly on your schoolwork.

Home: Your brother or sister tells your parents that you did something wrong.

Peer group: Someone doesn't play fair in a game or calls you a name.

COMMENTS

This skill may not be supported at home or "on the streets." Nevertheless, students need to be taught the importance of handling conflict in a peaceful way.

Skill 41: Problem Solving

STEPS	NOTES FOR DISCUSSION
1. Stop and say, "I have to calm down."	Discuss ways to calm down—for example, take three deep breaths, count to 10.
2. Decide what the problem is.	Stress the importance of reflecting on the reason the student is upset.
3. Think about different ways to solve the problem.	List and discuss a variety of alternatives and the consequences of each.
4. Choose one way.	Discuss how to weigh alternatives to pick the best choice.
5. Do it.	
6. Ask yourself, "How did this work?"	If one alternative doesn't work, the student should try another.

SUGGESTED SITUATIONS

School: You don't understand an assignment, or you forgot your lunch money.

Home: You broke a window at your house.

Peer group: You lost something you borrowed from a friend.

COMMENTS

When a problem arises in the classroom, teachers may lead the class in discussing alternative ways to deal with the problem and the possible consequences of each alternative. Students can then choose the best alternative. Using this problem-solving technique when classroom problems arise will promote students' ability to use this skill and teach them when to use it.

This is a good prerequisite skill for Accepting Consequences (Skill 42).

Skill 42: Accepting Consequences

STEPS	NOTES FOR DISCUSSION
1. Decide if you were wrong.	Discuss that it is okay to be wrong: Everyone makes mistakes, and it's not the end of the world.
2. If you were wrong, say to yourself, "I have to accept consequences."	Discuss the possible consequences of particular actions.
3. Say to the person, "Yes, I did _____ (describe what you did)."	Discuss how to describe the behavior without making excuses.
4. Say something else:	
a. How will you avoid this the next time?	Point out that this should be said in a friendly manner.
b. Apologize.	Emphasize sincerity.

SUGGESTED SITUATIONS

School: You forgot your homework assignment.

Home: Your parents tell you that you can't go to a movie because you didn't do your chores.

Peer group: You lost the money your friend asked you to keep for him/her.

COMMENTS

Because this skill involves some problem solving, it is best to teach Problem Solving (Skill 41) first.

Skill 43: Dealing with an Accusation

STEPS	**NOTES FOR DISCUSSION**
1. Stop and say, "I have to calm down."	Discuss ways to calm down— for example, take three deep breaths, count to 10.
2. Think about what the person has accused you of.	
3. Ask yourself, "Is this person right?"	If the person is correct, the student can use Accepting Consequences (Skill 42).
4. Think about your choices:	
a. Explain, in a friendly way, that you didn't do it.	Discuss the body language and nonverbal communicators that show a friendly attitude.
b. Apologize.	Emphasize sincerity.
c. Offer to make up for what happened.	Discuss how to make amends: earning the money to pay for a lost or broken item, giving the person something of your own, or giving back a stolen item.
5. Act out your best choice.	If one choice doesn't work, the student should try another one, but it should be an honest choice.

SUGGESTED SITUATIONS

School: A teacher has accused you of cheating.

Home: Your parents accuse you of breaking something.

Peer group: A friend accuses you of taking something that isn't yours.

COMMENTS

It is helpful to reinforce that everyone makes mistakes at times but that it is important to learn from these mistakes and not continue to make the same ones. Such a discussion may help students admit a mistake when accused.

133

Skill 44: Negotiating

STEPS	**NOTES FOR DISCUSSION**
1. Decide if you and the other person disagree.	Discuss signs of disagreement: Is the student getting angry? Is the other person getting angry?
2. Tell how you feel about the problem.	Stress saying this in a friendly way so the other person does not become more angry.
3. Ask the person how he/she feels about the problem.	
4. Listen to the answer.	Discuss the importance of not interrupting. Remind students to use the skill of Listening (Skill 1).
5. Suggest or ask for a compromise.	Discuss how to decide on something that will satisfy both the student and the other person.

SUGGESTED SITUATIONS

School: Your teacher gives you work you feel you can't do.

Home: Your parents want you to baby-sit, but you need to do your homework.

Peer group: Your friend wants to play one game, but you want to play another.

COMMENTS

This skill may be difficult for children younger than age 8. It is more appropriate for students in third through sixth grades.

Skill 45: Dealing with Boredom

STEPS	NOTES FOR DISCUSSION
1. Decide if you are feeling bored.	Discuss how to recognize signs of boredom (e.g., you don't know what to do or feel jittery inside).
2. Think of things you like to do.	Encourage students to generate and discuss personal lists of acceptable activities.
3. Decide on one thing to do.	
4. Do it.	
5. Say to yourself, "Good for me. I chose something to do."	Discuss ways of rewarding yourself.

SUGGESTED SITUATIONS

School: There are no playground games that interest you.

Home: It's a Saturday, and no one is around.

Peer group: You and your friends can't think of anything to do.

COMMENTS

This skill, similar to Deciding on Something to Do (Skill 12), is geared for use outside the academic learning setting. It is helpful for students to generate lists of acceptable activities they may engage in on the playground, at home, and in the neighborhood. These lists can be included in an individual prosocial skills folder.

Rewarding Yourself (Skill 35) is a part of this skill (Step 5). Self-reinforcement may be necessary until the skill can be reinforced by teachers or parents.

Skill 46: Deciding What Caused a Problem

STEPS	**NOTES FOR DISCUSSION**
1. Decide what the problem is.	Discuss how students can recognize a problem: by the way they feel inside, by what someone said to them, or by how someone acted toward them.
2. Think about what may have caused the problem.	Discuss how to evaluate possible causes of a problem: one's own behavior, someone else's behavior, or no one's fault.
3. Decide what most likely caused the problem.	Discuss how to determine the most likely cause.
4. Check it out.	Encourage students to ask someone, either the other person or an impartial judge.

SUGGESTED SITUATIONS

School: The teacher seems angry with you.

Home: Your parents have an argument, and you think it is about you.

Peer group: You feel angry at a friend but don't know why, or you feel that someone doesn't like you.

COMMENTS

This skill is intended to help students distinguish between the problems that they are responsible for and those due to factors outside their control. This is a good skill for students who have difficulty accepting that their own behavior may have caused or contributed to a problem.

Skill 47: Making a Complaint

STEPS	NOTES FOR DISCUSSION
1. Decide what the problem is.	Discuss how students can recognize a problem: by the way they feel inside, by what someone said to them, or by how someone acted toward them.
2. Decide whom to tell.	Talking about the problem with the other person is often the best way to begin finding a solution.
3. Choose a good time and place.	Discuss how to choose a good time: when the person isn't involved with something else or when the person is alone.
4. Tell the person your problem in a friendly way.	Tell students to wait until they are no longer angry or upset before talking about the problem. Discuss the body language and nonverbal communicators that show a friendly attitude.

SUGGESTED SITUATIONS

School: The teacher gives you an assignment that you know how to do, but it seems far too long.

Home: You feel your parents have been unfair because your brother is gone and you have to do his chores, too.

Peer group: A friend usually chooses what the two of you will do.

COMMENTS

Discuss the importance of stating the facts rather than blaming someone else. Students may also need instruction in distinguishing fact from opinion.

Skill 48: Answering a Complaint

STEPS	NOTES FOR DISCUSSION
1. Listen to the complaint.	Discuss proper body language while listening (ways to show that you aren't defensive).
2. Ask about anything you don't understand.	Discuss the body language and nonverbal communicators that show a friendly attitude.
3. Decide if the complaint is justified.	
4. Think about your choices:	
a. Apologize.	Emphasize sincerity.
b. Explain your behavior.	Even if a student did not intend to cause a problem, his/her behavior still might have caused difficulty. Sometimes giving a reason for acting a certain way will help others understand better. Discuss how to explain that an unjustified complaint is incorrect.
c. Suggest what to do now.	
d. Correct a mistake.	
5. Act out your best choice.	If one choice doesn't work, the student should try another one.

SUGGESTED SITUATIONS

School: The teacher complains that you are too loud or thinks you were the one who was making noises in class.

Home: Your parents complain that you haven't helped at home.

Peer group: A friend complains that you were teasing him/her.

COMMENTS

Discuss the difference between making excuses and explaining your behavior.

Skill 49: Dealing with Losing

STEPS	NOTES FOR DISCUSSION
1. Say to yourself, "Everybody can't win. It's okay that I didn't win this time."	Memorizing this statement will help the student control his/her impulses.
2. Think about your choices:	These choices will help the student get involved in another activity and not dwell on losing.
a. Ask to help someone.	Offer help to a teacher, your parents, or a friend.
b. Do an activity you like.	Students should generate and discuss personal lists of acceptable activities.
c. Do a relaxation exercise.	Teach the skill Relaxing (Skill 56).
3. Act out your best choice.	If one choice doesn't work, the student should try another one.

SUGGESTED SITUATIONS

School: You lose a contest or a raffle.

Home: You lose at a game with your brother or sister.

Peer group: Your team loses at basketball (or some other game).

COMMENTS

This is a good prerequisite skill for Being a Good Sport (Skill 50).

Skill 50: Being a Good Sport

STEPS	**NOTES FOR DISCUSSION**
1. Decide how you and the other person played the game.	Discuss evaluating your own and an opponent's performance (e.g., level of skill or effort).
2. Think of what you can honestly tell the other person:	Emphasize sincerity. Discuss the body language and nonverbal communicators that show a friendly, sincere attitude.
a. "Congratulations."	The student may also want to shake the person's hand.
b. "You played a good game."	
c. "You're getting a lot better at this game."	This is a way of encouraging another person. Students may want to comment on one thing the other person did particularly well.
3. Act out your best choice.	
4. Help the other person put equipment or materials away.	

SUGGESTED SITUATIONS

School: Your team loses at a group game during recess, or your team wins.

Home: You lose at a game with your brother or sister, or you win.

Peer group: You lose at a game with a friend, or you win.

COMMENTS

Students should learn the skill Dealing with Losing (Skill 49) before learning the present skill.

Skill 51: Dealing with Being Left Out

STEPS	NOTES FOR DISCUSSION
1. Decide what has happened to cause you to feel left out.	Discuss possible reasons a student may be ignored by peers.
2. Think about your choices:	
a. Ask to join in.	Teach the skill Joining In (Skill 17).
b. Choose someone else with whom to play.	Choose someone who may also be feeling left out or someone who is not with the group.
c. Do an activity you enjoy.	Students should generate and discuss personal lists of acceptable activities.
3. Act out your best choice.	If one choice doesn't work, the student should try another one.

SUGGESTED SITUATIONS

School: You are left out of a group game at recess.

Home: Your brother or sister is leaving you out of an activity with his or her friends.

Peer group: A group of friends are going to a movie or a birthday party, but you weren't invited.

COMMENTS

It is important to discuss the types of feelings that might result from being left out (feeling angry, hurt, or frustrated). Emphasize that it is better to deal with being left out by using the skill steps than to continue to feel angry or hurt.

Skill 52: Dealing with Embarrassment

STEPS	NOTES FOR DISCUSSION
1. Decide what happened to cause you to feel embarrassed.	Discuss how students can recognize signs of embarrassment (e.g., your face is flushed).
2. Think of what you can do to feel less embarrassed:	Discuss the possible consequences of each choice.
a. Ignore it.	
b. Decide what to do next time.	
c. Say to yourself, "It's over. People will forget it."	
3. Act out your best choice.	If one choice doesn't work, the student should try another one.

SUGGESTED SITUATIONS

School: You give the wrong answer to a question in class.

Home: You drop and break something belonging to your parents.

Peer group: You fall down on the playground or make some mistake when playing a game.

COMMENTS

It is important to let students know that everyone feels embarrassed at some time. Discussing when students (and group leaders!) are most likely to be embarrassed may lessen the intensity of real-life embarrassment.

Prior to teaching this skill, it is helpful to review Knowing Your Feelings (Skill 26).

Skill 53: Reacting to Failure

STEPS	NOTES FOR DISCUSSION
1. Decide if you have failed.	Discuss the difference between failing and not doing as well as hoped.
2. Think about why you failed.	Discuss reasons for failure: You didn't try as hard as you could have or weren't ready; it was a matter of chance.
3. Think about what you could do next time.	Suggest practicing more, trying harder, or asking for help.
4. Make your plan to do this.	This plan may be in written form, such as a contingency contract.

SUGGESTED SITUATIONS

School: You failed a test.

Home: You failed to complete your chores, so you couldn't do what you had planned.

Peer group: You failed to get someone to join in the activity you wanted to do.

COMMENTS

It is useful to discuss with students that human beings are not perfect and that everyone fails at something sometimes. Rather than dwell on the failure, it is more useful to think of ways to do better the next time.

Skill 54: Accepting No

STEPS	NOTES FOR DISCUSSION
1. Decide why you were told no.	Discuss the possible reasons for being told no in a particular situation.
2. Think about your choices:	Discuss the possible consequences of each choice.
a. Do something else.	Students should generate and discuss personal lists of acceptable activities.
b. Say how you feel in a friendly way.	Practice "I feel" statements with students. Discuss the body language and nonverbal communicators that show a friendly attitude.
c. Write about how you feel.	
3. Act out your best choice.	If one choice doesn't work, the student should try another one.

SUGGESTED SITUATIONS

School: The teacher says that you can't do an activity.

Home: Your parents say that you can't stay up late.

Peer group: A friend tells you he/she won't come over to your house.

COMMENTS

Writing about how you feel may not be appropriate for the child who does not have adequate writing skills or who is particularly frustrated with the writing process. Ask these students to generate other choices.

Skill 55: Saying No

STEPS	NOTES FOR DISCUSSION
1. Decide whether or not you want to do what is being asked.	Discuss when and with whom saying no is appropriate.
2. Think about why you don't want to do this.	Discuss reasons for saying no: You may get into trouble, or you may have something else you want to do.
3. Tell the person no in a friendly way.	Students should practice saying no in a friendly but firm manner, paying attention to body language and nonverbal communicators.
4. Give your reason.	Giving a reason may help the other person understand better.

SUGGESTED SITUATIONS

School: A friend wants you to skip school.

Home: Your brother or sister wants you to play a game, but you want to watch your favorite TV program.

Peer group: A friend wants you to play when you have work to do, or he/she wants you to come over after school, but you'd rather play basketball.

COMMENTS

Students need practice role-playing this skill with a variety of individuals assuming a variety of different roles. It should be emphasized that saying no to an adult who asks you to do something wrong or uncomfortable is very different from saying no to a parent who asks you to pick up your room or to a teacher who asks you to stop talking in class.

Skill 56: Relaxing

STEPS	**NOTES FOR DISCUSSION**
1. Decide if you need to relax.	Discuss how to recognize bodily cues of tension (e.g., feeling tense, jittery, or queasy).
2. Take three slow, deep breaths.	Teach students to breathe in through their noses and out through their mouths.
3. Tighten one part of your body, count to three, and relax.	Instruct students about which parts of their bodies to tighten and then relax (jaw, shoulders, hands, stomach, legs, feet).
4. Continue this for each part of your body.	Students will need to practice Step 3 before they can do this independently.
5. Ask yourself how you feel.	Discuss how students feel physically before and after tightening muscles.

SUGGESTED SITUATIONS

School: You feel nervous before a test.

Home: Your grandparents are coming, and you're excited.

Peer group: You are angry or upset with a friend, but you don't know why.

COMMENTS

Students may need a great deal of training in relaxation before they will be able to use this skill effectively. One good resource is *Relaxation: A Comprehensive Model for Adults, Children, and Children with Special Needs,* by Joseph R. Cautela and June Groden (Research Press, 1978).

Skill 57: Dealing with Group Pressure

STEPS	**NOTES FOR DISCUSSION**
1. Listen to what others want you to do.	Discuss possible reasons why the group may want someone to participate in particular actions.
2. Think about what might happen.	Discuss possible consequences of particular actions: Someone may be hurt, or you may get into trouble.
3. Decide what you want to do.	Discuss how difficult it is to resist pressure from a group of friends.
4. If you decide not to go along with the group, say to them, "No, I can't because _____ (give the reason)."	Discuss how giving a reason for not going along may help the group to think about what they want to do.
5. Suggest something else to do.	Help students generate and discuss a list of acceptable group activities.

SUGGESTED SITUATIONS

Peer group: The group is teasing someone or planning on taking something that belongs to someone else, and they want you to go along with them.

COMMENTS

Students need to be aware that this is a difficult, but necessary, skill to master. This skill should be role-played in a variety of situations and reviewed periodically throughout Skillstreaming instruction.

Skill 58: Dealing with Wanting Something That Isn't Yours

STEPS	NOTES FOR DISCUSSION
1. Say to yourself, "I want this, but I can't just take it."	Discuss how hard it may be to want something and not take it.
2. Say, "It belongs to _____."	Discuss how the other person might feel if the item were gone.
3. Think about your choices:	Discuss other alternatives, depending on the situation.
a. I could ask to borrow it.	
b. I could earn the money to buy it.	
c. I could ask the person to trade.	
d. I could do something else I like to do.	Help students generate and discuss personal lists of acceptable activities.
4. Act out your best choice.	If temptation continues after the student tries one choice, he/she should try another one.
5. Say, "Good for me. I didn't take it!"	Discuss ways of rewarding yourself.

SUGGESTED SITUATIONS

School: You see a notebook you'd really like to have.

Home: Your parents left money on the table.

Peer group: A friend has a game you would like to have, or you see candy in the pocket of a coat hanging in a locker.

COMMENTS

Self-reinforcement (Step 5) will be critical for many children. Because observers may not know that the student actually wanted to take something but succeeded in exerting self-control, outside reinforcement is unlikely.

Skill 59: Making a Decision

STEPS	NOTES FOR DISCUSSION
1. Think about the problem.	Discuss how students may want two conflicting things.
2. Decide on your choices.	Have students make a list of alternatives.
3. Think of the possible consequences of each choice.	Have students make a list of the consequences for each alternative, then discuss.
4. Make the best choice.	Discuss how to evaluate competing alternatives to make the best choice.

SUGGESTED SITUATIONS

School: Decide what group to play with.

Home: Decide how to spend your money.

Peer group: Decide whether to go to a movie or stay home and study for a test.

COMMENTS

Instruction should include generating alternatives and anticipating both short-term and long-term consequences.

Skill 60: Being Honest

STEPS	NOTES FOR DISCUSSION
1. Decide what might happen if you are honest.	Discuss impoliteness versus honesty: Students should not be honest just to hurt someone, such as saying that they don't like a person's clothes. Also discuss how others may respect or trust the student more in the future if he/she is honest now.
2. Decide what might happen if you aren't honest.	Discuss how punishing consequences are usually less severe if a person is honest in the beginning.
3. Think of how to say what you have to say.	Give examples: "I'm sorry, but I did _____"; "Yes, I did it, but I didn't mean to."
4. Say it.	Emphasize sincerity.
5. Say to yourself, "Good for me. I told the truth."	Discuss ways of rewarding yourself.

SUGGESTED SITUATIONS

School: You tore up your homework assignment or lost your reading book.

Home: You broke a window, or you were throwing a basketball in the house and broke a picture hanging on the wall.

Peer group: You borrowed someone's bike without asking permission.

COMMENTS

Rewarding Yourself (Skill 35) is a part of this skill (Step 5). Self-reinforcement may be necessary until the skill can be reinforced by teachers or parents.

CHAPTER 8
Refining Skill Use

Although Skillstreaming is a psychoeducational intervention derived from social learning theory, cognitive-behavioral interventions such as problem-solving, anger control, and verbal mediation are embedded in its instructional format. This chapter examines the role of these approaches in Skillstreaming, as well as that of skill combinations, skill shifting, social perceptions and behavioral flexibility, nonverbal behaviors, empathy, and supportive modeling.

COGNITIVE-BEHAVIORAL STRATEGIES

Kendall and Braswell (1985) define cognitive-behavioral approaches, as distinguished from other types of interventions, as follows:

> At the present juncture, the cognitive-behavioral approach does appear to be chiefly distinguished from the behavioral perspective by the emphasis on cognitive activities, such as beliefs, expectancies, self-statements, and problem solving; yet concern with overt behavior, both in treatment and as an indication of outcome (whether manifested in the use of behavioral contingencies or in explicit skills training), differentiates it from cognitive and insight-oriented approaches. (p. 3)

We believe incorporating elements of the cognitive-behavioral approach will promote the self-control needed by many students to change their typical manner of reacting, recall skill steps, and generalize the skills they learn. Knowledge of the following areas will guide group leaders in aspects to include in Skillstreaming instruction.

Problem Solving

Adolescents and younger children may, as Ladd and Mize (1983) point out, be deficient in such problem-solving competencies as "(a) knowledge of appropriate goals for social interaction, (b) knowledge of

151

appropriate strategies for reaching a social goal, and (c) knowledge of the contexts in which specific strategies may be appropriately applied" (p. 130). A major goal of providing instruction in problem solving, as stated by Cartledge and Feng (1996), is "to teach people how to think through and resolve interpersonal conflicts using a four-step process: (a) identifying and defining the problem, (b) generating a variety of solutions, (c) identifying potential consequences, and (d) implementing and evaluating a solution" (p. 62). Problem Solving (Skill 41) presents the specific steps for using this process in a social context. However, the cognitive aspect suggests that the general skill of problem solving might be useful in conjunction with other skills. Therefore, problem solving may be applied broadly as well as taught as one skill of many.

Anger/Impulse Control

Many students may know the desired and expected behavior and may, in fact, be likely to behave in this manner in many situations. However, when angry, anxious, or otherwise upset, they are unable to see beyond the emotion-producing event. Before many students will be able to recall the steps of a specific skill, they must use strategies to stop themselves from reacting in a perhaps well-established pattern of aggression or other unproductive behavior.

In contrast to the direct facilitation of prosocial behavior in Skill-streaming, Anger Control Training, developed by Feindler (Feindler, 1979; Feindler & Ecton, 1986), facilitates such skill behavior indirectly, by teaching ways to inhibit anger and loss of self-control. In this method, youngsters are taught how to respond to provocations to anger by (a) identifying their external and internal anger triggers; (b) identifying their own physiological/kinesthetic cues signifying anger; (c) using anger reducers to lower arousal via deep breathing, counting backwards, imagining a peaceful scene, or contemplating the long-term consequences of anger-associated behavior; (d) using reminders, or self-statements that are in opposition to triggers; and (e) self-evaluating, or judging how adequately anger control worked and rewarding oneself when it has worked well.

The majority of Skillstreaming skills that are used under stressful conditions include an anger or impulse control strategy—counting to five or taking three deep breaths, for example. Emphasizing these methods, taking additional time to teach them and reinforce their use, or using the Anger Control Training process just described will increase the likelihood of success in students' real-life skill use.

Verbal Mediation

Much of the early work on children's use of language to regulate their own behaviors was done by the Russian psychologist Luria (1961). This pattern of development is described by Little and Kendall (1979):

> The process of development of verbal control of behavior
> . . . seems to follow a standard developmental sequence.
> First, the initiation of motor behavior comes under control
> of adult verbal cues, and then the inhibition of responses
> is controlled by the speech of adults. Self-control emerges
> as the child learns to respond to his own verbal cues,
> first to initiate responses and then to inhibit them. (p. 101)

Verbal mediation, or saying aloud what would normally be said to oneself silently, is a valuable and necessary part of both modeling and role-playing. Saying the steps aloud as the models or role-players enact the behaviors demonstrates the cognitive processes underlying skill performance and facilitates learning. For example, in Joining In (Skill 17), the model might say, "I want to ask if I can play, but I'm afraid they might say no. But I'm going to take the chance. Okay, the first step is to watch."

This type of accompanying narration increases the effectiveness of the modeling display (Bandura, 1977), draws observers' attention to specific skill steps, and may facilitate skill generalization (Stokes & Baer, 1977). Verbal mediation may also be employed to demonstrate a coping model. For example, "They are all going to the party. I really want to go, but I can't—I wasn't invited. But feeling hurt won't get me invited. I need to think of my choices" (Skill 51: Dealing with Being Left Out).

Verbal mediation techniques have been used to teach impulse control in hyperactive children (Kendall & Braswell, 1985), anger control in adolescents (Goldstein & Glick, 1987), impulse control in aggressive youngsters (Camp & Bash, 1981), and academic behaviors through self-instruction training (Meichenbaum, 1977). By practicing talking themselves through a skill or saying aloud ways to control the impulse to react in an undesirable way, students learn to regulate their actions until these actions become nearly automatic. As stated by Camp and Bash (1985):

> A good deal of evidence suggests that adequate develop-
> ment of verbal mediation activity is associated with
> (1) internalization of the inhibitory function of language,
> which serves to block impulsive and associative responding
> in both cognitive and social situations, and (2) utilization
> of linguistic tools in learning, problem-solving, and fore-
> thought. (p. 7)

Many elementary-age children new to Skillstreaming will need to be taught the process of thinking aloud by having them practice while they are engaged in other types of activities (e.g., completing acade- mic tasks, doing a classroom chore). Activities useful in teaching ele- mentary students the technique of verbal mediation can be found in the Think Aloud programs (Camp & Bash, 1981, 1985).

FACTORS IN SUCCESSFUL SKILL USE

Skill Combinations

For many youngsters, relationships with adults and peers may pre- sent difficult interpersonal challenges—challenges that draw heavily upon their repertoire of interpersonal skills for solutions. Often com- petence in single skills is insufficient. For example, Hannah feels left out and is isolated from her classmates. She uses the skill of Joining In (Skill 17), but they continue to leave her out and refuse her friendly overtures. Darwin continues to be made fun of by his peers, and despite his efforts to ignore them (Responding to Teasing: Skill 38), they continue to taunt him. Despite her efforts and effective use of Ignoring Distractions (Skill 10), Lakeesha is still unable to complete her work on time. When Tanner uses Negotiating (Skill 44) to convince his mother to reduce his chores so he will have more time to practice basketball, his mother refuses. Yet another student successfully uses Introducing Yourself (Skill 14), but then doesn't know what to say next to the person she just met (Beginning a Conversation: Skill 15).

Many youths experience these reactions when challenged with complex social situations. Single-skill responses, even when per- formed correctly, prove inadequate. The target of skill use (parent, teacher, peer, etc.) does not respond in a manner that helps the student resolve the conflict or otherwise get his or her needs met. At other times the student may use a skill proficiently but attempt it with a person not in a position to accept this skill (e.g., starting a conversation with an adult in a manner more appropriate for use with a peer). In still other cases, a student may correctly use a skill but choose a poor time or misperceive the appropriateness of the social context in selecting one skill when another may have been more helpful. Instruction must therefore involve both individual skill competency and mastery of skill combinations.

The following edited transcript presents one example of instruction in skill combinations. Three skills—Saying No (Skill 55), Dealing with Another's Anger (Skill 32), and Using Self-Control (Skill 36)—are first modeled by the group leaders and then role-played by two group members. The steps in these three skills are presented in Table 3.

Leader: During the last several group meetings we have worked on only one skill at a time. Today we're going to do things a little differently. Sometimes using only one skill to deal with a problem isn't enough. Sometimes more than one skill is needed. We have worked on all of these skills: Saying No, Dealing with Another's Anger, and Using Self-Control. John, last week, when you did your homework assignment on Saying No, you told the rest of us that the skill didn't work too well for you—that when you used the skill with a friend who wanted you to steal money from your parents, it didn't work too well.

John: Emanuel won't take no. He kept on. We got in a fight.

Leader: And from what you told me, that wasn't what you wanted to have happen. I'm going to do a modeling display with Libby. She is going to try to get me to take something from the convenience store after school. I'm going to say no, but Libby is going to keep pressuring me to steal. In fact, she's going to get really angry with me, so I'll not only have to say no, but I'll have to deal with Libby's anger, too. But Libby will keep on, and

Table 3   A Sample Skill Sequence

Skill 55: Saying No

1. Decide whether or not you want to do what is being asked.

2. Think about why you don't want to do this.

3. Tell the person no in a friendly way.

4. Give your reason.

Skill 32: Dealing with Another's Anger

1. Listen to what the person has to say.

2. Think about your choices:

> a. Keep listening.
>
> b. Ask why the person is angry.
>
> c. Give the person an idea to fix the problem.
>
> d. Walk away for now.

3. Act out your best choice.

Skill 36: Using Self-Control

1. Stop and count to 10.

2. Think of how your body feels.

3. Think about your choices:

> a. Walk away for now.
>
> b. Do a relaxation exercise.
>
> c. Write about how you feel.
>
> d. Talk to someone about it.

4. Act out your best choice.

then I'll have to use self-control to keep from getting so angry myself, so I don't do something I'm sorry for later. That's the sequence of skills we're going to model. Then some of you will have the chance to try it, too. *(To Libby)* Are you ready? We're in the convenience store, over by the candy aisle.

Libby: Hey, the guy who is supposed to be at the counter isn't there. I'm hungry. Let's take some of this stuff. I'll go by the counter and watch, and you take some.

Leader: *(Thinking aloud while looking at the steps to the skill of Saying No)*

"Step 1: Decide whether or not you want to do what is being asked." I don't want to do this.

"Step 2. Think about why you don't want to do this." I know if I steal I'll get caught and get into big trouble.

"Step 3. Tell the person no in a friendly way." *(To Libby)* I'm not going to take anything.

(To herself) "Step 4: Give your reason." *(To Libby)* It's wrong, and we would get into big trouble. Let's get out of here.

Libby: Come on! It's only candy. It's not like they would put us in jail even if we were caught. But we won't be. Just put it in your backpack. The guy is busy over there. Now, take some!

Leader: Libby, I won't steal. Let's leave.

Libby: Are you ever a chicken liver. Who would even know? No one. Now, I'm telling you to take some. Do it! Do it now, or I'll tell everyone at school what a pansy you are. And then you'll be in big trouble. You know what happens to pansies, don't you?

Leader: *(Thinking aloud while looking at the skill steps to Dealing with Another's Anger)*

I can tell she's really angry. "Step 1: Listen to what the person has to say." I have listened to what she had to say. I don't think continuing to listen would help, and I know she's angry because I won't do what she wants me to do—to steal.

"Step 2: Think about your choices." I could use my allowance and just buy the candy for her. Or I could walk away. I'm going to walk out of the store and wait for Libby outside.

"Step 3: Act out your best choice."

(Walks off to the side.)

Libby: And where do you think you are going? I told you what I would do, and I'll do it. You're a joke! Nothing but a joke!

Leader: *(Thinking aloud and looking at the skill steps to Using Self-Control)*

Now I'm getting angry. "Step 1: Stop and count to 10." 1 . . . 2 . . . 3 . . . 4 . . . 5 . . . 6 . . . 7 . . . 8 . . . 9 . . . 10.

"Step 2: Think of how your body feels." I feel like I could explode.

"Step 3: Think about your choices." I could walk away, or I could try to find someone to talk to about this. I think I'll go home and talk to my sister. Maybe Libby will forget about it by tomorrow.

"Step 4: Act out your best choice." Libby, I'm going home. See you tomorrow.

(To the group) How did I do with this combination of skills? *(Students respond.)* Yes, I followed the steps of Saying No. When that didn't work, and Libby got really angry, I switched to the skill of Dealing with Another's Anger. Then when I started to get angry, too, I switched to the skill of Using Self-Control. And I ended up not losing control. There are other ways I could have done this, with other combinations of skills. What would be a situation that each of you have that's pretty complicated, starting with the skill of Saying No?

(Group members identify situations.) John, would you like to go first? You told us about the problem, and this would be a good situation. John, who in the group reminds you most of Emanuel?

John: Logan does.

Leader: All right. John and Logan, why don't you come up here. Logan, you are trying to convince John to steal money from his parents so that the two of you can go to the concert. When he says no, you're going to get angry with him, and we want to see a little bit of anger. John, you'll have to deal with his anger. Then, when you start to get angry or upset yourself, you'll need to use self-control. The skills and steps are up here on the chart to help you. We'll watch John go through all three of these skills. Are you ready? Okay. Logan, you start to encourage John to steal from his parents when he doesn't have the money to go to the concert.

Logan: So, you don't have the money. You can take it from your mom. Just take it from her purse. She'll never know.

John: *(Thinking aloud and looking at the skill steps to Saying No)*

"Step 1: Decide whether or not you want to do what is being asked." He wants me to steal from my mom. I can't do it.

"Step 2: Think about why you don't want to do this." She'll know it's gone, and she needs the money for other stuff.

"Step 3: Tell the person no in a friendly way." *(To Logan)* I want to go to the concert. But I can't steal from my mom.

(To himself) "Step 4: Give your reason." *(To Logan)* She'd know the money was gone.

Logan: Come on. How would she know you took it? Just say you didn't do it. No problem.

John: I won't steal.

Logan: It's not like really stealing. It's your mom. Come on. Take the money. Oh, yeah, I know you just don't want to go. You're just makin' up excuses.

Leader: John, Logan seems to be getting angry now.

John: *(Thinking aloud and looking at the skill steps for Dealing with Another's Anger)*

"Step 1: Listen to what the person has to say." I guess I'll listen to what he says.

Logan: I thought you were my best friend, but you won't go. And this is a great concert. Man, you're off my list. You acted like you were my best bud. You liar.

John: *(To himself)* "Step 2: Think about your choices." I could keep listening. I could ask why, or I could give him an idea. I'll try that.

"Step 3: Act out your best choice." *(To Logan)* I am your best friend, and I do want to go. I just don't have the money. Maybe I could ask my mom, maybe do some of her chores.

Logan: The concert's on Saturday, jerk. And your mom won't give it to you . . . you already said. You're a mama's boy, won't steal from her!

John: *(Thinking aloud and looking at the skill steps for Using Self-Control)*

"Step 1: Stop and count to 10." 1 . . . 2 . . . 3 . . . 4 . . . 5 . . . 6 . . . 7 . . . 8 . . . 9 . . . 10.

"Step 2: Think of how your body feels." My stomach is all jumpy.

"Step 3: Think about your choices." I could just walk. Or I could talk to someone.

"Step 4: Act out your best choice." It's not fair to say stuff about my mom. I'm going to leave. *(Walks away.)*

Leader: Let's get some feedback.

Other skill combinations may be used. Hannah, for example, who tried Joining In (Skill 17) but continued to be rejected by her peers, might need to use Expressing Your Feelings (Skill 27) following the group's rejection and then perhaps Suggesting an Activity (Skill 23) with a peer outside of the original group. Darwin, who continued to be made fun of despite his proficient use of Responding to Teasing (Skill 38), may have been more effective using the combination of Dealing with Fear (Skill 34) and Making a Complaint (Skill 47). Likewise, Lekeesha may find that if Ignoring Distractions (Skill 10) doesn't help her complete her work, she might use the skills of Completing Assignments (Skill 6) or Asking for Help (Skill 2). Tanner, whose use of Negotiating (Skill 44) failed with his mother, may need to use the skill combination of Reacting to Failure (Skill 53) and Problem Solving (Skill 41).

Other helpful skill combinations include the following:

- Joining In (Skill 17) and Dealing with Being Left Out (Skill 51)

- Dealing with an Accusation (Skill 43) and Accepting Consequences (Skill 42)

- Deciding What Caused a Problem (Skill 46) and Negotiating (Skill 44)

- Asking Permission (Skill 37), Accepting No (Skill 54), and Dealing with Boredom (Skill 45)

- Knowing Your Feelings (Skill 26) and Expressing Your Feelings (Skill 27)

- Setting a Goal (Skill 13), Dealing with Fear (Skill 34), and Contributing to Discussions (Skill 7)

Skillstreaming instruction should include modeling and role-playing such skill combinations. The real-life situations students face are complex and often not easily resolved with use of a single skill. Such instruction will better prepare students for skill use in the real world.

Skill Shifting

Sometimes during the course of a Skillstreaming session devoted to a given skill, the need may arise for instruction in a different skill.

When this is the case, the group leader should either shift to teaching the new skill on the spot or make note of the need to do so in the near future. For example, in a session devoted to Dealing with Your Anger (Skill 31), one student developed a role-play related to having difficulty with an academic assignment. Although this student often did become angry during such situations, instruction in the skill of Asking for Help (Skill 2) was also necessary to teach her to deal effectively with this type of event.

Students will often find it valuable if they become proficient in knowing when and how to shift from one skill to another. Thus, group instruction should help students discern when a skill is unsuccessful, when an alternative skill should be attempted, and which specific skill to try. In one group, for example, students were attending a schoolwide assembly. Joe had used the skill Asking a Favor (Skill 19) with Paul by asking him to move over so that Joe could see better. Paul not only refused to move, he also began to tease Joe. Joe needed to shift to Responding to Teasing (Skill 38) to deal with his immediate problem, but he also needed to think of another skill to use so he would be able to see the assembly. Problem Solving (Skill 41) or Making a Complaint (Skill 47) might have been useful for Joe to try.

Social Perceptions and Behavioral Flexibility

Even if a student becomes proficient in a given skill, the student may misread the context in which the prosocial behavior is desirable or acceptable. A major emphasis in psychology for the past 15 years has been the importance of the situation or setting as perceived by the individual in determining behavior. Morrison and Bellack (1981), for example, state that individuals must not only possess the ability to enact given behavioral skills, but must also know when and how these responses should be applied. These authors further state that in order to use this knowledge, individuals must have the "ability to accurately 'read' the social environment" (p. 70). This ability, they suggest, includes awareness of the norms and conventions in operation at a given time as well as understanding of the message given from the other person. The work of Dil (1972), Emery (1975), and Rothenbert (1970) suggest that emotionally disturbed and "socially maladjusted" youngsters are characteristically deficient in such social perceptiveness. Argyle (1981) additionally observes:

It has been found that people who are socially inadequate are unable to read everyday situations and respond appropriately. They are unable to perform or interpret nonverbal signals, unaware of the rules of social behavior, mystified by ritualized routines and conventions of self-presentation and self-disclosure, and are hence like foreigners in their own land. (p. 37)

Argyle (1981) and Backman (1979) have emphasized this social-perceptual deficit in their work with aggressive individuals. Yet we believe that students can be taught to read the context (situation and setting) of the social situation accurately and adjust their behavior accordingly. Brown and Fraser (1979) propose three salient dimensions of accurate social perceptiveness:

1. The setting of the interaction and its associated rules and norms

2. The purpose of the interaction and its goals, tasks, and topics

3. The relationship of the participants—their rules, responsibilities, expectations, and group membership

Attention to setting demands is drawn in some of the skill steps (e.g., choosing a good time and place).

Emphasis must be placed, therefore, not only on Skillstreaming skill performance, but also on such questions as the following: What is expected behavior (or the expected skill to use) in this setting? Which skill should I use with this person, considering his or her role? and What signs are there that this is a good time to use the skill? Inviting students to consider such questions will result in more successful skill use and guide students in developing the flexibility needed to adjust skill use across settings, situations, and people.

Nonverbal Behaviors

Nonverbal communicators such as body posture and movements, facial expressions, and voice tone and volume give others messages either consistent with or contradictory to verbal content. Consider, for example, a student who is told to leave the playground for breaking the rules. Often it is not the breaking of the rule per se that results in the playground supervisor's action. Rather, one hears comments about such students like "She was defiant" or "He didn't seem sorry for what he did." When the playground supervisor is further questioned regarding the student's defiance or failure to apologize, nonverbal evidence may be called upon (e.g., "She just stood there" or "He didn't look sorry!"). Understanding the influence of nonverbal language is an important factor in learning prosocial behaviors. In brief, skill-deficient students will need to be made more aware of the ways in which nonverbal communicators send clear and definite messages.

Empathy

Chronically aggressive or other skill-deficient youth have been shown to display a pattern of personality traits high in egocentricity and low in concern for others (Slavin, 1980). Expression of empathic understanding can serve both as an inhibitor of negative behaviors and as a facilitator of positive actions. As stated by Goldstein and Michaels (1985):

> Responding to another individual in an empathic manner and assuming temporarily their perspective decreases or inhibits one's potential for acting aggressively toward the other (Feshbach, 1982; Feshbach & Feshbach, 1969). Stated otherwise, empathy and aggression are incompatible interpersonal responses, hence learning to be more skilled in the former serves as an aid to diminishing the latter. (p. 309)

Results of a number of studies inquiring into the interpersonal consequences of empathic responding show that empathy is a consistently potent promoter of interpersonal attraction, dyadic openness, conflict resolution, and individual growth (Goldstein & Michaels, 1985). In other words, students who are able to show empathy are far less likely to act out aggressively toward others, are more accepted and sought after in social situations, are more able to participate in resolving interpersonal disputes, and are more satisfied with themselves.

Some helpful methods of encouraging empathy include (a) instructing students in skills such as Expressing Concern for Another

(Skill 30) and Expressing Your Feelings (Skill 27); (b) providing opportunities for role reversal during role-plays, followed by actors' expression of feelings; (c) providing opportunities for observers to take the perspective of others (e.g., the main actor) during feedback sessions; and (d) encouraging empathy toward others through the modeling and discussion of appreciation for individual differences.

Supportive Modeling

Typically, aggressive youth are regularly exposed to highly aggressive models. Parents, siblings, and peers are often frequently chronically aggressive individuals themselves (Knight & West, 1975; Loeber & Dishion, 1983; Robins, West, & Herjanic, 1975). At the same time, relatively few prosocial models that might help counteract the effects of aggressive modeling exist for these youngsters to observe and imitate. When prosocial models are available, they apparently can make a tremendous difference in the social development of such youth. Werner and Smith (1982), in their longitudinal study of aggressive and nonaggressive youth *Vulnerable but Invincible,* clearly demonstrate that youth growing up in a community characterized by high crime, high unemployment, high secondary school dropout rates, and high levels of aggressive models were able to develop into effective, satisfied, prosocially oriented individuals if they had sustained exposure to at least one significant prosocial model—be it parent, relative, teacher, coach, neighbor, or peer.

The classroom teacher can be a powerful model for students. Needless to say, a powerful negative effect can be exerted on students if the teacher models prosocial skill deficiencies. Throughout the course of the school day, the teacher should make a sustained effort to model desirable, prosocial behaviors and to use the behavioral steps for selected skills when it is appropriate to do so. When frustrated or angry with an individual student's behavior, for example, the teacher can greatly affect student learning if he or she models the steps of Dealing with Your Anger (Skill 31) in a clear and deliberate manner.

CHAPTER 9
Managing Behavior Problems

Problems can and do occur in the Skillstreaming group, just as they may in any group teaching endeavor. Students may be unmotivated to participate as requested, actively resist meaningful group involvement, or fail to see the relevance of the skills to their everyday lives. Their resistive behavior may interfere not only with their skill acquisition, but also with the learning of others in the group.

As the Skillstreaming session unfolds, one or more students may display resistive behavior. One student refuses to participate in feedback or role-plays, despite the teacher's repeated requests. In another group, a student becomes disruptive by repeatedly commenting that "This is silly" and "This is just stupid." In yet another group, a student becomes angry at another group member and attempts to instigate a fight. We urge as a first step in managing such resistive and problematic behavior that group leaders ask themselves, Why at this moment is the student engaging in that particular behavior?

Dreikurs, Grunwald, and Pepper (1971) offer four reasons for misbehavior: attention, power, revenge, and inadequacy. Is the student's goal to seek attention or to belong? To control the group? To ruin the teaching opportunity? To avoid participation? Group leaders need to make a guess, a hypothesis, a diagnosis. The diagnosis will often suggest the cure. Perhaps one's causal hypothesis is that the student is displaying the particular resistive behavior to avoid a task he perceives as too complicated (e.g., one that has too many steps). In this case, the teacher may need to simplify the task. Another student may be experiencing anxiety as she realizes that her turn to role-play is approaching. In this situation, the teacher will likely need to offer reassurance. Still another student may not be receiving the desired amount of attention from others. Another may have been engaging in undesirable behaviors to belong and to be perceived as "cool." In these last two examples, the teacher may need to restructure the lesson to allow students to gain attention or belonging by being a helper or an actor in the next role-play.

The present chapter offers suggestions for increasing student motivation and reducing student resistance. Just as one type of reinforcer may be rewarding for one child but not for another, a particular management strategy is likely to be more effective for one child than for another. Therefore, we will describe a range of strategies to be used when conducting Skillstreaming groups and urge that teachers and other group leaders individualize these methods, using the techniques that appear to work best.

STUDENT MOTIVATION

Motivation is not an easy task. A great many of the youths offered the opportunity to learn from Skillstreaming—a technique for teaching *prosocial* skills—are highly competent in the regular use of *antisocial* behavior. Further, this predilection may be frequently encouraged, supported, and rewarded by many of the significant people in these students' lives—family, peers, and others.

Two types of motivators are at the teacher's disposal. *Extrinsic motivators* are tangible rewards provided contingent upon performance of desired behaviors. Such rewards take many forms. In the early years of the behavior modification movement, the use of extrinsic, tangible reinforcers was sometimes denounced as "bribery." The youth, it was asserted, should want to engage in the desired behavior for its own sake and not for the external rewards it would bring. Some intervenors still offer such protests (e.g., Kohn, 1986), but most agree that use of a combination of external and internal motivators is the most effective strategy.

Tangible motivators are, in fact, widely used in American schools and other institutions serving children and youth. The stars and stickers of the preschool and primary years take the form of points, pizza and popcorn parties, and special privileges and activities in the later grades. Extrinsic rewards appear to be especially useful in eliciting initial involvement in learning unfamiliar skills.

It has been the consistent experience of many teachers of Skill-streaming, however, that using only external rewards—whether in the form of tangible reinforcers, a token economy, a levels system, or other incentives—is insufficient on a sustained basis. We and others believe that substantial payoffs must be inherent in the activity itself. In Skillstreaming, such *intrinsic motivators* reside within the skills themselves, especially those students select themselves and use successfully in their real-world settings. Our earlier discussion of the process we call "negotiating the skill curriculum" is central here (see chapter 4). When youths have the opportunity to select the skills they feel *they* need, a major step toward participation motivation has been taken. When such student-selected (or, to perhaps a somewhat lesser degree, teacher-selected) skills yield positive outcomes in interactions with family, peers, or significant others, motivation is further enhanced.

In addition to regular negotiation of the skill curriculum, we have used a second tactic to augment intrinsic motivation. It is to communicate to the students, both during the initial structuring of the Skillstreaming group and periodically as the sessions unfold, that the goal of Skillstreaming is to teach alternatives, not substitutes. Many students who are selected to participate have been admonished, reprimanded, and punished literally hundreds of times for behaviors their parents, teachers, or others deemed inappropriate. In one way or another, they have been told, "Stop doing that, and do this instead (e.g., "Stop talking and listen"; "Stop hitting and talk out the problem").

Although we agree that it is certainly desirable to decrease inappropriate behavior, we believe a more successful means of reaching this goal is to expand the child's behavioral repertoire, or range of possible responses. If, for example, someone wrongly accuses the student of stealing something, and the only response to accusations he or she has learned, practiced, and been rewarded for is fighting, the student will fight again. The student has, in effect, no choices. If Skillstreaming teaches the student that accusations may also be responded to by explanation, investigation, negotiation, walking away, and other means, at least some of the time he or she may use one of these more desirable ways in lieu of counterattack. The very fact that reprimands, punishments, and the like have had to be used hundreds of times is stark testimony to their lack of enduring effect.

If the student has skill response choices, then some of the time, at least, he or she will use them.

One additional motivational concern exists. Youngsters who frequently behave in their everyday lives in an angry, aggressive, intimidating, bullying, and threatening manner may also do so in the Skillstreaming group. If such behaviors are not dealt with—immediately, swiftly, and successfully—other students will avoid the group. The Skillstreaming teacher functions not only as an instructor, model, and role-play/feedback guide, but also as a protector. In creating a safe learning environment, the teacher must immediately correct any efforts to bully, intimidate, or otherwise treat others in an inappropriate, aggressive manner. Such vigilance and responsiveness not only serve to protect the victim but also, if done constructively, offer an additional teaching opportunity for the attacker. No matter how skilled the leader is in modeling, conducting role-playing, and so forth, if the group is not safe, learning cannot take place.

For example, suppose in the group Sue gives feedback to Linda, who has just completed a role-play, in a negative, offensive manner. The first problem is Sue, whose intimidating behavior is one of the things that brought her to the Skillstreaming group. The second problem is the role-play observers. Observers who have not yet role-played may be thinking that they will be treated similarly when it is their turn. The third problem is Linda, who is getting feedback that will discourage rather than encourage her to use the skill. So how can the leader serve as a protector for all of these students? One way to do so would be to prompt Sue to restate the feedback in a helpful way. If that response is not in her skill repertoire, the leader could whisper to Sue what to say and have Sue repeat it. This teaches Sue a little about giving constructive feedback and lets her know that intimidating comments are not acceptable. Linda gets more appropriate feedback, which will help encourage real-world skill use. The observers get the message that if Sue puts them down the leader will come to their aid. In an active manner, the leader protects and instructs all of the group members.

CREATING A POSITIVE LEARNING CLIMATE

The atmosphere of the Skillstreaming group, and the classroom as well, should be positive. By this we mean that the teacher should openly notice the children following group rules, making prosocial choices, and "being good," rather than catching them breaking rules. A benefit of this approach is the fact that when a teacher sees a child behaving appropriately and states approval of that behavior publicly, children engaging in unacceptable behavior are likely to stop that behavior and engage in the one that received teacher approval (Kounin, 1970).

Psychologists and educators have long known that the better the relationship between the helper and client (student), the more positive and productive the outcome of their interaction. In fact, it has been demonstrated that a positive relationship is a potent factor in effecting long-term behavior change. The techniques next described draw primarily upon the relationship between teacher and student and can often be combined with other management techniques for maximum effect. Specifically, these include empathic encouragement, threat reduction, prompting, simplifying, and capturing teachable moments.

Empathic encouragement

Empathic encouragement is a strategy in which the teacher first shows that he or she understands the difficulty the student is experiencing and then urges the student to participate as instructed. Often this additional one-to-one attention will motivate the child to participate and follow the teacher's guidance. In applying this technique, the teacher first listens to the student's explanation of the problem and expresses an understanding of the student's feelings and behavior (e.g., "I know it's difficult. Learning something new can be frustrating."). If appropriate, the teacher responds that the child's view is a valid alternative for dealing with the problem. The teacher then restates his or her own view with supporting reasons and probable outcomes, and urges the student to try out the suggestion (e.g., "But if you don't try the skill, you won't know if you can do it. Let's give it a try.")

> EXAMPLE. While two students were role-playing Responding to Teasing (Skill 38), Michelle leaned back in her chair and began to sneer in an angry manner. After several minutes of being ignored, Michelle became even more restless and began muttering loudly enough to be quite distracting to the group. The leader began by taking Michelle aside and saying, "You appear quite angry. What's

the problem?" Michelle responded by stating that it was stupid to ignore someone who was teasing her because that wouldn't make the person stop. The only thing that would get the others to stop was to beat them up. The teacher expressed understanding of how horrible it can feel to be teased but pointed out that fighting seems to result in being physically hurt and getting into trouble as well: "Sometimes kids tease so that they can get someone into trouble. The goal we talked about is to deal with teasing in a way where you won't get hurt and you'll also stay out of trouble." Michelle stood quietly, but her anger appeared to lessen. "Well, let's not decide if this is a useful skill for you until you try it out in a role-play. Is that reasonable?" Michelle replied that this would be okay, and she and the teacher rejoined the group.

Threat reduction

This technique is helpful in dealing with a student's anxiety. Children who find role-playing or other types of participation threatening may react with inappropriate or disruptive behaviors or withdraw from the learning process. To deal with this problem, the teacher should provide reassurance or even physical contact (e.g., an arm around the student, a pat on the back). The teacher should also encourage group members to express support for role-players and others who participate.

Other strategies for threat reduction include postponing the student's role-playing until last and clarifying and restructuring those aspects of the task that the student experiences as threatening.

EXAMPLE. Sam experienced anxiety because he couldn't think of a role-play situation. The teacher responded by asking the group, "Let's think of some situations in which Sam could use the skill. Then, Sam, you may choose one of these situations to role-play."

Prompting

Prompting may prevent the student from acting in a disruptive or aggressive manner due to fear of failing. One of the teacher's main functions is to anticipate student difficulties during the group and be ready to prompt a desirable response. During role-plays, for example, students practicing a new skill may forget a step or several steps, or they may not know how to behave in order to carry out a particular step. The teacher may give instructional comments (e.g., "You're now ready to . . ."), offer hints to elicit the behavior, or coach the student from start to finish. We are reminded that an important function of role-playing is to practice the proficient display of the behavioral steps. If students are allowed to fail, they have had only more practice at failing.

> EXAMPLE. Todd stood up in front of the group to role-play the skill of Joining In (Skill 17). He continued to stand there while the two co-actors played the game Todd had planned to join. The teacher then said, "Todd, do you remember what to do first?" Todd shook his head and replied no. The teacher responded: "Look up at the chart. Decide if you want to join in." To provide for a successful role-play, in this case the teacher found it necessary to give Todd a verbal prompt for each skill step while pointing to the step on the chart.

Simplifying

Simplifying, or asking less at one time, is another way to increase the likelihood that students will experience success in the Skill-streaming group. Students' abilities to handle particular group tasks will vary. Some may have difficulty following a series of instructions, or understanding instructions, or knowing what to say during feedback. Methods of simplifying include the following:

- Have the student role-play one behavioral step at a time. Reward minimal student accomplishment.

- Shorten the role-play.

- Have the student read a prepared script portraying the behavioral steps.

- Ask the student to take the role of co-actor before that of main actor.

> EXAMPLE. When it was Alisha's turn to role-play Setting a Goal (Skill 13), she began to talk in a silly, high-pitched

voice, digressing from the steps. When prompted by the teacher to look at the first step and try it out, she continued to act the clown. Instead of requesting that Alisha return to her seat and try this another day, the teacher restated the first behavioral step by saying to Alisha, "Is there something, one thing, you would like to do better with in math? You do a terrific job with the skills we have worked on so far, and now we're getting into multiplication. Would learning how to multiply be a goal you might want to set?" Alisha responded that this would be okay, she guessed. "Great. Then you've done the first step. You've decided on a goal. We'll work on the second step, the steps to achieve this goal, during another session." Alisha calmly returned to her seat.

Capturing teachable moments

Capturing teachable moments employs Skillstreaming to better manage the Skillstreaming group. Many problematic behaviors, including withdrawal, disruptiveness, threatening, and so forth may be viewed as behavioral excess—too much talking, too much bullying, and so on. Each such behavior, however, may equally well be construed as behavioral deficiency—too little listening to others, too little empathy, and so on. Thus, an additional way to reduce problem behaviors is to replace them with desirable ones. The Skillstreaming curriculum consists of just such alternatives. Skills may be taught as previously scheduled (as part of regular sessions) or at spontaneous times that help students reduce behavior problems (i.e., teachable moments).

> **EXAMPLE.** In one group session, Leroy, who was angry because of an incident that had occurred on the playground during noon recess, verbally began to attack Justin. While the teacher first needed to clarify that Leroy would not be allowed to physically harm Justin and take steps to make certain the learning setting remained safe for all group members, the incident created the opportunity to learn. Here was the chance to teach Leroy an alternative, more prosocially skilled way of handling the same situation. In such a situation, Leroy could be reminded of a skill previously practiced (Making a Complaint: Skill 47), handed the

Skill Card depicting the steps, encouraged to try out the skill, and prompted through skill use. Likewise, Justin could be given a Skill Card for Dealing with an Accusation (Skill 43) and asked to respond to Leroy by using the skill steps.

SUPPORTIVE INTERVENTIONS

The Skillstreaming curriculum will be more readily learned by youngsters in need of such instruction when presented in an encouraging, supportive environment. At times, however, more structured and directive interventions may be necessary. The following interventions are designed to support students' desirable behaviors in a unobtrusive manner within the instructional setting while, in most cases, allowing instruction to continue. These interventions include behavioral redirection, surface management, and limit setting.

Behavioral Redirection

One way to encourage a student's appropriate behavior while preventing the occurrence of negative actions is to employ behavioral redirection. For example, a student who frequently disrupts the Skillstreaming group by standing up and walking around may be asked to assist the teacher in pointing out the skill steps as they are being role-played. Another example would be requesting that a student who inappropriately brings a toy to the group take other classroom materials and put them on the teacher's desk, replacing the toy on the way. Still another student who feels the need to dominate conversation in the group may be asked to dictate his or her ideas into a tape recorder after the session.

This technique allows the teacher to emphasize the student's positive, helping actions without having to ignore the student's negative behaviors or deal with them in a manner disruptive to the learning of others.

Surface Management

Several techniques for managing mild and commonly occurring misbehaviors have been suggested by Redl and Wineman (1957). These methods, termed "surface management" techniques, have been used successfully to deal with problematic behaviors in Skillstreaming groups.

Planned ignoring

Mild misbehaviors can best be dealt with by simply ignoring them. Many times drawing attention to such behaviors is more distracting to the learning process than the occurrence of the behaviors themselves. Positively reinforcing concurrent appropriate behavior adds to the elimination of the inappropriate action. This strategy is most effective when the group leader plans in advance which mild behaviors will be ignored.

> **EXAMPLE.** Paul frequently played with his clothing, rolling up his shirt or picking at his shoes during the sessions despite the teacher's requests for him to stop. Because Paul's behavior did not appear to distract others, the teacher decided to ignore it to see if, with lack of attention, the behavior would diminish.

Proximity control

In proximity control, the teacher moves closer to (stands near, sits next to) the student who is misbehaving. Often simply moving closer to the student who is engaging in problematic or distracting behavior will draw the student's attention back to the learning situation. For students who do not mind being touched, a hand on the shoulder is an effective way of drawing the student back to task.

> **EXAMPLE.** While the group was providing feedback to the role-players, Tommy began making noises. The leader quietly moved away from the front of the group, stood next to Tommy, and touched his shoulder while continuing to elicit feedback about the role-play.

Signal interference

Signal interference includes nonverbal communicators that let the student know a behavior is unacceptable. This may include eye contact, hand gestures, clearing one's throat, or frowning. Some students who engage in mildly disruptive behavior may not even realize they are doing something distracting to others. In such cases, prearranging with the child a specific signal (e.g., a word or gesture) to cue the student that the behavior is occurring has been a useful strategy.

Example. While the group leaders modeled the skill, Michelle started tapping her foot against Tommy's chair. Tommy then hit his foot against Michelle's chair. The group leader caught Michelle's eye and shook her head "no."

Interest boosting

When a student's attention appears to be drifting away from an activity, it is often helpful to redirect the student's interest. This can be done by involving the student more directly in the activity, asking for the student's input, or directing a high-interest question to the group.

Example. Brian was getting restless—moving his chair, turning around—while a student was reporting performance on a homework assignment. The teacher quickly summarized the student's performance, provided positive feedback, and involved Brian by asking him in what other situations the skill could be used.

Humor

At times something very clever or humorous may be expressed by a student in the Skillstreaming group. Such a humorous moment can quickly ease a tense situation. As long as the humor is not at the expense of a specific individual or group, or the student is not being rewarded for being a class clown, it is fine to go ahead and laugh with the youngsters.

Example. The group had been through a difficult lesson the day before. While the group was getting ready to begin the next day, one student told a silly knock-knock joke, and all the other group members laughed. Instead of reprimanding the student, the teacher laughed along with the others for a few moments and then began the instruction.

Restructuring the classroom program

Sometimes the classroom schedule must be abandoned in favor of dealing with a problem that has just occurred. If the class appears tense and upset due to a playground problem, for example, requiring the students to participate in practice of Beginning a Conversation

(Skill 15) clearly will not meet their immediate needs. Instead, the teacher should abandon the preplanned lesson and restructure the program (e.g., change the skill to be taught).

> **EXAMPLE.** The students came to the Skillstreaming group very agitated and loudly complaining that the playground supervisor was unfair in taking a certain disciplinary action. Even though the teacher's plan for the day was to work on a different skill, he abandoned this plan and introduced the more timely skill of Making a Complaint (Skill 47).

Removing seductive objects

It is natural for students to be distracted by interesting objects and toys. Including the rule of leaving toys and other objects at one's desk may prevent such distractions from occurring during Skillstreaming groups.

> **EXAMPLE.** Troy brought a flashlight to the group and began showing it to others before instruction started. The teacher asked Troy to finish showing the flashlight and then directed him to put it either in his desk or in the teacher's desk for safekeeping.

Temporary removal

When a student's behavior is not easily controlled within the instructional setting, it may be best for the student to take a break. Redl and Wineman (1957) describe this approach as "antiseptic bouncing." It is not intended as a punitive measure, but as a strategy for removing the student from a situation before he or she loses control. With this technique, the student is asked to leave the room to get a drink of water, run an errand, and so forth.

> **EXAMPLE:** Randa couldn't seem to settle down in the group. She continually moved about in her chair, talking to the students sitting next to her. The teacher called Randa away from the group and requested that she take a book back to the library right away.

In some cases, a student may know he or she is emotionally unable to handle the classroom or group setting and may request a time-out or cooling-off period. Referred to by Grayson, Kiraly, and McKinnon (1996) as the *cooling-off approach,* this method allows the student to spend time alone in a nonstressful setting or time with an adult to discuss the student's concerns. This form of therapeutic crisis intervention may avert more serious behavior difficulties. The teacher needs to monitor the student's use of cooling-off periods carefully to judge that it is not employed to avoid a particular classroom activity, subject, or Skillstreaming task.

> **EXAMPLE.** Billy became gradually more agitated in the group. When the teacher inquired whether he was having a problem, Billy asked to sit on a rug in the reading area for 2 or 3 minutes. After that, he calmly returned to the group.

Reality appraisal

This technique involves giving students an explanation of why a behavior is not acceptable, or "telling it like it is." The approach also helps students understand the consequences of their behavior.

> **EXAMPLE.** During feedback, most of the students began talking all at once. The group leader responded, "If everyone is going to talk at once, we can't hear anyone's ideas."

Limit Setting

There are times when the more unobtrusive strategies just described will be unsuccessful and an even more structured approach is needed. The following five-step method, designed to deal with behavioral concerns while continuing to support the student who is acting out, will protect the learning of others.

Step 1: Reward positive behavior

Foremost among behavior management techniques for dealing with problematic behavior in the classroom is positive reinforcement, discussed further in the next section of this chapter. Many disruptions can be reduced or even eliminated by applying positive reinforcement to such desirable class behaviors as listening, participating, and following the group guidelines. Positive reinforcement also has a powerful effect on a student who is behaving inappropriately if other children who are engaging in desirable behavior are rewarded. For example, if those who are listening are reinforced with verbal praise, a ripple effect is created, and the inattentive child will most likely begin to listen as well (Kounin, 1970). This strategy allows the teacher to control the group in a positive, helping way and decreases the impulse to nag children to pay attention.

Step 2: Offer positive consequences

Reminding students of the positive consequences of desirable behavior will often encourage them to stop an undesirable behavior and engage in a more desirable one. Offering positive consequences means the student is told that a specific desirable behavior will earn a given reward. Examples include the following: "When you listen, you may have a turn" and "When you put your materials away, you may join the group." Some behaviors may need a tangible positive consequence: "When you wait your turn, you'll earn a point" (or token, or ticket). Reminding students to engage in a specific appropriate behavior to earn a privilege or reward lets them know that positive actions lead to good things—and it does so in an encouraging, helpful manner. It is important to present the positive consequences for stopping an undesirable action before informing the student of any negative consequences.

Step 3: Inform the student of negative consequences

The majority of minor behavioral difficulties (e.g., inattention, noise making, etc.) will likely be remedied by employing Steps 1 and 2 of this plan. However, if a student's inappropriate behavior does not cease, it may be necessary to inform the student of the negative consequences if he or she chooses to continue the undesirable behavior. Examples of such negative consequences include sitting away from the group for a minute, not earning points or other rewards that have been structured within the plan, or not having a privilege such as extra recess time. Such consequences should be as logically related to the misbehavior as possible. For example, if the child misuses classroom materials, he or she would then lose the privilege of using these materials for the rest of the day. Informing the student of a negative consequence thus provides a warning of what will happen if the student continues to engage in that behavior. A more complete discussion of consequences is presented later in this chapter.

Step 4: Instruct the student to make a choice

After the student is informed of both positive and negative consequences, he or she is instructed to make a choice—either stop the behavior and earn the positive reinforcement or continue the behavior and accept the negative consequences. When students are given a choice, power struggles are eliminated. We cannot make students behave in the way we would like them to behave; however, we can structure the system of rewards and negative consequences to encourage students to make prosocial choices.

Often it is helpful to allow the student time to make the choice. Informing the student that he or she will have 2 minutes to make the choice to put materials away or 1 minute to make the choice of whether or not to stop disrupting the group allows the teacher to leave the student alone, lessens the potential for a power struggle, and allows the student to maintain his or her dignity.

Step 5: Enforce positive or negative consequences

Either the positive or negative consequences are next carried out. If the student chooses negative consequences by continuing the inappropriate behavior, these are delivered in a calm and firm manner. For example, if the student continues to disrupt the Skillstreaming group by making noises and the consequence for this behavior is to sit away from the group for 2 to 3 minutes, then the student is required to follow through. Once a negative consequence has been enforced, and repeated if necessary, the teacher should reevaluate the structure of the learning environment, making accommodations for that student—for example, seating the student closer to a group leader or implementing a behavior management plan according to the procedures described in the following section of this chapter.

If the student makes the choice to stop the behavior as requested, then the student should receive the positive consequence (e.g., allowing the student to remain with the group or continue to use class materials). It is important to stress that once a student has earned a reward for a given positive behavior (e.g., points for listening) the reward should not be taken away as a negative consequence for another undesirable behavior. Loss of a reward previously earned may result in more severe maladaptive behavior, such as aggression or loss of motivation to earn the reward.

EXAMPLE. When Sam began disrupting the group by making silly comments and laughing, the group leader rewarded those students who had been listening with both verbal praise and "participation tickets" (Step 1). Sam continued the behavior, and the leader responded, "Sam, when you show that you are listening, you may have a turn to role-play" (Step 2). Sam stopped the comments and laughter, and was selected as the next role-player. If he had continued, the leader would have calmly walked over to Sam, saying, "Sam, you need to stop the silly comments. It's distracting all of us. If you stop, you will earn some participation tickets to use for extra recess time this afternoon" (Step 2). "If you continue, you will not earn your tickets for participating, and you'll need to sit away from the group" (Step 3). "You will need to decide what you are going to do. You have 2 minutes to make your choice" (Step 4). Depending upon the choice Sam made, the positive or negative consequences would be enforced.

BEHAVIOR MANAGEMENT

Both student behaviors promoting skill learning as well as behaviors inhibiting such progress can be directed with behavior management techniques (i.e., behavior modification). The effectiveness of behavior modification technology rests upon a firm experimental foundation.

Beyond the repeated demonstration that "they work," these techniques are relatively easy to learn and use; may be teacher-, peer-, parent-, and/or self-administered; are generally cost-effective; yield typically unambiguous behavior-change results; and have a long history of successful application (with aggressive youngsters in particular). For these reasons, the techniques can maximize time and opportunity for student learning.

Behavior modification techniques are derived from formal learning theory, systematically applied in an effort to change observable behavior, and rigorously evaluated by experimental research. These procedures are based on the core premise that behavior is largely determined by its environmental consequences (Ferster & Skinner, 1957; Skinner, 1938, 1953). Operationally, this premise has been employed in techniques that contingently present or withdraw rewards or punishments (i.e., environmental consequences) to alter the behavior preceding these consequences. It is this contingent quality that has led to the use of the term *contingency management* to describe most of the activities in which the behavior modifier engages.

Providing Positive Reinforcement

A major way to substitute appropriate for inappropriate behaviors is to present positive reinforcement to the student following and contingent upon the occurrence of appropriate behavior. A *positive reinforcer* is any event that increases the subsequent frequency of a behavior it follows. Teachers and other school-based contingency managers have worked successfully with four types of positive reinforcers: material, social, activity, and token. A list of commonly used reinforcers is presented in Table 4.

Material reinforcers (sometimes called *tangible reinforcers*) are actual goods or objects presented to the individual contingent upon enactment of appropriate behaviors. A specific type of material reinforcer is the Skill Award (see Figure 7, p. 76, for an example). An important subcategory of material reinforcement, *primary reinforcement,* occurs when the contingent event presented satisfies a basic biological need. Food is one such primary reinforcer.

Social reinforcers—most often expressed in the form of attention, praise, or approval—are particularly powerful and are frequently used in the Skillstreaming group. Both teacher experience and extensive experimental research testify to the potency of teacher-dispensed social reinforcement in influencing a broad array of personal, interpersonal, and academic student behaviors.

Activity reinforcers are those events the youngster freely chooses when an opportunity exists to engage in several different activities. Given freedom to choose, many youngsters will watch television rather than complete their homework. The parent wishing to use this activity reinforcer may specify that the youngster may watch television for a given time period contingent upon the prior completion of the homework. Stated otherwise, the opportunity to perform a higher probability behavior (given free choice) can be used as a reinforcer for a lower probability behavior.

Token reinforcers, usually employed when more easily implemented social reinforcers prove insufficient, are symbolic items (chips, stars, points, etc.) provided contingent upon the performance

Table 4 Commonly Used Reinforcers

MATERIAL REINFORCERS

Objects

Food (peanuts, raisins,
    apples, cereal)
Stars/stickers
Pictures to color
Letters of praise to the
    principal or parent
Ribbons
Pencils, paper, colorful
    folders
Coupons for McDonald's
"Good Work" buttons
Comic books
Posters
A photograph of the student
Awards
Small toys or trinkets

SOCIAL REINFORCERS

Nonverbal Encouragers

Smiling
Nearness to the student
Thumbs up
Looking interested
Giving a hug
Applause
Nodding
Giving a pat on the back
Giving a "high five"
Arm around the student

Verbal Encouragers

Thank you.
You really paid attention.
That's right.
Good thinking.
I'm pleased that you chose
    to do that.
Bravo.
I like the way you're being
    a good sport (or other
    behavior).
Wow!
Fantastic.
Terrific.
Good answer.
That was a very kind (friendly,
    caring) thing to do.
You did a great job.
I like that.

ACTIVITY REINFORCERS

Reading comics
Using the teacher's
    equipment or materials
Having one-to-one time
    with an adult
Going early to lunch
Tutoring a younger child
Taking free time in the library
Completing duties for the
    teacher (e.g., running
    errands)

ACTIVITY REINFORCERS
(continued)

Helping in the principal's office

Coloring

Computer time

Resting

Sharpening pencils

Working with shoes off

Chewing gum

Cooking

Looking through magazines or catalogues

Placing desk anywhere in the room for a work period

Playing with Legos

Listening to a record

Using the tape recorder

Drawing, painting

Taking a 10-minute break

Watering the plants

Completing a task to "beat the timer"

Earning a piece of a model car (completing the model when all pieces are earned)

Listening to a story on the tape recorder

Listening to a book on the computer

Dictating a story onto a tape

Using a lap-top computer for an assignment

Doing an assignment on the chalkboard

Playing a game with a friend

Taking extra recess or gym time with a friend

Bringing a guest to class

Using the telephone

Ordering a video for the entire class

Earning additional recess, computer lab, or gym time for the entire class

Taking a field trip

Lunch with the teacher

Having a class party (e.g., Jell-O party, popcorn party)

Having a class break or free time

Daydreaming

TOKEN REINFORCERS
(for general exchange)

Points

Tickets

Chips

Puzzle pieces (when the puzzle is together, then an activity is earned)

Coupons

of appropriate or desirable behaviors. Tokens thus obtained are exchangeable for a wide range of material or activity reinforcers. A *token economy* is a system by which specific numbers of tokens are contingently gained and exchanged for the backup material or activity reinforcers.

In making decisions about which type of reinforcer to use with a given youngster, the teacher should keep in mind that social reinforcement (e.g., attention, praise, approval) is easiest to implement on a continuing basis and is most likely to lead to enduring behavior change. Therefore, it is probably the type of reinforcement the teacher will wish to use most frequently. Unfortunately, in the initial stages of a behavior-change effort—especially when aggressive, disruptive, and other inappropriate behaviors are probably being richly rewarded by teacher and peer attention as well as by tangible reinforcers—the teacher will likely need to rely more on material and activity reinforcers.

Alternatively, a token reinforcement system may prove effective as the initial reinforcement strategy. Children's reinforcement preferences change over time, and teacher views of the appropriate reward value of desirable behaviors also change over time. Both variables are easily reflected in token-level adjustments. Those interested in a more detailed discussion of token-economy procedures may wish to refer to Ayllon and Azrin (1968), Kazdin (1975), Morris (1976), or Kaplan and Carter (1995). Some issues to be considered prior to implementing a token system are presented by Kaplan and Carter (1995) and are summarized as follows:

1. Identify what the student needs to do, the specific behaviors, to earn tokens. A list of these contingent behaviors needs to be posted (e.g., somewhere in the classroom, on the student's desk) to remind him or her of the expectations.

2. Decide what the tokens will be. Tokens should be age-appropriate and might include check marks, play money, stickers, tickets, and so forth. Provisions need to be made to prevent students from having tokens that they have not earned (e.g., accept only tokens validated with the teacher's signature).

3. Determine how many tokens the students will earn for given behaviors and how much they will be charged (in tokens) for the reinforcers.

4. Determine the back-up reinforcers—for example, prizes, entitlements (privileges students normally receive without having to earn them), other privileges.

5. Decide who will give the tokens (typically the teacher, associate, peer tutor).

6. Determine when the tokens will be given. Typically the token should be given as soon after the behavior is demonstrated as possible and according to the reinforcement schedule that is being followed with a particular student.

7. Determine how the tokens will be given (e.g., Given directly to the student? Marked on a card? Placed in a bank?). This system should be kept simple and time-efficient.

8. Determine when the tokens will be redeemed. The primary consideration should be the student's needs (i.e., how long the student is able to wait before receiving the reinforcer). Activities or privileges that may be disruptive to the instructional setting will require additional consideration.

Tokens, as well as other tangible rewards, should be combined with social reinforcers. It is critical to remember that, with few exceptions, reliance on material, activity, or token reinforcement eventually should give way to reliance upon more "real-life" social reinforcement.

The potency, or strength, of many reinforcers is increased when the reward, in addition to being inherently desirable, also brings reinforcement from peers and others (e.g., ordering a video to watch as a group, earning extra gym or recess time for the class). A further benefit of certain activity reinforcers (e.g., playing a game with peers, helping in the principal's office) is the degree to which the activity, while serving as a reward, also helps the student practice one or more Skillstreaming skills.

Identifying reinforcers

Identifying positive reinforcers for given youngsters is often necessary prior to presenting such events contingently upon the occurrence of desirable behaviors. Given that almost any event may serve as a reinforcer for one individual but not another, how can the teacher decide which reinforcers may best be used with a particular youngster? Simply, the youngster can be asked straightforwardly which items he or she would like to earn. Often, however, this approach will be insufficient because youngsters are unaware of the full range of reinforcers available to them. When they are aware, they may discount in advance the possibility that a reinforcer will actually be given. When this is the case, other identification procedures must be employed. Carr (1981) and others have reported three procedures typically used for this purpose. First, the teacher can often make an accurate determination of whether a given event is functioning as a reinforcer by carefully *observing effects* on the youngster. The event probably is reinforcing if the youngster (a) asks that the event be repeated, (b) seems happy during the event's occurrence, (c) seems unhappy when the event ends, or (d) will work in order to earn the event. If one or more of these reactions are observed, chances are good that the event is a positive reinforcer and that it can be contingently provided to strengthen appropriate, nonaggressive, or interactive behaviors.

Second, *observing choices* can also be helpful. As noted earlier in connection with activity reinforcers, when a youngster is free to choose among several equally available activities, which one the child chooses and how long he or she engages in it are clues to whether an event is reinforcing.

Finally, a small number of *questionnaires* have been effectively used to identify positive reinforcers. Examples of such questionnaires include Tharp and Wetzel's (1969) Mediation-Reinforcer Incomplete Blank, which consists of incomplete sentences that the youngster finishes by specifying particular reinforcers and identifying the mediator of such reinforcers (e.g., parent, peer, teacher). Homme, Csanyi, Gonzales, and Rechs (1970) offer the Reinforcing Event Menu, in which the youngster selects from a set of pictures those reinforcers for which he or she would most like to work.

As noted earlier, which objects or activities will in fact be reinforcing for a given child will vary from child to child and from time to time. In addition, the strength of selected reinforcers often decreases the more frequently they are used. Some teachers therefore find it useful to create a "reinforcement menu," or a list of rewards from which the student can choose. Such a menu may be in the form of an actual list, or it may be in the form of "coupons" for tangible and activity rewards. Each coupon may be a voucher for a particular amount of a given reinforcer (e.g., 5 minutes of computer time, 5 minutes playing with the gerbil). Using a reinforcement menu prevents students from becoming satiated with one reward when it is offered over a period of time and also allows them to make their own reinforcement choices.

Factors in presenting positive reinforcers

As noted earlier, a basic principle of contingency management is that the presentation of a reinforcing event contingent upon the occurrence of a given behavior will function to increase the likelihood of the reoccurrence of that behavior. Research has demonstrated a number of considerations that influence the success of this reinforcement effort and that should be reflected in the actual presentation of reinforcers.

Contingency. Although this rule for reinforcer presentation may seem obvious, it is sometimes forgotten or inadequately implemented. The connection between the desirable behavior and the subsequent reward should be made explicit to the youngster. As is true for all contingency management efforts, this description should be behaviorally specific—that is, the connection between particular behavioral acts and reinforcement should be emphasized over behaviorally ambiguous concepts like "good behavior" or "being well-behaved." Instead, comments like "Good job taking turns" and "Good listening" will help the youngster understand what has gained him or her the desired reinforcement.

Immediacy. Related to the communication of the behavioral reinforcement contingency is the fact that the more immediately the reinforcer follows the desirable behavior, the more likely it is to be effective. Rapid reinforcement augments the message that the immediately preceding behavior is desirable, whereas delayed reinforcement increases the risk that an inappropriate behavior will occur between the positive behavior and the reinforcement. Thus, the following sequence will occur: A (desirable behavior), B (undesirable behavior), and C (reinforcement intended for A that in actuality reinforces B).

Consistency. The effects of positive reinforcement on behavior are usually gradual, not dramatic, working slowly to strengthen behavior over a period of time. Thus, it is important that positive reinforcement be presented consistently. Consistency means not only that the teacher must be consistent, but also that the teacher must attempt to match his or her reinforcement efforts with similar efforts from as many other important persons in the youngster's life as possible. This means, ideally, that when the youngster enacts the behavior to be reinforced—in school in the presence of other teachers, at home in the presence of parents or siblings, or at play in the presence of peers—such reinforcement will be forthcoming.

Frequency. When first trying to establish a new appropriate behavior, the teacher reinforces all or almost all instances of that behavior. This high frequency of reinforcement is necessary to establish the behavior in the individual's behavioral repertoire. Once it seems clear that the behavior has actually been acquired, the teacher thins the reinforcement schedule, decreasing presentation so that only some of the youngster's desirable behaviors are followed by the reinforcement. This schedule, known as *partial reinforcement,* contributes to the continuation of the appropriate behavior because it parallels the sometimes reinforced/sometimes not reaction the youngster's appropriate behavior will elicit in other settings from other people. Partial reinforcement of the youngster's appropriate behaviors may be on a fixed-time schedule (e.g., at the end of each Skillstreaming session), on a fixed-number-of-response schedule (e.g., every fifth instance of the appropriate behavior), or on variable-time or number-of-response schedules. In any event, the basic strategy for reinforcement frequency remains a rich level for initial learning and partial reinforcement to sustain performance.

Amount. In our preceding discussion of frequency of reinforcement, we began to distinguish between learning (i.e., acquiring knowledge about how to perform new behaviors) and performance (i.e., overtly using these behaviors). The amount of reinforcement provided influences performance much more than it does learning. Youngsters will learn new appropriate behaviors just about as fast for a small reward as for a large reward, but they are more likely to perform the behaviors on a continuing basis when large rewards are involved. Yet rewards can be too large, causing a *satiation effect* in which youngsters lose interest in seeking the reinforcement because it is "too much of a good thing." Or rewards can be too small: too little time on the playground, too few tokens, too thin a social reinforcement schedule. The optimal amount can be determined empirically. If a youngster has in the past worked energetically to obtain a particular reinforcer but gradually slacks off and seems to lose interest in obtaining it, a satiation effect has probably occurred, and the amount of reinforcement should be reduced. On the other hand, if a youngster seems unwilling to work for a reinforcer believed desirable, it can be given once or twice for free—that is, not contingent on a specific desirable behavior. If the youngster seems to enjoy the reinforcer and even wishes more of the same, the amount used may have been too little. The amount can be increased and made contingent; observations will then show whether it is yielding the desired effect. If so, the amount of reinforcement offered is appropriate.

Variety. A type of reinforcement satiation parallel to a satiation effect due to excessive reinforcement occurs when the teacher uses the same approving phrase or other reward over and over again. Youngsters may perceive such reinforcement as mechanical, and they may thus lose interest in or decrease responsiveness to it. By varying the content of the reinforcer, the teacher can maintain its potency. Thus, instead of repeating "Nice job" four or five times, using a mix of comments (e.g., "Well done," "Good work," "You really listened") is more likely to yield a sustained effect.

Pairing with praise. Earlier, we noted that social reinforcement is most germane to enduring behavior change, though there are circumstances under which material, activity, or token reinforcers are at least initially more appropriate. To aid in the desired movement toward social reinforcement, the teacher pairs all presentations of material, activity, or token rewards with some expression of social reinforcement: an approving comment, a pat on the back, a wink, a smile, and so forth. A major benefit of this tactic is noted by Walker (1979):

> By virtue of being consistently paired with reinforcement delivery, praise can take on the reinforcing properties of

the actual reinforcer(s) used. This is especially important since teacher praise is not always initially effective with many deviant children. By systematically increasing the incentive value of praise through pairing, the teacher is in a position to gradually reduce the frequency of (material, activity, or token) reinforcement and to substitute praise. After systematic pairing, the teacher's praise may be much more effective in maintaining the child's appropriate behavior. (p. 108)

Positive reinforcement for prevention

These rules for maximizing the effectiveness of positive reinforcement are essentially remedial in nature. They are efforts to substitute appropriate prosocial behaviors for already existing aggressive, disruptive, antisocial, withdrawn, or asocial behaviors. Positive reinforcement may also be used for preventive purposes. Sarason et al. (1972) urge teachers to present positive reinforcement openly to specific youngsters in such a manner that the entire class is aware of it. As they comment:

> Positive reinforcement for productive activity for the whole group is a powerful preventive technique. It can eliminate or reduce the great majority of behavior problems in classrooms. Try to praise the children who are paying attention. Attend to those who are sitting in their seats, doing their work in a nondisruptive manner. "That's right, John, you're doing a good job." "You watched the board all the time I was presenting the problem. That's paying attention."... These responses not only reinforce the child to whom they are directed, but they also help to provide the rest of the class with an explicit idea of what you mean by paying attention and working hard. Young children, especially ... learn to model their actions after the positive examples established and noted by the teacher. (p. 18)

Such open attempts to "catch them being good" are strongly recommended for the Skillstreaming group.

Shaping

The first time a student practices an unfamiliar behavior, the performance may be rough or imperfect. This is true for classroom behaviors such as participating or paying attention, which may not have been exhibited often by a particular student. Therefore, even a partial or flawed performance should be reinforced in early sessions. As the student becomes more confident and skilled in performing the behavior, rewards are given for the improved skill behaviors and eliminated for the earlier and less adequate approximations. Gradually, the rewarded performance will come to approximate the target behavior. The student's performance is thus "shaped" by the teacher. Social behavior can be shaped according to the following guidelines, developed by Sloane (1976):

1. Find some behavior in which the child is currently engaging that is a better approximation of your goal for him than his usual behavior and reinforce this approximation each time it occurs.

2. When an approximation has become more frequent for several days, select a slightly better one for reinforcement and stop reinforcing the first.

3. Each approximation should be only slightly different from the last one.

4. Let a new approximation receive many reinforcements before moving on to another approximation.

5. Never look a gift horse in the mouth, but reinforce any behavior that is better than that currently required. (p. 68–70)

Group reinforcement

Children are very responsive to the influence of their peers. This phenomenon can be used to encourage the performance of infrequent but desirable behaviors. In using group reinforcement, the teacher provides a reward (e.g., food, activity) to the entire group contingent upon the cooperative behavior of individual group members. If the reward is meaningful and desirable to the entire group,

group members are likely to put pressure on one another to behave appropriately.

> **EXAMPLE.** For the last three sessions, Tammy has made statements about how "stupid and dumb" she thought the Skillstreaming group was. When Tammy made these remarks, other students joined in by adding their own derogatory comments. The group leader decided to deal with this problem by telling the students that if, for the next three sessions, they encouraged each other's participation in the activities, they would have a popcorn party and watch one of their favorite videos. The teacher prepared a small chart on which he wrote the dates of the next three sessions and a space for marking how frequently encouraging statements were offered. The party was a desirable enough group reinforcer that when Tammy began her usual comments the other students insisted that she stop disrupting the group.

Removing Positive Reinforcement

The teacher's behavior management goal with youngsters displaying aggressive or other problematic behaviors is, in a general sense, twofold. Both sides of the behavioral coin—appropriate and inappropriate, prosocial and antisocial, desirable and undesirable—must be attended to. In a proper behavior-change effort, procedures are simultaneously or sequentially employed to reduce and eliminate the inappropriate, antisocial, or undesirable components of the youngsters' behavioral repertoires and to increase the quality and frequency of appropriate, prosocial, or desirable components. This latter task is served primarily by the direct teaching of prosocial behaviors via Skillstreaming participation and by the contingent presentation of positive reinforcement following skill use. Conversely, the contingent removal of positive reinforcement in response to aggressive, disruptive, or other negative behaviors is the major behavior management strategy for reducing or eliminating such behaviors. Therefore, in conjunction with the procedures discussed previously for presenting positive reinforcement, the teacher should also simultaneously or consecutively employ one or both of the following techniques for removing positive reinforcement.

Extinction

Extinction is the withdrawal or removal of positive reinforcement for aggressive or other undesirable behaviors that have been either deliberately or inadvertently reinforced in the past. This technique is the procedure of choice with milder forms of aggression (e.g., sarcasm, put-downs, or other low-level forms of verbal aggression).

Knowing when to use extinction. Determining when to use extinction is, of course, in part a function of each teacher's guiding group management philosophy and tolerance for deviance. Each teacher will have to decide individually the range of undesirable behaviors that can be safely ignored. Taking a rather conservative stance, Walker (1979) suggests that extinction "should be applied only to those inappropriate behaviors that are minimally disruptive to classroom atmosphere" (p. 40). Others are somewhat more liberal in its application (e.g., Carr, 1981). In any event, it is clear that the first step in applying extinction is knowing when to use it.

Providing positive reinforcement for appropriate behaviors. As noted earlier, attempts to reduce inappropriate behavior by reinforcement withdrawal should always be accompanied by efforts to increase appropriate behaviors by reinforcement provision. This combination of efforts will succeed especially well when the appropriate and inappropriate behaviors involved are opposite from, or at least incompatible with, each other (e.g., reward in-seat behavior, ignore out-of-seat behavior; reward talking at a conversational level, ignore talking loudly).

Identifying the positive reinforcers maintaining inappropriate behaviors. The reinforcers maintaining inappropriate behaviors are the ones to be withheld. The teacher should discern what the youngster is working for; what payoffs are involved; and what reinforcers are being sought or earned by aggression, disruptiveness, and similar behaviors. Very often, the answer will be attention. Looking, staring, yelling at, talking to, or turning toward are common teacher and peer reactions to a youngster's inappropriate behaviors. The withdrawal of such positive social reinforcement by ignoring the behaviors (by turning away and not yelling, talking, or looking at the perpetrator) are the teacher and peer behaviors that will effect extinction. Ignoring someone who would normally receive one's attention is itself a talent, as the following extinction rules illustrate.

Knowing how to ignore low-level aggressive behaviors. Carr (1981) has suggested guidelines for ignoring low-level aggressive behaviors (e.g., verbal comments). First, do not comment to the child that you are ignoring him or her. Long (or even short) explanations provided to youngsters about why teachers, peers, or others are going to avoid attending to given behaviors provide precisely the type of social reinforcement extinction is designed to withdraw. Such explanations are to be avoided. Ignoring behavior should simply occur with no forewarning, introduction, or prior explanation. Second, do not look away suddenly when the child behaves inappropriately. Doing so may communicate the message that "I really noticed and was impelled to action by your behavior," the exact opposite of an extinction message. As Carr recommends, "It is best to ignore the behavior by reacting to it in a matter of fact way by continuing natural ongoing activities" (p. 38).

These guidelines should be followed only with behaviors that are not harmful to others. Observed incidents of verbal and physical aggression (or harassment) must be dealt with quickly and consistently in order to maintain an a safe school environment. Thus, extinction is not supported as a method for dealing with behaviors that could cause harm to the student or others (Hartwig & Ruesch, 1994).

Using extinction consistently. As is true for the provision of reinforcement, removal of reinforcement must be consistent. Within a given Skillstreaming group, this rule of consistency means that the teacher and students must act in concert and that the teacher must be consistent across time. Within a given school, consistency means that, to the degree possible, all teachers having significant contact with a given youngster must strive to ignore the same inappropriate behaviors. In addition, to avoid the youngster's making a type of "I can't act up here, but I can out there" discrimination, parent conferences should be held to bring parents, siblings, and other significant real-world figures in the youngster's life into the extinction effort. As Karoly (1980) notes, when consistency of nonattending is not reached, the behavior will be intermittently or partially reinforced, a circumstance that we noted earlier would lead to its becoming highly resistant to extinction.

Using extinction for a long enough period of time. Disruptive behaviors often have a long history of positive reinforcement. Especially if much of that history is one of intermittent reinforcement, efforts to undo them must be sustained. Teacher persistence in this regard will usually succeed. There are, however, two types of events to keep in mind when judging the effectiveness of extinction efforts. The first is what is known as the *extinction burst*. When extinction is first introduced, it is not uncommon for the rate or intensity of the aggressive behavior to increase sharply before it begins its more gradual decline toward zero. It is important that the teacher not be discouraged during this short detour. In fact, the meaning of the increase is that extinction is beginning to work. In addition, inappropriate behaviors that have been successfully extinguished will reappear occasionally for reasons that are difficult to determine. Like the extinction burst, this *spontaneous recovery* is transitory and will disappear if the teacher persists in the extinction effort.

Time-out

In time-out, a youngster who engages in aggressive or other inappropriate behavior is physically removed from all sources of reinforcement for a specified time period. As with extinction, the purpose of time-out is to reduce the undesirable behavior. It differs from extinction in that extinction involves removing reinforcement from the person, whereas time-out usually involves physically removing the person from the reinforcing situation.

In school-based practice, time-out has typically taken three forms. *Isolation time-out* requires that the youngster be removed from the classroom to a time-out room. *Exclusion time-out* is somewhat less restrictive but also involves removing the youngster from sources of reinforcement; it is perhaps the most common form of time-out used in elementary school classrooms. Here the youngster is required to go to an area of the classroom and perhaps to sit in a "quiet chair" (Firestone, 1976), which is sometimes behind a screen. The youngster is not removed from the classroom but is excluded from classroom activities for a specified time period. *Nonexclusion time-out* (also called *contingent observation*), the least restrictive time-out variant, requires the youngster to sit and watch on the periphery of classroom activities, to observe the appropriate behaviors of other youngsters. This variant combines time-out with modeling opportunities and thus may be the preferred approach for Skillstreaming group use. All three of these variants of time-out may be effectively employed to deal with problematic behavior in the Skillstreaming group. The implementation of time-out in any of its forms optimally employs the procedures next described.

Knowing when to use time-out. Extinction, it will be recalled, is the recommended procedure for undesirable behaviors that can be safely ignored. Behaviors potentially injurious to other youngsters require a more active teacher response, possibly time-out. Exclusion or nonexclusion time-out is also the procedure to use for less severe forms of problematic behavior when the combination of extinction and positive reinforcement for more positive behaviors has been attempted and failed.

Whenever possible the student should be verbally directed to use the time-out area. If he or she refuses to go, the rest of the class or group may be removed instead of the problematic student. This will leave the student with the same response—time-out from positive reinforcement. In certain severe cases, it may be necessary to move a student physically to time-out. Such physical intervention should be used only as a last resort to protect the safety of the child or others. This may be the case for youngsters aged 2 to 12 who display high rates of potentially dangerous or aggressive behaviors.

Providing positive reinforcement for appropriate behaviors. As is the case for extinction, positive reinforcement for appropriate behaviors should accompany time-out. When possible, the behaviors positively reinforced should be opposite to, or at least incompatible with, those for which the time-out procedure is used. Carr (1981) recommends an additional basis combining these two techniques:

> Although one important reason for using positive reinforcement is to strengthen nonaggressive behaviors to the point where they replace aggressive behaviors, there is a second reason for using reinforcement procedures. If extensive use of positive reinforcement is made, then time-out will become all the more aversive since it would involve the temporary termination of a rich diversity of

positive reinforcers. In this sense, then, the use of positive reinforcement helps to enhance the effectiveness of the time-out procedure. (pp. 41–42)

Arranging an effective time-out setting. The majority of school buildings do not have a small, well-ventilated, well-lit room, easily monitored by an adult, for a youngster to sit in during isolation time-out. However, if such a room is available, the time-out period should be as brief as possible (e.g., until the student is calm). Time-out must be a boring environment, with all reinforcers removed. When using exclusionary time-out there should be no attractive or distracting objects or opportunities—no toys, books, posters, people, windows to look out, sounds to overhear, or other obvious or not-so-obvious potential reinforcers.

Sending a youngster to time-out. The teacher can take a number of actions when initiating time-out to increase the likelihood of its effectiveness. As for positive reinforcement, immediacy is an issue. Time-out is optimally instituted immediately following the aggressive or other behavior one is seeking to modify. Having earlier explained to the target youngster the nature of time-out, as well as when and why it will be used, the teacher should initiate the procedure in a more-or-less automatic manner following the undesirable behavior—that is, in a way that minimizes social reinforcement. Concretely, this means sending the youngster to time-out without a lengthy explanation but with a brief description of the precipitating behavior. This process is best conducted in a calm and matter-of-fact manner. To minimize reinforcement of aggression during this process, it is best if the distance between the teaching setting and time-out room or area is small: The shorter the distance and the briefer the transportation time, the less opportunity exists for inadvertent social reinforcement by the teacher. In addition to these considerations, the effectiveness of time-out is further enhanced by its consistent application, when appropriate, by the same teacher on other occasions as well as by other teachers.

Maintaining a youngster in time-out. The skilled contingency manager must deal with two questions during a youngster's period in time-out: What is the youngster doing? and How long should time-out last? Answering the first question by monitoring the youngster makes certain that the time-out experience is not in fact pleasant or positively reinforcing. For example, rather than being a removal from positive reinforcement, time-out may in reality help a youngster avoid an aversive situation from which he or she would prefer to escape. Similarly, if monitoring reveals that the youngster is singing or playing, time-out will be less effective. Unless the situation can be made essentially nonreinforcing, a different behavioral intervention may be required.

With regard to duration, most successful time-out implementations have been from 2 to 20 minutes long, with clear preference for the shorter time spans in this range. If time-out periods are longer than necessary, the student may calm down and then act up again out of boredom or frustration. When experimenting to find the optimal duration for any given youngster, it is best, as White, Nielson, and Johnson (1972) have shown, to begin with a short duration (e.g., 3 to 5 minutes) and to lengthen the time until an effective span is identified rather than to shorten an initially longer span. This latter approach would, again, risk the danger of introducing an event experienced as positive reinforcement by the youngster when the intention is quite the opposite.

Releasing a youngster from time-out. We noted earlier in connection with extinction that withdrawal of positive reinforcement frequently leads to an extinction burst, in which more intense or more frequent problem behaviors appear before they begin to subside. This same pattern is evident with withdrawal from positive reinforcement—that is, time-out. The first few times a youngster is directed to use time-out, what might be termed a *time-out burst* of heightened aggression or other problem behaviors may occur. These outbursts will usually subside, especially if the teacher requires the time-out to be served and the outburst does not result in the suspension of the time-out.

The student's release from time-out should be conducted in a matter-of-fact manner, and the student should be quickly returned to regular Skillstreaming activities. Lengthy teacher explanations or moralizing are, once again, tactically erroneous provisions of positive reinforcement that communicate to the youngster that acting out in the classroom will bring a short period of removal from reinforcement and then a (probably longer) period of undivided teacher attention. However, it is important once the student returns to ongoing activities that the teacher quickly reinforce the student for subsequent positive behaviors. The Skillstreaming group must be a positive place—a place where the student wants to be—or time-out will be perceived as a reward instead of a negative consequence.

Prosocial alternatives. The responsible group leader will plan instruction in specific skills that could serve as prosocial ways of dealing with the problem that led to the use of time-out. For example, the student could be guided through the steps of Problem Solving (Skill 41) to reduce the likelihood that the event will reoccur. In addition, the leader must attempt to deescalate future occurrences of such behavior through techniques like prompting.

Punishment versus Consequences

It is a common finding that, when punishment does succeed in altering behavior, such effects are often temporary. In part because of this temporary effect, but more so for even more important reasons, a number of contingency management researchers have assumed an antipunishment stance, seeing little place for punishment, especially in the contemporary classroom. This view corresponds to punishment research demonstrating such undesirable side effects as withdrawal from social contact, counteraggression toward the punisher, modeling of punishing behavior, disruption of social relationships, failure of effects to generalize, selective avoidance (refraining from inappropriate behaviors only when under surveillance), and stigmatizing labeling effects (Azrin & Holz, 1966; Bandura, 1973). Nelsen, Lott, and Glenn (1993) state:

> Most teachers mean well when they administer punishment. They believe punishment is the best way to motivate students to behave properly. If the misbehavior stops for a while because of punishment, they may have been fooled into thinking they were right. However, when they become aware of the long-range effects of punishment on students, they naturally want to learn more respectful methods of motivating students to behave properly. (p. 78)

An encouraging environment teaches students to respect themselves and others and treats all students with dignity. Rarely are students exposed to punishment; however, clear and consistent limits on unacceptable behavior are set and enforced so all students have the opportunity to learn. Such limits involve the administration of *logical consequences.* Logical consequences (Dreikurs & Cassel, 1972) differ from punishment in several important ways. Such consequences are related to the misbehavior (punishment rarely is); are planned, explained, and agreed upon by students in advance (there is often no forewarning with punishment); administered in a neutral way (not in anger, as punishment often is); and given consistently. In addition, they are reasonable and demonstrate respect by giving students a choice (i.e., engage in the inappropriate behavior and receive an unpleasant consequence, or engage in the appropriate behavior and receive positive reinforcement).

When planning logical consequences, teachers will need to keep in mind that these consequences must be reasonable, related to the misbehavior, and respectful to the student (Nelsen et al., 1993). Examples of logical consequences include the following:

- For choosing to talk instead of completing a class assignment, the student must complete the work during an enjoyable activity.

- For choosing to fight when provoked at recess, the student must stay on a specific area of the playground where there is increased supervision.

- For choosing to take a notebook belonging to someone else, making restitution.

Individual Behavior Plans

At times, more systematic, structured behavior management plans are needed to create a desired change in individual children's problematic behaviors. A student for whom it is frequently necessary to use time-out, for example, can often benefit from an individual behavior plan. When indicated by the intensity or frequency of the behavior, such a plan can be designed by following these steps:

1. Identify the target behavior to be changed. To do this, list the student's problematic behaviors. Then choose one behavior to decrease in frequency. This may be the behavior that bothers

the teacher the most, the one that would be the easiest to change, or the one creating the greatest problem for the student.

2. Determine the positive behavior that is incompatible with the undesirable one. For example, if the undesirable behavior is not following directions, the incompatible behavior would be following directions.

3. Obtain baseline data to determine (a) how frequently the undesirable behavior occurs, (b) how frequently the incompatible behavior occurs, and (c) under what conditions each behavior occurs. This process need not be complicated. For example, you may list the undesirable behavior and the incompatible behavior and make a tally mark for each occurrence of the behavior on a given day. Or you may find an A–B–C format useful (specifying the *antecedent* conditions under which the behavior occurred, the specific *behavior* exhibited by the child, and the *consequences* that the child receives as a result of that behavior). The A–B–Cs can be written on a sheet of paper and quickly documented whenever the behavior of concern and the incompatible behavior are observed.

4. Determine an effective reinforcer and deliver it consistently when the incompatible or desirable behavior occurs.

5. Deciding on the frequency of reinforcement delivery is next: If the reward is given immediately following the performance of the desirable behavior, it is more likely that the behavior will be repeated. Consequently, some type of small reinforcement (e.g., verbal encouragement along with a point or token) should be given immediately following the behavior the teacher wants to increase. A larger reward (e.g., a special privilege) may then be given at a later time—for example, after the student earns a certain number of points or tokens. A chart or graph of points earned for the positive behavior will inform the student of progress made.

6. Once the individual plan has been implemented, monitor behavior change. Teacher observations and recording the frequency of both the problematic and incompatible, desirable behaviors will provide information on the degree to which desired behavioral changes are in fact occurring.

CHAPTER 10
Teaching for Skill Generalization

As the social skills movement in general and Skillstreaming in particular have matured, and evidence regarding effectiveness has accumulated, it has become clear that skill acquisition is a reliable finding across both training methods and populations. However, generalization is quite another matter. Both generalization to new settings (transfer) and over time (maintenance) have been reported to occur in only a minority of cases. The main concern of any teaching effort is not how students perform in the teaching setting, but how well they perform in their real lives. This chapter is devoted to examining approaches to enhance skill generalization.

INTERVENTION AS INOCULATION

Many traditional interventions have reflected a core belief in personality change as both the target and outcome of effective treatment, as well as a strong tendency to ignore environmental influences on behavior. In brief, these approaches have viewed intervention as a sort of "psychological inoculation." It has been assumed that the positive changes believed to have taken place within the individual's personality would enable the client to deal effectively with problematic events wherever and whenever they might occur. That is, transfer and maintenance would occur automatically.

TRAIN AND HOPE

Research on psychotherapy was initiated in the 1950s and grew both in quantity and scope during the 1960s and 1970s. Much of the outcome research at that time included systematic follow-up probes, which sought to ascertain whether gains present at the end of the formal intervention had generalized across settings and/or time. Stokes and Baer (1977) described this time as one in which transfer and maintenance were hoped for and noted if they did occur.

The overwhelming result of these investigations was that, much more often than not, transfer and maintenance of intervention gains did not occur. Treatment and training did not often serve as an inoculation; gains did not persist automatically; transfer and maintenance did not necessarily follow (Goldstein & Kanfer, 1979; Keeley, Shemberg, & Carbonell, 1976). The failure of the inoculation model, as revealed by evidence accumulated during the train-and-hope phase, led to a third phase—the energetic development, evaluation, and use of procedures explicitly designed to enhance transfer and maintenance of intervention gains.

DEVELOPMENT OF TRANSFER AND MAINTENANCE ENHANCERS

The effort to develop means of maximizing transfer and maintenance has resulted in considerable success. A variety of useful techniques have been developed, evaluated, and incorporated into practice. These procedures, which collectively constitute the current technology of transfer and maintenance enhancement, are listed in Table 5 and are examined in detail in the remainder of this section.

Provision of General Principles

Transfer of training may be facilitated by providing the student with the general mediating principles that govern satisfactory performance on both the original and the transfer task. The student can be given the rules, strategies, or organizing principles that lead to successful performance. The general finding that understanding the principles underlying successful performance can enhance transfer to new tasks and contexts has been reported in a number of domains of psychological research, including studies of labeling, rules, advance organizers, and learning sets. It is a robust finding, with empirical support in both laboratory and psychoeducational settings.

No matter how competently Skillstreaming leaders seek to create in the role-play setting the "feel" of the real-life setting in which the

---

Table 5 Transfer- and Maintenance-Enhancing Procedures

Transfer

1. Provision of general principles (general case programming)
2. Overlearning (maximizing response availability)
3. Stimulus variability (training sufficient exemplars, training loosely)
4. Identical elements (programming common stimuli)
5. Mediated generalization (self-recording, self-reinforcement, self-punishment, self-instruction)

Maintenance

1. Thin reinforcement (increase intermittency, unpredictability)
2. Delay reinforcement
3. Fade prompts
4. Provide booster sessions
5. Prepare for real-life nonreinforcement
6. Program for reinforcement in the natural environment
7. Use natural reinforcers

---

student will need to use the skill, and no matter how well the co-actor in a given role-play matches the actual qualities the real target person possesses, there will always be differences between role-play and real world. Even when the student has role-played the skill a number of times, the demands of the actual situation will depart at least in some respects from the demands portrayed in the role-play. And the real parent, real peer, or real teacher is likely to respond at least somewhat differently than did the student's role-play partner. When the student has a good grasp of the principles underlying a situation (demands, expected behaviors, norms, purposes, rules) and the principles underlying the skill (why *these* steps, in *this* order, toward *which* ends), successful transfer of skilled performance becomes more likely.

Overlearning

Transfer of training has been shown to be enhanced by procedures that maximize overlearning or response availability: The likelihood that a response will be available is clearly a function of its prior use. We repeat and repeat foreign language phrases we are trying to learn, we insist that our child spend an hour per day in piano practice, and we devote considerable time practicing to make a golf swing smooth and "automatic." These are simply expressions of the response-availability notion—that is, the more we have practiced responses (especially *correct* ones), the easier it will be to use them in other contexts or at later times. We need not rely solely on everyday experience to find support for this conclusion. It has been well established empirically that, other things being equal, the response emitted most frequently in the past is more likely to be emitted on subsequent occasions. However, it is not sheer practice of attempts at effective behaviors that is of most benefit to transfer, but practice of *successful* attempts. Overlearning involves extending learning over more trials than would be necessary merely to produce initial changes in the individual's behavior. In all too many instances of teaching, one or two successes at a given task are taken as evidence to move on to the next task or the next level of the original task. This is an error if one wishes to maximize transfer via overlearning. To maximize transfer, the guiding rule should not be "practice makes perfect" (implying that one simply practices until one gets it right and then moves on), but "practice of perfect" (implying numerous overlearning trials of correct responses after the initial success).

Youths who have just received good feedback from group members and leaders about their role-play (all steps followed and well portrayed) may object to the request that they role-play the skill a second or third time. Although valid concerns exist about the consequences of boredom when teaching a group of often restless children, the value of skill repetition cannot be overstressed. Often leaders, not students, are most bothered or bored by the repetition. To assuage any student concerns, leaders can point to the value for professional athletes of warm-ups, shoot-arounds, batting practice, and other repetitive practice. Such practice makes core skills nearly automatic and frees the player to concentrate on strategy.

In many real-life contexts, people and events actually work against the student's use of prosocial behaviors. It is therefore quite common and appropriate for a Skillstreaming group to spend two, three, or even more sessions role-playing a single skill. To reduce the possible interference of new learning on previously learned materials, a second skill should be introduced only when the student can recall the steps of the first skill, has had opportunities to role-play it, and has shown some initial transfer outside of the group teaching setting (e.g., a successfully completed homework assignment).

Stimulus Variability

In the previous section, we addressed enhancement of transfer by means of practice and repetition—that is, by the sheer number of correct skill responses the student makes to a given situation. Transfer is also enhanced by the variability or range of situations to which the individual responds. Teaching related to even two situations is better than teaching related to one. As noted several years ago, "The implication is clear that in order to maximize positive transfer, training should provide for some sampling of the population of stimuli to which the response must ultimately be given" (Goldstein, Heller, & Sechrest, 1966, p. 220). As Kazdin (1975) comments:

> One way to program response maintenance and transfer
> of training is to develop the target behavior in a variety of
> situations and in the presence of several individuals. If the
> response is associated with a range of settings, individuals,
> and other cues, it is less likely to be lost when the situations
> change. (p. 21)

Epps, Thompson, and Lane (1985) discuss stimulus variability for transfer enhancement as it might operate in school contexts under the rubrics "train sufficient examples" and "train loosely." They observe that generalization of new skills or behaviors can also be facilitated by training students under a wide variety of conditions. Manipulating the numbers of leaders, settings, and response classes involved in the intervention promotes generalization by exposing students to a variety of situations. If for purposes of overlearning students are asked to role-play a given skill correctly, let us say, three times, each attempt should involve a different co-actor, a different constructed setting, and, especially, a different need for the same skill.

Identical Elements

In perhaps the earliest experimental work dealing with transfer enhancement, Thorndike and Woodworth (1901) concluded that, when one habit had a facilitative effect on another, it was to the degree that the habits shared identical elements. Ellis (1965) and Osgood (1953) later emphasized the importance for transfer of similarity between characteristics of the training and application tasks. As Osgood (1953) noted: "The greater the similarity between practice and test stimuli, the greater the amount of positive transfer" (p. 213). This conclusion rests on solid experimental support.

In Skillstreaming, the principle of identical elements is implemented by procedures that increase the "real-lifeness" of the stimuli (places, people, events, etc.) to which the leader is helping the student learn to respond with effective, satisfying behaviors. Two broad strategies exist for attaining such high levels of correspondence between in-group and extra-group stimuli. The first concerns the place in which Skillstreaming takes place. Typically, we remain in the school or institution and by use of props and imagination try to recreate the feel of the real-world context in which the student plans to use the skill. Whenever possible, however, the Skillstreaming group leaves the formal teaching setting and meets in the actual locations in which the problem behaviors occur: "Fight on the playground? Let's have our session there." "Sitting alone at lunch? Let's move to the lunchroom." "Argument with a teacher in the hallway? Today's group will meet out there."

In addition to implementing identical elements via in vivo locations, Skillstreaming employs the principle of transfer enhancement by having co-trainees in the group be the same people the youngster interacts with on a regular basis outside of the group. It is especially valuable to employ such a strategy when the others involved are persons one is not getting along with well and with whom more prosocially skilled interactions are desired. Suppose, for example, you are starting two Skillstreaming groups of eight children each. Two of the 16 children fight a lot. For most interventions, for behavior management purposes and for purposes of being better able to carry out the goals of the interventions, one youth would be placed in one group, the second in the other. Not so in Skillstreaming. If students fight, put them in the same group and hope that conflict occurs during a group session. These two youths are real-world figures for one another. They employ poor quality prosocial (and "high quality" antisocial) behaviors in their chronic inability to get along outside the group. What a fine opportunity their participation in the same group presents to teach them positive alternatives for dealing with their real-life difficulties.

Thus, if given the choice in starting a single Skillstreaming group, we would select all of its members from one class or unit, rather than one or a few each from more than one class or unit. Live together, play together, go to class together, fight together—you learn Skillstreaming together. For the same reason, when implementing Skillstreaming in residential, agency, or institutional settings, our teaching groups are most often constructed to directly parallel the facility's unit, crew, cottage, or ward structure.

Mediated Generalization

The one certain commonality, by definition present in both teaching and application settings, is the target student. Mediated generalization—mediated by the student, not by others—is an approach to transfer enhancement that relies on instructing the student in a series of context-bridging, self-regulation competencies (Neilans & Israel, 1981). Operationally, it consists of instructing the student in self-recording, self-reinforcement, self-punishment, and self-instruction. Epps et al. (1985), working in a special education setting, have structured these generalization-mediating steps as follows.

Self-recording

1. The teacher sets up the data collection system—that is, selects a target behavior, defines it in measurable terms, and decides on an appropriate recording technique.

2. The teacher tries out the data collection system.

3. The teacher teaches the student how to use the data collection system.

4. The teacher reinforces the student for taking accurate data.

We have found this technique to be beneficial for several reasons: First, the group leader can become aware of the student's functioning in all school settings (i.e., implementing self-recording procedures may give the teacher an indication of the frequency with which the student actually attempts the skill). Second, skill performance may not always result in positive reinforcement from others, but having the student record performance lets the student know that the teacher will later reinforce these efforts. Finally, many students are far more motivated to use newly learned skills when they, rather than an outside observer, monitor and record their performance. (Figure 6, on p. 75, presents a sample Self-Recording Form).

Self-reinforcement

The steps in self-reinforcement are summarized by Epps et al. (1985) as follows:

1. The teacher determines how many points a student has earned, and the student simply records these.

2. The teacher tells the student to decide how many points should be awarded for appropriate behavior.

3. The student practices self-reinforcement under teacher supervision.

4. The student employs self-reinforcement without teacher supervision.

Frequently, environmental support is insufficient to maintain newly learned skills. In fact, as mentioned earlier, many real-life environments actually discourage children's efforts at prosocial behavior. For this reason we have found it useful to include the teaching of self-reinforcement procedures.

Self-recording forms provide a reinforcing function. Self-reinforcement may also consist of verbal praise, in addition to (and later in lieu of) earning points. For example, if the student follows all the steps of a particular skill especially well, self-reinforcement might take the form of saying something positive (e.g., "Good for me" or "I did a good job"). Teachers can help encourage students by having them rehearse self-rewarding statements following completion of homework assignments or after spontaneous skill use. Videotaping role-play efforts can be very reinforcing; in addition, being able to review performance helps students assess their skill proficiency.

Self-punishment

Self-punishment is taught in a manner directly parallel to that just described for self-reinforcement (Epps et al., 1985). It is important to note that, when self-punishment is used with elementary-age children, the language needs to stress the child's accountability—for example, "You didn't earn your points" as opposed to "I am taking points away." Some practitioners may condone taking away points the student has already earned; however, at this age level removing previously earned points may result in behaviors even more problematic than the one the teacher had hoped to remediate. Thus, self-punishment as described here refers to the student's failure to earn points if he or she does not display a desired behavior.

Self-instruction

According to Epps et al. (1985), self-instruction involves the following steps:

1. The teacher models the appropriate behavior while talking through the task aloud so that the student can hear.

2. The student performs the task with overt instructions from the teacher.

3. The student performs the task while talking aloud the self-instructions (overt instructions).

4. The student performs the task with silent (covert) self-instructions.

In recent years, the cognitive behavior modification therapies, especially those relying heavily on self-instructional processes, have grown in popularity. Self-mediated approaches to generalization have grown as well. Verbal self-mediation, discussed in more detail in chapter 8, is emphasized during the modeling and role-play portions of the Skillstreaming groups.

MAINTENANCE-ENHANCING PROCEDURES

The persistence, durability, or maintenance of behaviors developed by skills training approaches is primarily a matter of the manipulation of reinforcement both during the original teaching and in the youngster's natural environment. There are several ways of manipulating such maintenance-enhancing reinforcement. We will first examine what can be done during the Skillstreaming session, then turn to ways to increase generalization beyond the Skillstreaming group.

During the Skillstreaming Session

Thinning of reinforcement

A rich, continuous reinforcement schedule is optimal for the establishment of new behaviors. Maintenance of learned behaviors will be enhanced if the reinforcement schedule is gradually thinned. Thinning of reinforcement proceeds best by moving from a continuous (every trial) schedule, to some form of intermittent schedule, to the level of sparse and infrequent reinforcement characteristic of the natural environment. In fact, the maintenance-enhancing goal of such a thinning process is to make the reinforcement schedule indistinguishable from that typically found in real-world contexts.

Delay of reinforcement

Resistance to extinction is also enhanced by delay of reinforcement. As Epps et al. (1985) note:

> During the early stages of an intervention, reinforcement should be immediate and continuously presented contingent on the desired response. . . . After the behavior becomes firmly established in the student's repertoire, it is important to introduce a delay in presenting the reinforcement. Delayed reinforcement is a closer approximation to reinforcement conditions in the natural environment. (p. 21)

Delay of reinforcement may be implemented, according to Sulzer-Azaroff and Mayer (1991), by (a) increasing the size or complexity of the responses required before reinforcement is provided; (b) adding a time delay between the response and the delivery of reinforcement; and (c) in token systems, increasing the interval between the receipt of tokens and the opportunity to spend them and/or requiring more tokens in exchange for a given reinforcer.

Fading of prompts

Prompting may involve describing the specific types of situations in the real world in which students should use a given skill (i.e., instructed generalization; Stokes & Baer, 1977). Students can be encouraged to use a particular skill, or verbally prompted, in a variety of real-life settings. Historically, teachers have used this principle of generalization by prompting students during "teachable moments," or times the skill is actually needed. When potential problems arise in the classroom, the teacher can elicit a prosocial response by suggesting a particular skill. For example, Todd, who often became disruptive in the classroom, had completed all of his academic assignments and was sitting quietly at his desk; rather than waiting for Todd to become disruptive, the teacher suggested that he use Deciding on Something to Do (Skill 12). This proactive approach turns naturally occurring problem situations into realistic learning opportunities, thus providing more opportunities for practice. Furthermore, it helps create a positive environment for learning ways to deal with interpersonal problems.

Another way of prompting skill use is to provide written prompts in the form of cue cards or cue posters. Cue cards list the behavioral steps of a skill, along with a space for the student to check each step, either as each is enacted or after all steps are completed. The card may also include a place for self-evaluation. The student may tape the card to his or her desk, if it is a skill that is to be used in the classroom, or keep it in a pocket or folder if it is for use in another setting (e.g., on the school bus, on the playground, in another classroom, at home). For example, Michelle needed to practice Staying Out of Fights (Skill 40) on the playground and in the school hallways. Her cue card is shown in Figure 8.

Figure 8   Michelle's Cue Card

Staying Out of Fights

☐ 1. Stop and count to 10.

☐ 2. Decide what your problem is.

☐ 3. Think about your choices:

Walk away.

Talk to the person.

Ask someone for help.

☐ 4. Act out your best choice.

How did I do?

Displaying a cue poster of a given skill will help students remember to practice it. Placed wherever it is most appropriate, the cue poster presents the title of the skill and its behavioral steps. If students have been instructed in the skills of Playing a Game (Skill 18) and Dealing with Losing (Skill 49), for example, displaying cue posters for these skills in the area of the classroom used for free-time activities may remind the students of these particular skills and skill steps.

Maintenance may be enhanced by the gradual removal of such suggestions, reminders, coaching, or instruction. Fading of prompts is a means of moving away from artificial control (the teacher's) to more natural (self) control of desirable behaviors. As is true for all the enhancement techniques examined here, fading of prompts should be carefully planned and systematically implemented.

Booster sessions

Periodically, it may be necessary to reinstate instruction in order for certain prosocial behaviors to continue in the natural environment. Booster sessions between teacher and student, either on a preplanned schedule or as needed, have often proven valuable in this regard (Feindler & Ecton, 1986; Karoly & Steffen, 1980).

Preparation for real-life nonreinforcement

Both teacher and student may take energetic steps to maximize the likelihood that reinforcement for appropriate behaviors will occur in the natural environment. Nevertheless, on a number of occasions, reinforcement will not be forthcoming. Thus, it is important for the student to be prepared for this eventuality. As described previously in this chapter, self-reinforcement is one option when desirable behaviors are performed correctly but are unrewarded by external sources.

The student may also be prepared for nonreinforcement in the natural environment by completing graduated homework assignments. It becomes clear at times as Skillstreaming homework is discussed that the real-life figure is too difficult a target, too harsh, too unresponsive, or simply too unlikely to provide reinforcement for competent skill use. When this is the case, with the newly learned skill still fragile, we have redirected the homework assignment toward two or three more benevolent target figures. When the student finally does use the skill correctly with the original target figure and receives no reinforcement, his or her previously reinforced trials help minimize the likelihood that the behavior will be extinguished.

Contingency contracting. Contingency contracting, an additional type of homework, is an agreement between the teacher and student stating a behavioral goal the student will work to achieve and the reward that will be earned for achieving that goal. The goal and reward are negotiated by the teacher and student. Typically, both parties agree to carry out an action—the student to perform a selected behavior or skill (for a given length of time or a predetermined number of times) and the teacher to provide the mutually agreed upon reinforcement (e.g., a class popcorn party).

Homme et al. (1970) present several rules to follow when implementing contingency contracts. These include the following:

1. Initial contracts should require a small amount of behavior change.

2. The payoff (reward) should be given immediately after the performance of the task.

3. Frequent rewards should be provided.

4. Contracts should reward accomplishments rather than obedience.

5. The terms should be clearly stated.

6. Contracts should be fair.

7. Contracts should be reviewed regularly.

8. Contracts should be phrased in a positive manner.

9. Contracting should be carried out consistently.

Further, contracts should be in writing, not merely verbal; signed by both teacher and student; have beginning and ending dates; and, if appropriate, specify a reward for a particular behavior or skill performance, a bonus reward for extraordinary performance, and a penalty for the absence of behavior change. (Figure 5, on p. 74, presents a sample Skill Contract.)

Social skills games. A variety of games can be developed and used to enhance skill learning. Group games, in and of themselves, require students to practice a variety of social skills (e.g., joining in, sharing, being a good sport). Types of games that lend themselves well to Skillstreaming include board games and role-play games.

Cartledge and Milburn (1980) make several important points worth considering when using social skills games:

1. The connection between performing a skill in the game setting and in real life needs to be made explicit.

2. The winner (if there is one) should be determined on the basis of performance, rather than solely on the basis of chance.

3. If rewards are used they should be given for appropriate (skilled) participation rather than for winning.

4. Participants should not be "out" in a game without provisions for being allowed to participate again within a short period of time.

5. If teaming is required, skill-deficient children should be included on the same team as skill-competent children.

Skill of the Week. One enjoyable activity that has the potential to enhance skill maintenance is a "Skill of the Week" bulletin board. One skill that has been taught in the Skillstreaming group is chosen each week. This may be the skill students are working on at the time or a skill for which review is needed. The class may want to draw pictures or write descriptions of times when they can use the skill and display these along with the title of the skill. Any awards students receive may be displayed on this board. A large picture may be drawn and divided into 20 or so "puzzle pieces"; when any student uses the skill, he or she may color in one section of the puzzle. When the puzzle is completely colored in, perhaps the class will have a "Skill of the Week" party. This strategy emphasizes the use of prosocial skills, reminds students to use a selected skill, and publicly reinforces skill use.

Prosocial skills folders. All students in the Skillstreaming group should keep a prosocial skills folder. This is simply a way of organizing materials—cue cards, homework assignments, skill contracts, awards, self-monitoring forms, lists of appropriate alternative activities for use with particular skills, and the like. Students will then have an easy record of the behavioral steps to the skills they have practiced in the past.

Beyond the Skillstreaming Session

The maintenance-enhancing techniques examined thus far are directed toward the student. But maintenance of appropriate behaviors also may be enhanced by efforts directed toward others, especially those in the student's natural environment who function as the main providers of reinforcement.

Programming for reinforcement in the natural environment

The student's larger interpersonal world includes a variety of people—parents, siblings, peers, teachers, neighbors, classmates, and others. By their responsiveness or unresponsiveness to the student's newly learned skills, to a large extent they control the destiny of these behaviors. We all react to what the important people in our lives think or feel about our behavior. What they reward, we are more likely to continue doing. What they are indifferent or hostile to will tend to fall into disuse.

During the past several years, we and others have suggested the increased involvement of educators, agency and institutional staff, parents, and peers in students' acquisition and maintenance of skills. Our earlier suggestion that support staff be trained as "transfer coaches" is one way we have served this goal (see chapter 4).

Parents have been a second target for procedures designed to enhance the likelihood that prosocial skills, once learned, will be maintained. The School-Home Note (Figure 9) is intended to encourage parents to reward student skill performance. Each time a new skill is presented, students' parents are sent this note, informing them of the purpose and value of the skill, its steps, and any homework assigned (often involving the parents themselves). In addition, the note asks parents for feedback on student skill performance and for suggestions to foster teacher-parent collaboration. In addition, the Parent/Staff Skill Rating Form (Figure 10) is designed to permit parents to document student skill use between the introduction of new skills. To increase the student's use of skills outside of school, this report is sent home with the name of the skill and the specific steps listed. Parents are asked to sign and return the report when they have observed the child using the skill in the home or neighborhood environment.

In a major program elaboration, also designed primarily to increase skill maintenance, Skillstreaming sessions were also provided to parents themselves (Goldstein et al., 1989). These parent groups met independently of those held for their adolescent children three out of every four sessions, the fourth being a joint meeting.

We have also conducted major Skillstreaming teaching programs for the peers of group members. In one instance, the peers involved were fellow members of the youngsters' juvenile gangs (Goldstein et al., 1994). In the second, the peers were fellow residents in a state facility for juvenile delinquents (Gibbs et al., 1995). In both instances, research evaluations demonstrated, as was the case for parent training, that enhancing the skills of people significant in students' lives enhances the students' own skill use.

FIGURE 9   **School-Home Note**

Student: _____ Date: _____

DESCRIPTION OF LESSON

Skill name: _____

Skill steps:

Skill purpose, use, value: _____

_____

DESCRIPTION OF SKILL HOMEWORK

_____

_____

REQUEST TO PARENTS

1. Provide skill homework recognition and reward.

2. Respond positively to your child's skill use.

3. Return this School-Home Note with your comments
    (on the back) about quality of homework done and ques-
    tions/suggestions for the teacher.

4. Please sign and return this form to _____

    by _____

Signature: _____ Date: _____

FIGURE 10 **Parent/Staff Skill Rating Form**

Date: _____

_____

(student's name)

is learning the skill of _____

The steps involved in this skill are:

1. Did he or she demonstrate this skill in your presence?
   ☐ yes   ☐ no

2. How would you rate his or her skill demonstration?
   (check one)
   ☐ poor   ☐ below average   ☐ average
   ☐ above average   ☐ excellent

3. How sincere was he or she in performing the skill?
   (check one)
   ☐ not sincere   ☐ somewhat sincere   ☐ very sincere

Comments: _____

_____

Please sign and return this form to _____

by_____

Signature: _____ Date:_____

We consider these research outcomes an important reflection of the belief held by many that attempts to alter problem behaviors must be directed both to the youths themselves and to the people who constitute the youths' system.

Using natural reinforcers

A final and especially valuable approach to maintenance enhancement is the use of reinforcers that occur naturally and readily in the student's real-world environment. Stokes and Baer (1977) observe that

> perhaps the most dependable of all generalization programming mechanisms is the one that hardly deserves the name: the transfer of behavioral control from the teacher-experimenter to stable, natural contingencies that can be trusted to operate in the environment to which the subject will return, or already occupies. To a considerable extent, this goal is accomplished by choosing behaviors to teach that normally will meet maintaining reinforcement after the teaching. (p. 353)

Galassi and Galassi (1984) offer the following similar comment:

> We need to target those behaviors for changes that are most likely to be seen as acceptable, desirable, and positive by others. Ayllon and Azrin (1968) refer to this as the "Relevance of Behavior Rule." "Teach only those behaviors that will continue to be reinforced after training." (p. 10)

Alberto and Troutman (1982) suggest a four-step process to facilitate the use of natural reinforcers:

1. Observe which specific behaviors are regularly reinforced and how they are reinforced in the major settings that constitute the student's natural environment.

2. Instruct the student in a selected number of such naturally reinforced behaviors (e.g., certain social skills, grooming behaviors).

3. Teach the student how to recruit or request reinforcement (e.g., by tactfully asking peers or others for approval or recognition).

4. Teach the student how to recognize reinforcement when it is offered, because its presence in certain gestures or facial expressions may be quite subtle for many students.

✧◆✧

In summary, although the technology described in this chapter is still evolving, the call in the 1960s for transfer and maintenance enhancers has been largely answered. We recommend the use of all of these strategies in Skillstreaming instruction. We also contend that skill generalization will be further promoted if the student is concurrently taught the supportive psychological competencies previously discussed in chapter 8 (i.e., problem solving, anger/impulse control, and verbal mediation).

Skillstreaming Research: An Annotated Bibliography

Training and treatment approaches that aspire to help people lead more effective and satisfying lives must not be permitted to endure simply on the basis of the faith and enthusiasm of their proponents. Whether psychoeducational or of another type, such interventions must be subjected to careful, objective, and continuing evaluation. Only those approaches that research demonstrates to be effective deserve continued use and development. Those that fail such evaluations justly must not survive.

The present appendix references and briefly describes studies examining the effectiveness of Skillstreaming. Generally, these investigations combine to support the effectiveness of Skillstreaming with diverse trainee groups and diverse skill-training targets. Continuing tests of Skillstreaming's efficacy are necessary. But on the basis of this evidence, we confidently recommend its continued and expanded use.

❖◆❖

Beeker, M., & Brands, A. (1986). Social skills training in retardates. *Bedragstherapie, 19,* 3–14.

A series of studies employing Skillstreaming with mentally retarded individuals. Authors report substantial levels of enhanced skill competency and interpersonal interaction.

Berlin, R.J. (1979). *Teaching acting-out adolescents prosocial conflict resolution with Structured Learning Therapy.* Unpublished doctoral dissertation, Syracuse University.

Trainees: Adolescent boys with history of acting-out behaviors (N=42)

Skill(s): Empathy

Experimental design: (1) Skillstreaming for empathy in conflict situations, (2) Skillstreaming for empathy in nonconflict situations, versus (3) No-treatment control by (a) High Interpersonal Maturity Level versus (b) Low Interpersonal Maturity Level

Results: Skillstreaming for empathy (conflict) significantly > Skillstreaming for empathy (non-conflict) or controls on acquisition. High I level significantly > Low I level. No significant generalization effects.

Bleeker, D.J. (1980). *Structured Learning Therapy with skill-deficient adolescents.* Unpublished master's thesis, Syracuse University.

Trainees: Adolescent boys identified as disruptive in regular junior high school (N=55)

Skill(s): Responding to a complaint

Experimental design: A 2 × 2 plus control factorial design reflecting high versus low perceived (by the trainee) similarity between Skillstreaming trainer and generalization test figure by high versus low objective similarity, plus brief instructions control

Results: Significant effects for both Skillstreaming and similarity

Bryant, S.E., & Fox, S.K. (1995). Behavior modeling training and generalization: Interaction of learning point type and number of modeling scenarios. *Psychological Record, 45,* 495–503.

Trainees: Undergraduate volunteers (N=80)

Skill(s): Cooperative problem solving

Experimental design: One versus three modeling exposures by rule code versus summary label skill step presentation

Results: Significant interaction effect on skill generalization attributable to the superiority of the multiple model plus rule code condition

Cobb, F. M. (1973). *Acquisition and retention of cooperative behavior in young boys through instructions, modeling, and structured learning.* Unpublished doctoral dissertation, Syracuse University.

Trainees: First-grade boys (N=80)

Skill(s): Cooperation

Experimental design: (1) Skillstreaming for cooperation, (2) instructions plus modeling of cooperation, (3) instructions for cooperation, (4) attention control, (5) no-treatment control

Results: Skillstreaming significantly > all other conditions on both immediate and delayed tests of cooperative behavior

Coleman, M., Pfeiffer, S., & Oakland, T. (1991). *Aggression Replacement Training with behavior disordered adolescents.* Unpublished manuscript, Department of Special Education, University of Texas.

An evaluation of the effectiveness of a 10-week Aggression Replacement Training program used with behavior-disordered adolescents in a residential treatment center. Results indicated significant increases in skill knowledge but not actual overt skill behaviors.

Cross, W. (1977). *An investigation of the effects of therapist motivational predispositions in Structured Learning Therapy under task versus relationship stress conditions.* Unpublished doctoral dissertation, Syracuse University.

Trainees: College undergraduates (N=120)

Skill(s): Skillstreaming group leadership skills

Experimental design: Task-motivated versus relationship-motivated trainers by task-relevant versus relationship-relevant trainee-originated trainer stress plus no-treatment control

Results: Relationship-motivated trainers significantly >
task-motivated trainers on Skillstreaming effectiveness
under task threat conditions

Curulla, V.L. (1990). *Aggression Replacement Training in the
community for adult learning disabled offenders.* Unpublished
manuscript, Department of Special Education, University of
Washington, Seattle.

Trainees: Young adult offenders in a community
treatment center (N=67)

Skill(s): "Tendency toward recidivism" skills

Experimental design: Compared (1) Aggression Replacement
Training, (2) Aggression Replacement Training absent its
Moral Education component, (3) no-training control

Results: Significant reduction in tendency toward recidivism
in (1), but not (2) or (3)

Cutierrez, M.C., & Hurtado, S. (1984). Effects of transfer enhancers
on generalization of social skills in handicapped adolescents.
Revista de Analisis del Comportamiento, 21, 81–88.

Trainees: Physically handicapped adolescents (N=15)

Skill(s): Social competency subset

Experimental design: Three training conditions: (1) Skillstreaming plus transfer enhancers, (2) Skillstreaming,
(3) wait-list control

Results: For skill acquisition, both (1) and (2) > (3). For skill
maintenance at 4-week follow-up probe, (1) > (2) and (3).

Davis, C. (1974). *Training police in crisis intervention skills.*
Unpublished manuscript, Syracuse University.

Description of a training program utilizing Skillstreaming
to develop skills among a 225-person urban police force for
the competent handling of family fights, rapes, accidents,
suicides, and variety of other crises common in everyday
police work. Skills taught included (1) preparing to deal
with threats to your safety, (2) calming the emotional
aspects of the crisis, (3) gathering relevant information,
and (4) taking appropriate action.

Dominquez, Y.A., & Garrison, J. (1977). Towards adequate psychiatric classification and treatment of Mexican American patients. *Psychiatric Annals, 7,* 86–96.

Responding to the several ways in which the core procedures of the Skillstreaming approach were selected for use in response to characteristic learning styles of low-income populations, this article recommends Skillstreaming as one of four intervention methods for bridging the gap between primarily Anglo middle class therapists and primarily lower class Chicano patients.

Edelman, E. (1977). *Behavior of high versus low hostility-guilt Structured Learning trainers under standardized client conditions of expressed hostility.* Unpublished master's thesis, Syracuse University.

Trainees: Nurses and attendants at state mental hospital (N=60)

Skill(s): Structured Learning trainer group leadership behaviors

Experimental design: Skillstreaming trainers high versus low in hostility-guilt by (1) high, (2) low, or (3) no expressed client hostility

Results: High hostility-guilt trainers responded to trainee hostility with significantly less counterhostility than did low hostility-guilt trainers. Low hostility-guilt trainers significantly > counterhostility to hostile than neutral trainees; no similar effect for high hostility-guilt trainers.

Epstein, M., & Cullinan, D. (1987). Effective social skills curricula for behavior-disordered students. *Pointer, 31,* 21–24.

A comparative description of six social skills curricula for secondary and elementary behavior-disordered students.

Figueroa-Torres, J. (1979). Structured Learning Therapy: Its effects upon self-control of aggressive fathers from Puerto Rican low socioeconomic families. *Hispanic Journal of Behavioral Sciences, 14,* 345–354.

Trainees: Family-abusing fathers (N=60)

Skill(s): Self-control

Experimental design: Skillstreaming for self-control versus no treatment

Results: Skillstreaming-trained fathers significantly > controls on self-control on acquisition and minimal generalization criteria

Fleming, D. (1977). *Teaching negotiation skills to preadolescents.* Unpublished doctoral dissertation, Syracuse University.

Trainees: Adolescents (N=96)

Skill(s): Negotiation

Experimental design: High self-esteem versus low self-esteem adolescents by adult Skillstreaming trainer versus peer Skillstreaming trainer by presence versus absence of pre-Skillstreaming enhancement of expectancy for success

Results: All Skillstreaming groups showed significant increase in negotiation skill acquisition but not transfer. No significant effects observed between trainer type or between esteem level effects.

Fleming, L.R. (1977). *Training aggressive and unassertive educable mentally retarded children for assertive behaviors, using three types of Structured Learning Therapy.* Unpublished doctoral dissertation, Syracuse University.

Trainees: Mentally retarded children (N=96)

Skill(s): Assertiveness

Experimental design: (1) Skillstreaming for assertiveness plus fear-coping training, (2) Skillstreaming for assertiveness plus anger-coping training, (3) Skillstreaming for assertiveness, (4) attention control by aggressive versus unassertive children

Results: All three Skillstreaming groups significantly > controls on increase in assertiveness. No significant in vivo transfer effects.

Friedenberg, W.P. (1971). *Verbal and nonverbal attraction modeling in an initial therapy interview analogue.* Unpublished master's thesis, Syracuse University.

Trainees: Psychiatric inpatients (all male, mostly schizophrenic; N=60)

Skill(s): Attraction

Experimental design: High versus low attraction to interviewer displayed via nonverbal cues by high versus low attraction to interviewer displayed via verbal cues

Results: Significant modeling effect for attraction for the high-high group (high modeled attraction using both the verbal and nonverbal cues) as compared to the other three conditions

Gibbs, J.C., Potter, G.B., & Goldstein, A.P. (1995). *The EQUIP program: Teaching youth to think and act responsibly through a peer-helping approach.* Champaign, IL: Research Press.

EQUIP is a multimethod intervention for delinquent youth consisting of a positive peer culture, Aggression Replacement Training, and means to correct disordered, criminal thinking. This book describes these procedures in "how-to" detail and presents an extensive and successful evaluation of their efficacy when used with a sample of incarcerated delinquents.

Contents: (1) Introduction and Description; (2) Developing a Positive Youth Culture; (3) Equipping with Mature Moral Judgment; (4) Equipping with Skills to Manage Anger and Correct Thinking Errors; (5) Equipping with Social Skills; (6) Program Implementation; (7) Developing a Positive Staff Culture; (8) Program Adaptations and Expansions

Gibbs, J.C., Potter, G.B., Goldstein, A.P., & Brendtro, L.K. (1996). Frontiers in psychoeducation: The EQUIP model with antisocial youth. *Reclaiming Children and Youth, 4,* 22–29.

A discussion of the intervention challenges presented by antisocial youth, the development of earlier psychoeducational methods, and the rationale that led to the construction of the EQUIP approach, which combines skills-oriented and peer-oriented components.

Gilstad, R. (1977). *Acquisition and transfer of empathic responses by teachers through self-administered and leader-directed Structured Learning Training and the interaction between training method and conceptual level.* Unpublished doctoral dissertation, Syracuse University.

Trainees: Elementary school teachers (N=60)

Skill(s): Empathy

Experimental design: Skillstreaming for empathy training conducted by a trainer in "standard" Skillstreaming groups versus Skillstreaming for empathy self-instructional training format by high versus low conceptual level trainees, plus attention control

Results: Both Skillstreaming groups significantly > control on empathy acquisition and transfer criteria. No significant effects between Skillstreaming conditions or between conceptual levels.

Glick, B., & Goldstein, A.P. (1987). Aggression Replacement Training. *Journal of Counseling and Development, 65,* 356–362.

A description of the Skillstreaming, anger control training, and moral reasoning training components of Aggression Replacement Training, including the institutional evaluation studies on juvenile delinquent populations conducted to ascertain its effectiveness.

Golden, R. (1975). *Teaching resistance-reducing behavior to high school students.* Unpublished doctoral dissertation, Syracuse University.

Trainees: High school students (N=43)

Skill(s): Resistance-reducing behavior (reflection of the other's feeling plus appropriate assertiveness regarding one's own view in an interpersonal conflict situation with authority figures)

Experimental design: (1) Discrimination training ("good" modeled skill behavior versus "bad" modeled skill behavior) for resistance-reducing behavior, (2) Skillstreaming for resistance-reducing behavior, (3) no-treatment control by internal versus external locus of control

Results: Both discrimination training and Skillstreaming significantly > controls on resistance-reducing behavior on both acquisition and generalization criteria. No significant locus of control effects.

Goldstein, A.P. (1973). A prescriptive psychotherapy for the alcoholic patient based on social class. In *Proceedings of the Second Annual Alcoholism Conference of NIAAA.* Washington, DC: U. S. Department of Health, Education and Welfare.

An overview of the development of Skillstreaming and relevant evaluative research, with special emphasis upon its implications for alcoholic patients.

Goldstein, A.P. (1973). *Structured Learning Therapy: Toward a psychotherapy for the poor.* New York: Academic.

A comprehensive statement of the origin and rationale for Structured Learning Therapy and a full presentation of relevant evaluative research. Modeling scripts from both inpatient and outpatient studies are presented.

Contents: (1) Psychotherapy: Income and Outcome; (2) Personality Development and Preparation for Patienthood; (3) Language and Malcommunication; (4) Psychopathology and Sociopathology; (5) Structured Learning and the Middle-Class Patient; (6) Structured Learning and the Lower-Class Inpatient; (7) Structured Learning and the Lower-Class Outpatient; (8) Structured Learning and the Working-Class Paraprofessional; (9) Future Directions; (10) Appendix: Modeling Scripts

Goldstein, A.P. (1981). *Psychological skill training: The Structured Learning technique.* New York: Pergamon.

A comprehensive description of Skillstreaming research and application with diverse trainee populations. Trainer manuals for implementing this approach are also provided.

Contents: (1) Introduction; (2) Origins of Structured Learning; (3) Mental Hospital Patient Trainees; (4) Adolescent Trainees; (5) Child Trainees; (6) Change Agent Trainees; (7) Other Trainees; (8) Issues in Skill Training: Resolved and Unresolved

Goldstein, A.P. (1985). Prosocial education: Aggression replacement via psychological skills training. *International Journal of Group Tensions, 15,* 6–26.

Prosocial education is the intentional teaching of a curriculum of effective interpersonal, conflict management, and anger control skills. This paper describes the rationale underlying this strategy and means for its implementation.

Goldstein, A.P. (1985). Structured Learning Therapy. In D. Larsen (Ed.), *Giving psychology away.* San Francisco, Brooks/Cole.

A review of prescriptive need for new interventions to serve underserved populations. Describes how and why Skillstreaming was developed to meet the psychoeducational needs of low-income trainee populations.

Goldstein, A.P. (1986). Teaching prosocial skills to antisocial youth. In C.M. Nelson, R.B. Rutherford, & B.T. Wolford (Eds.), *Special education and the criminal justice system.* Columbus, OH: Charles E. Merrill.

A review of the educational and correctional philosophy underlying a psychoeducational intervention orientation toward changing antisocial behavior. Described are the Skillstreaming and Aggression Replacement Training implementations of this philosophy.

Goldstein, A.P. (1988). *The Prepare Curriculum: Teaching prosocial competencies.* Champaign, IL: Research Press.

A major expansion of the Skillstreaming approach, this 10-course curriculum collectively proposes that a diverse array of prosocial competencies can be taught, learned, and effectively employed in various settings by diverse trainees.

Contents: (1) Introduction; (2) Problem-Solving Training; (3) Interpersonal Skills Training; (4) Situational Perception Training; (5) Anger Control Training; (6) Moral Reasoning Training; (7) Stress Management Training; (8) Empathy Training; (9) Recruiting Supportive Models; (10) Cooperation Training; (11) Understanding and Using Groups; (12) Transfer and Maintenance; (13) Classroom Management; (14) Future Directions

Goldstein, A.P. (1989). Refusal skills: Learning to be positively negative. *Journal of Drug Education, 19,* 271–277.

A description of the application of the Skillstreaming method and curriculum to the problem of alcohol or drug refusal by adolescents. In effect, responding to the failure of a "just say no" philosophy, the goal is to teach youth how to say no in challenging situations.

Goldstein, A.P. (1989). Teaching alternatives to aggression. In D. Biklen, D.L. Ferguson, & A. Ford (Eds.), *Schooling and disability.* Chicago: The National Society for the Study of Education.

A review of psychoeducational philosophy and procedures for use in expanding the behavioral repertoires of chronically aggressive youngsters, thus making alternatives to aggression more available and more likely.

Goldstein, A.P. (1991). El curriculum de preparation. *Revista de Analisis del Comportemiento, 4,* 108–129.

A description in Spanish of the background, methods, constituent courses, and range of applicability of the Prepare Curriculum.

Goldstein, A.P. (1992). Teaching prosocial behavior to low-income youth. In P. Pedersen & J. Carey (Eds.), *Multicultural counseling in schools.* Fairfield, CT: Greenwood.

An examination of the developmental life path typical for low-income youth and the manner in which this path leads to particular channels of accessibility for learning. The Skillstreaming, Aggression Replacement Training, and Prepare Curriculum methods are each described, as is their compatibility with a low-income learning style.

Goldstein, A.P. (1993). Interpersonal skills training interventions. In A.P. Goldstein & C.R. Huff (Eds.), *The gang intervention handbook.* Champaign, IL: Research Press.

A review of the Skillstreaming approach—its rationale, procedures, and curriculum—and the main expansions of this intervention (Aggression Replacement Training, Prepare Curriculum) as they have been and might be employed with gang youth.

Goldstein, A.P. (1995). Coordinated multitargeted skills training: The promotion of generalization enhancement. In W. O'Donohue & L. Krasner (Eds.), *Handbook of psychological skills training: Clinical techniques and applications*. Boston: Allyn & Bacon.

An examination of the problem of generalization failure, which has plagued interventions of all kinds, including those oriented toward teaching prosocial skills. Reviewed are the content and research base of procedures for the enhancement of both setting generalization (transfer) and temporal generalization (maintenance) of newly learned skills.

Goldstein, A.P., Amann, L., & Reagles, K.W. (1990). *Refusal skills: Preventing drug use in adolescents*. Champaign, IL: Research Press.

A presentation of procedures and materials needed to focus Skillstreaming efforts on refusal skills needed by adolescents being pressured to use drugs or alcohol. Designates 20 of the 50 Skillstreaming skills for adolescents as core refusal skills.

Contents: (1) Introduction; (2) Issues in Drug Use; (3) The Refusal Skill Curriculum; (4) Refusal Skill Training Procedures; (5) Transfer and Maintenance; (6) Skillstreaming Curriculum for Adolescents; (7) Commonly Abused Drugs

Goldstein, A.P., Blake, G., Cohen, R., & Walsh, W. (1971). The effects of modeling and social class structuring in paraprofessional psychotherapist training. *Journal of Nervous and Mental Disease, 153,* 47–56.

Trainees: Nurses and attendants (N=135)

Skill(s): Attraction, empathy, warmth

Experimental design: High, low, and no attraction modeling by middle, low, and no social class structuring

Results: Significant modeling by social-class structuring interaction effects for attraction, empathy, and warmth.

Goldstein, A.P., Blancero, D.A., Carthen, W., & Glick, B. (1994). *The prosocial gang: Implementing Aggression Replacement Training*. Thousand Oaks, CA: Sage.

A description of the use of Aggression Replacement Training, an expansion of Skillstreaming, with 10 criminally oriented youth gangs. Comparison of treated versus untreated gang youth reveals significant benefits from participation, including reduced recidivism.

Contents: (1) Gangs in the United States; (2) Gang Aggression; (3) A Historical Review; (4) Aggression Replacement Training: Background and Procedures; (5) Aggression Replacement Training: Evaluations of Effectiveness; (6) Gangs in the Hood; (7) The Program: Management and Evaluation; (8) Future Perspectives: Enhancing Generalization of Gain

Goldstein, A.P., Coultry, T., Glick B., Gold, D., Reiner, S., & Zimmerman, D. (1985). Entrenaminto en sustitucion de agresion: Un modelo de intervencion integral endelincuencia. *Revista de Analisis del Comportamiento, 2,* 325–335.

Aggression Replacement Training—both methods and evaluation research—is described as it has been and might be profitably used with delinquent youth.

Goldstein, A.P., Coultry, T., Glick B., Gold, D., Reiner, S., & Zimmerman, D. (1986). Aggression Replacement Training: A comprehensive intervention for the acting-out delinquent. *Journal of Correctional Education, 37,* 120–126.

Aggression Replacement Training—both methods and evaluation research—is described as it has been and might be profitably used with delinquent youth.

Goldstein, A.P., Erne, D., & Keller, H. (1985). *Changing the abusive parent.* Champaign, IL: Research Press.

Child abuse is a major and growing social problem. This book describes the development and application of a Skillstreaming approach to teaching parenting skills to chronically abusive parents.

Contents: (1) Child Abuse: The Problem; (2) Child Abuse: Intervention Approaches; (3) An Introduction to Structured Learning; (4) Preparing for Structured Learning; (5) Conducting the Structured Learning Group; (6) Structured Learning

Skills for Abusive Parents; (7) A Typical Structured
Learning Session; (8) Managing Problem Behaviors;
(9) Structured Learning in the Agency Context;
(10) Structured Learning Research

Goldstein, A.P., Gershaw, N.J., Glick, B., Sherman, M., & Sprafkin,
R.P. (1978). Training aggressive adolescents in prosocial
behavior. *Journal of Youth and Adolescence, 7,* 73–92.

A comprehensive review of research employing Skillstreaming with aggressive adolescent trainees. Study
designs and findings are presented and examined. The
value of prescriptively designed practice and research
is emphasized. Special emphasis is placed upon transfer
of training, particularly reasons for its infrequency and
possible means for its enhancement.

Goldstein, A.P., Gershaw, N.J., Klein, P., & Sprafkin, R.P. (1980).
*Skillstreaming the adolescent: A structured learning approach
to teaching prosocial skills.* Champaign, IL: Research Press.

A practitioner-oriented trainer's manual presenting the
background, procedures, materials, and measures necessary to organize and manage Skillstreaming groups for
adolescents.

Contents: (1) A Prescriptive Introduction; (2) Structured
Learning: Background and Development; (3) Structured
Learning Procedures for Adolescents; (4) Selection and
Grouping of Trainees; (5) Structured Learning Skills for
Adolescents; (6) Structured Learning in Use; (7) Manage-
ment of Problem Behavior in a Structured Learning
Group; (8) Structured Learning Research: An Annotated
Bibliography

Goldstein, A.P., Gershaw, N.J., Klein, P., & Sprafkin, R.P. (1983).
Structured Learning: A psychoeducational approach to teaching
social competencies. *Behavior Disorders, 8,* 161–170.

A presentation of the Skillstreaming method—its history,
development, procedures, and curriculum—as it might
optimally be employed with troubled and troubling youth.

Goldstein, A.P., Gershaw, N.J., & Sprafkin, R.P. (1975). Structured Learning Therapy: Skill training for schizophrenics. *Schizophrenia Bulletin, 14,* 83–88.

A description of the procedures that constitute Skillstreaming and their evaluation. Relevant modeling tapes and related materials are also described. This article places special emphasis on the community-relevant needs of a variety of types of schizophrenic patients and the manner in which daily living skill deficits may be systematically reduced by the use of this approach.

Goldstein, A.P., Gershaw, N.J., & Sprafkin, R.P. (1976). *Skill training for community living: Applying Structured Learning Therapy.* New York: Pergamon.

A detailed, applied presentation regarding the use of Skillstreaming with adult psychiatric patients and similar trainees.

Contents: (1) Introduction; (2) Trainer Preparation and Training Procedures; (3) Inpatient and Outpatient Trainees; (4) Modeling Tapes; (5) Skillstreaming Research; (6) Supplement A: Trainer's Manual; (7) Supplement B: Trainee's Notebook; (8) Supplement C: An Advanced Skillstreaming Session; (9) Supplement D: Resistance and Resistance Reduction; (10) Supplement E: Skill Surveys

Goldstein, A.P., Gershaw, N.J., & Sprafkin, R.P. (1979). *I know what's wrong, but I don't know what to do about it.* Englewood Cliffs, NJ: Prentice Hall.

A self-administered version of Skillstreaming, presented in stepwise, concrete detail. Oriented in content and procedures toward the general adult population.

Contents: (1) How to Use This Book; (2) Knowing What's Wrong: Diagnosing the Problem; (3) Getting Ready: Preparing to Change Your Behavior; (4) What to Do about It: Changing Your Behavior; (5) Personal Skills in Action: Guidelines, Steps and Examples; (6) Making Changes Stick; (7) More Personal Skills

Goldstein, A.P., Gershaw, N.J., & Sprafkin, R.P. (1979). Structured
Learning Therapy: Training for community living. *Psychotherapy:
Theory, Research and Practice, 16,* 199–203.

An examination of existing approaches to the resocialization
of mental hospital patients, which, while often yielding
positive changes at the termination of treatment, typically
do not result in enduring transfer of such changes into
community functioning. Skillstreaming is described as an
intervention deliverable in association with transfer-
enhancing features, thus overcoming this typical weakness
in generalization.

Goldstein, A.P., Gershaw, N.J., & Sprafkin, R.P. (1985). Structured
Learning: Research and practice in psychological skills training. In L. L'Abate & M.A. Milan (Eds.), *Handbook of social skills
training and research.* New York: Wiley.

Explores the history and development of psychological
skills training in general and the Skillstreaming approach
in particular, including its constituent methods, curriculum,
and research evaluations.

Goldstein, A.P., Gershaw, N.J., & Sprafkin, R.P. (1995). Teaching
the adolescent: Social skills training through Skillstreaming.
In G. Cartledge & J.F. Milburn (Eds.), *Teaching social skills to
children and youth.* Boston: Allyn & Bacon.

A description of the Skillstreaming method as utilized with
adolescent populations. Examined are the developmental
relevance of this approach, methods and application, curriculum, means for enhancing trainee motivation, and the
Aggression Replacement Training and Prepare Curriculum
expansions of the approach.

Goldstein, A.P., & Glick, B. (1987). *Aggression Replacement Training:
A comprehensive intervention for aggressive youth.* Champaign,
IL: Research Press.

A description of a major expansion of the Skillstreaming
approach. Skillstreaming teaches youths skill alternatives
to aggression. Anger control training inhibits use of the

alternative antisocial behaviors. Moral Education provides the concern with the rights of others that encourages use of the skills taught. This book describes this three-part approach and provides evaluation results for two investigations of its effectiveness with incarcerated delinquents.

Contents: (1) Juvenile Delinquency: Incidence and Interventions; (2) The Behavioral Component of ART: Structured Learning; (3) Trainer's Manual for Structured Learning; (4) The Affective Component of ART: Anger Control Training; (5) Trainer's Manual for Anger Control Training; (6) The Cognitive Component of ART: Moral Education; (7) Trainer's Manual for Moral Education; (8) Program Description and Evaluation; (9) Future Directions; (10) Administrator's Manual for ART

Goldstein, A.P., & Glick, B. (1987). Angry youth—reducing aggression. *Corrections Today, 49,* 38–42.

A description of the purposes, methods, curricula, and evaluations of Aggression Replacement Training as used with juvenile delinquent populations.

Goldstein, A.P., & Glick, B. (1994). Aggression Replacement Training: Curriculum and evaluation. *Simulation and Gaming, 25,* 9–26.

A description of the history, development, and evaluation of Aggression Replacement Training (i.e., Skillstreaming, anger control training, and Moral Education). Its curriculum, methods, and outcomes in institutional, community, and school settings are presented.

Goldstein, A.P., & Glick, B. (1995). Aggression Replacement Training for delinquents. In R.R. Ross, D.H. Antonowicz, & G.A. Dhlival (Eds.), *Going straight: Effective delinquency prevention and offender rehabilitation.* Ottawa, Canada: AIR Training and Publications.

A review of research examining the effectiveness of Aggression Replacement Training used with juvenile delinquents in residential, community, and school settings. Conclusion: "With considerable reliability [ART] appears to promote skills acquisition and performance, improve anger control, decrease the frequency of acting-out behaviors, and increase the frequency of constructive, prosocial behaviors."

Goldstein, A.P., & Glick, B. (1995). Artful research management: Problems, process and products. In B. Glick & A.P. Goldstein (Eds.), *Managing delinquency programs that work.* Laurel, MD: American Correctional Association.

A review of research on Aggression Replacement Training, with particular emphasis on problems that may arise, and solutions that may work, when one organizes and conducts an extended intervention evaluation program. Considered are matters of program planning, training, monitoring, supervision, maintenance of motivation, coordination of functions, data collection and analysis, and results dissemination.

Goldstein, A.P., Glick, B., Irwin, M.J., Pask-McCartney, C., & Rubama, I. (1989). *Reducing delinquency: Intervention in the community.* New York: Pergamon.

A description of the use of Aggression Replacement Training with 24 juvenile delinquent youth and, for a subsample, their families (parents and siblings). Results of this project indicated that on several criteria, including recidivism, administering the intervention to both the delinquent trainees and their family members yielded significantly greater skill generalization than did working with the youths only or with a wait-list control.

Contents: (1) Community-Based Intervention: A Review; (2) Aggression Replacement Training: Background and Procedures; (3) The Youth Program; (4) The Family Program; (5) Program Evaluation; (6) Administration of Community-Based Programs; (7) Future Perspectives

Goldstein, A.P., & Goedhart, A.W. (1973). The use of Structured Learning for empathy enhancement in paraprofessional psychotherapist training. *Journal of Community Psychology, 1,* 168–173.

EXPERIMENT I

Trainees: Student nurses (N=74)

Skill(s): Empathy

Experimental design: (1) Skillstreaming for empathy (professional trainers), (2) Skillstreaming for empathy (paraprofessional trainers), (3) no-training control

Results: Both Skillstreaming conditions significantly > no-training control on both immediate and generalization measures of empathy

EXPERIMENT II

Trainees: Hospital staff (nurses, attendants, occupational therapists, recreational therapists; N=90)

Skill(s): Empathy

Experimental design: (1) Skillstreaming plus transfer training for empathy, (2) Skillstreaming for empathy, (3) no-training control

Results: Significant Skillstreaming effect for immediate empathy measurement (Groups 1 and 2 > 3); significant transfer effect for generalization empathy measure (Group 1 > 2 and 3)

Goldstein, A.P., Goedhart, A., Hubben, J., Martens, J., Schaaf, W., Van Belle, H., & Wiersema, H. (1973). The use of modeling to increase independent behavior. *Behaviour Research and Therapy, 11,* 21–42.

EXPERIMENT I

Trainees: Psychiatric outpatients (all psychoneurotic or character disorders; N=90)

Skill(s): Independence (assertiveness)

Experimental design: (1) Independence modeling, (2) dependence modeling, (3) no modeling

Results: Warm and no-structuring modeling conditions significantly > cold structuring and control on independence for males and females

EXPERIMENT II

Trainees: Psychiatric outpatients (all psychoneurotic or character disorders; N=60)

Skill(s): Independence (assertiveness)

Experimental design: Independence modeling plus (1) structuring model as warm, (2) structuring model as cold, (3) no structuring of model by male versus female plus a no-structuring/no-modeling control

Results: Warm and no-structuring modeling conditions significantly > cold structuring and control on independence for males and females

EXPERIMENT III

Trainees: Psychiatric inpatients (all schizophrenic; N=54)

Skill(s): Independence (assertiveness)

Experimental design: Presence versus absence of independence modeling by presence versus absence of instructions to behave independently

Results: Significant main and interaction effects for modeling and instructions on independence as compared to no-modeling/no-instructions conditions

Goldstein, A.P., Goedhart, A.W., & Wijngaarden, H.R. (1973). Modeling in de psychotherpie bij patienten uit de lagere sociale klasse. In A.P. Cassee, P.E. Boeke, & J.T. Barendregt (Eds.), *Klinische Psychologie in Nederland.* Deventer: Van Loghum Slaterus.

A presentation (in Dutch) of the origin, rationale, and current status of Skillstreaming. The particular usefulness of this approach with low-income Dutch and American patient populations is stressed.

Goldstein, A.P., Green, D.J., Monti, P.J., & Sardino, T.J. (1977). *Police crisis intervention.* New York: Pergamon.

An applied text oriented toward law enforcement and criminal justice personnel concerned with effective handling of diverse order maintenance and police service matters.

Contents: (1) Introduction; (2) Crisis Intervention Manual for Police; (3) Family Disputes; (4) Mental Disturbance; (5) Drug and Alcohol Intoxication; (6) Rape; (7) Suicide; (8) A Method for Effective Training: Structured Learning; (9) Structured Learning Manual for Police Trainers

Goldstein, A.P., Hoyer, W., & Monti, P.J. (Eds.). (1979). *Police and the elderly.* New York: Pergamon.

The special needs and problems of elderly citizens as related to the role of police is the primary focus of this book. Among the topics addressed are means by which police, other criminal justice personnel, and the elderly themselves can assist in preventing crime against the elderly and minimizing its psychological import when it does occur. Use of Skillstreaming to train police in these roles is systematically presented.

Contents: (1) The Elderly: Who Are They? (2) Fear of Crime and the Elderly; (3) Minority Elderly; (4) Crime Prevention with Elderly Citizens; (5) Police Investigation with Elderly Citizens; (6) Assisting the Elderly Victim; (7) Training the Elderly in Mastery of the Environment; (8) Training Police for Work with the Elderly

Goldstein, A.P., & Pentz, M.A. (1984). Psychological skill training and the aggressive adolescent. *School Psychology Review, 13,* 311–323.

Reviews the history of psychological skills training and the evaluation research reported in the literature focused on the effectiveness of this method. Problems of trainee motivation, prescriptive utilization, and the facilitation of generalization are discussed.

Goldstein, A.P., & Sorcher, M. (1973). Changing managerial behavior by applied learning techniques. *Training and Development Journal, March,* 36–39.

An examination of inadequacies characterizing most managerial training approaches, including the singular focus on attitude change rather than behavior change, unresponsiveness to changing characteristics of the

American work force, and insufficient attention to the implications of research on human learning for managerial training. The manner in which Skillstreaming seeks to correct these inadequacies and provide an effective approach to training managers is presented.

Goldstein, A.P., & Sorcher, M. (1974). *Changing supervisor behavior.* New York: Pergamon.

An applied presentation of Skillstreaming, oriented toward the teaching of supervisory skills, especially in industry. Relevant evaluative research in an industrial context is reported.

Contents: (1) Supervisor Training: Perspectives and Problems; (2) A Focus on Behavior; (3) Modeling; (4) Role-Playing; (5) Social Reinforcement; (6) Transfer Training; (7) Applied Learning: Application and Evidence

Greenleaf, D. (1992). The use of programmed transfer of training and Structured Learning Therapy with disruptive adolescents in a school setting. *Journal of School Psychology, 20,* 122–130.

Trainees: Adolescent boys with history of disruptive behavior (N=43)

Skill(s): Helping others

Experimental design: Skillstreaming versus no Skillstreaming by transfer programming versus no transfer programming plus attention control

Results: Skillstreaming showed significantly greater skill acquisition, minimal generalization, and extended generalization than either no Skillstreaming or attention control. Transfer programming did not augment this significant transfer effect.

Gutride, M.E., Goldstein, A.P., & Hunter, G.F. (1973). The use of modeling and role playing to increase social interaction among schizophrenic patients. *Journal of Counseling and Clinical Psychology, 40,* 408–415.

Trainees: Psychiatric inpatients (all "asocial, withdrawn"; N=133)

Skill(s): Social interaction (an array of conversational and physical approach skill behaviors)

Experimental design: Skillstreaming versus no Skillstreaming by psychotherapy versus no psychotherapy by acute versus chronic

Results: A substantial number of significant interaction and main effects for Skillstreaming across several social interaction behavioral criteria

Gutride, M.E., Goldstein, A.P., & Hunter, G.F. (1974). Structured Learning Therapy with transfer training for chronic inpatients. *Journal of Clinical Psychology, 30,* 277–280.

Trainees: Psychiatric inpatients (all "asocial, withdrawn"; N=106)

Skill(s): Social interaction in a mealtime context

Experimental design: (1) Skillstreaming plus transfer training, (2) Skillstreaming plus additional Skillstreaming, (3) Skillstreaming, (4) companionship control, (5) no-treatment control

Results: A substantial number of significant effects for Skillstreaming across several social interaction behavioral criteria. Significant effects are mainly for Groups 1, 2, and 3 compared to the control conditions, rather than between the Skillstreaming conditions.

Guzzetta, R.A. (1974). *Acquisition and transfer of empathy by the parents of early adolescents through Structured Learning Training.* Unpublished doctoral dissertation, Syracuse University.

Trainees: Mothers of early adolescents (N=37)

Skill(s): Empathy

Experimental design: (1) Skillstreaming for empathy taught to mothers and their children together, (2) Skillstreaming for empathy taught to mothers and their children separately, (3) Skillstreaming for empathy taught to mothers only, (4) no-training control

Results: All three Skillstreaming conditions showed significantly greater acquisition and transfer of empathy than did no-training control mothers. No significant difference existed between Skillstreaming conditions.

Hayman, P.M., & Weiss-Cassady, D.M. (1981). Structured Learning Therapy with mentally ill criminal offenders. *Journal of Offender Counseling, Services and Rehabilitation, 6,* 41–51.

Trainees: Mentally ill incarcerated offenders (N=22)

Skill(s): Social competency subset

Experimental design: A 12-session series of Skillstreaming meetings provided to six trainees. Pre-post changes compared to 16 no-treatment controls

Results: Treatment versus no-treatment significant differences on skill acquisition and on change measure of psychopathology

Healy, J.A. (1975). *Training of hospital staff in accurate effective perception of anger from vocal cues in the context of varying facial cues.* Unpublished master's thesis, Syracuse University.

Trainees: Nurses and attendants (N=44)

Skill(s): Recognition of vocal cues of anger

Experimental design: (1) Skillstreaming for vocal and facial cues, (2) Skillstreaming for vocal cues with exposure to but no training for facial cues, (3) Skillstreaming for vocal cues, (4) no-training control

Results: All Skillstreaming groups significantly > controls on vocal training and test cues; no significant generalization to new (untrained) vocal cues

Healy, J.A. (1979). *Structured Learning Therapy and the promotion of transfer of training through the employment of overlearning and stimulus variability.* Unpublished doctoral dissertation, Syracuse University.

Trainees: Unassertive adolescents in regular junior high school (N=84)

Skill(s): Assertiveness

Experimental design: A 3 × 2 plus control factorial design reflecting the presence versus absence of stimulus variability by three levels of overlearning, plus brief instructions control

Results: Significant effect for overlearning, not for stimulus variability

Hollander, T.G. (1970). *The effects of role playing on attraction, disclosure, and attitude change in a psychotherapy analogue.* Unpublished doctoral dissertation, Syracuse University.

Trainees: V.A. hospital psychiatric inpatients (all males; N=45)

Skill(s): Attraction to the psychotherapist

Experimental design: Role-play versus exposure versus no-treatment control

Results: No significant role-playing effects for attraction or disclosure

Hoyer, W.J., Lopez, M., & Goldstein, A.P. (1982). Predicting social skill acquisition and transfer by psychogeriatric inpatients. *International Journal of Behavioral Geriatrics, 1,* 43–46.

Trainees: Elderly institutionalized psychiatric patients (N=47)

Skill(s): Social competency subset

Experimental design: A multiple regression analysis examining several potential predictors of skill acquisition and competence consequent to participation in a series of Skillstreaming sessions

Results: Mental status measures were the best predictors of skill acquisition. Mental status combined with trait anxiety were the best predictors of skill maintenance.

Hummel, J. (1979). *Session variability and skill content as transfer enhancers in Structured Learning training.* Unpublished doctoral dissertation, Syracuse University.

Trainees: Aggressive preadolescents (N=47)

Skill(s): Self-control, negotiation

Experimental design: Skillstreaming-variable conditions versus Skillstreaming-constant conditions by self-control skill versus negotiation skill versus both

Results: Skillstreaming-variable conditions significantly > Skillstreaming-constant conditions on both acquisition and transfer dependent measures across both skills singly and combined

Jennings, R.L., & Davis, C.G. (1977). Attraction enhancing client behaviors: A structured learning approach for "Non Yavis, Jr." *Journal of Consulting and Clinical Psychology, 45,* 135–144.

Trainees: Emotionally disturbed lower socioeconomic children and adolescents (N=40)

Skill(s): Interviewee behaviors (initiation, terminating silences, elaboration, and expression of affect)

Experimental design: (1) Skillstreaming for interviewee behaviors versus (2) minimal treatment control in a $2 \times 2 \times 4$ factorial design reflecting (a) repeated measures, (b) treatments, and (c) interviewers

Results: Skillstreaming significantly > minimal treatment control on interview initiation and terminating silences. No significant effects on interview elaboration or expression of affect. Skillstreaming significantly > minimal treatment control on attractiveness to interviewer on portion of study measures.

Jones, Y. (1990). *Aggression Replacement Training in a high school setting.* Unpublished manuscript, Center for Learning & Adjustment Difficulties, Brisbane, Australia.

Trainees: Chronically aggressive high-school age male students (N=45)

Skill(s): Self-control and aggression management subset

Experimental design: Compared (1) Aggression Replacement Training, (2) Moral Education, and (3) no-training control

Results: Compared to the two control conditions, students completing the Aggression Replacement Training program showed a significant decrease in aggressive incidents, a significant increase in coping incidents, and acquired more social skills. Students in Condition 1 also improved on self-control and impulsivity.

Lack, D.Z. (1971). *The effect of a model and instructions on psychotherapist self-disclosure.* Unpublished master's thesis, Syracuse University.

Trainees: Mental hospital attendants (N=60)

Skill(s): Self-disclosure

Experimental design: Presence versus absence of modeled self-disclosure by presence versus absence of instructions to self-disclose

Results: Significant modeling and instruction effects for self-disclosure

Lack, D.Z. (1975). *Problem-solving training, Structured Learning training, and didactic instruction in the preparation of parapro-fessional mental health personnel for the utilization of contingency management techniques.* Unpublished doctoral dissertation, Syracuse University.

Trainees: Nurses and attendants (N=50)

Skill(s): Contingency management

Experimental design: Skillstreaming for problem solving and contingency management versus Skillstreaming for contingency management by instruction for problem solving and contingency management versus instruction for contingency management plus no-training control

Results: Significant Skillstreaming effects for problem solving

Leeman, L.W., Gibbs, J.C., Fuller, D., & Potter, G. (1991). Evaluation of a multi-component treatment program for juvenile delinquents. *Aggressive Behavior, 19,* 281–292.

Trainees: Incarcerated male juvenile offenders (N=57)

Skill(s): Interpersonal and self-management

Experimental design: Compared (1) EQUIP program (positive peer culture, Aggression Replacement Training, and means to correct disordered criminal thinking), (2) motivational control group, and (3) no-training control group

Results: EQUIP > both control groups on such institutional behaviors as self-reported misconduct, staff-field incident reports, unexcused absences from school, and recidivism rate at both 1-month and 1-year follow-up

Liberman, B. (1970). *The effect of modeling procedures on attraction and disclosure in a psychotherapy analogue.* Unpublished doctoral dissertation, Syracuse University.

Trainees: Alcoholic inpatients (N=84, all males)

Skill(s): Self-disclosure; attraction to the psychotherapist

Experimental design: High versus low modeled self-disclosure by high versus low modeled attraction plus neutral-tape and no-tape controls

Results: Significant modeling effect for self-disclosure; no modeling effect for attraction

Litwak, S.E. (1977). *The use of the helper therapy principle to increase therapeutic effectiveness and reduce therapeutic resistance: Structured Learning Therapy with resistant adolescents.* Unpublished doctoral dissertation, Syracuse University.

Trainees: Junior high school students (N=48)

Skill(s): Following instructions

Experimental design: (1) Skillstreaming for following instructions—trainees anticipate serving as Skillstreaming trainers and (2) Skillstreaming for following instructions—no trainee anticipation of serving as trainers versus (3) no-treatment control by three parallel conditions involving a skill target not concerned with resistance reduction (i.e., expressing a compliment)

Results: Group 1 significantly > Group 2 significantly > Group 3 on both skills on immediate posttest and transfer measures

Lopez, M.A. (1974). *The influence of vocal and facial cue training on the identification of affect communicated via paralinguistic cues.* Unpublished master's thesis, Syracuse University.

Trainees: Nurses and attendants (N=52)

Skill(s): Recognition of vocal cues of depression

Experimental design: (1) Skillstreaming for vocal and facial cues, (2) Skillstreaming for facial cues, (3) Skillstreaming for vocal cues, (4) no-training control.

Results: Skillstreaming for vocal cues plus either facial cue training (Group 1) or Skillstreaming for facial cues (Group 2) significantly > Skillstreaming for vocal cues (Group 3) or no-training control (Group 4) on posttest and generalization criteria

Lopez, M.A., Hoyer, W., & Goldstein, A.P. (1979). *Effects of over-learning and incentive on the acquisition and transfer of interpersonal skills with institutionalized elderly patients.* Unpublished manuscript, Syracuse University.

Trainees: Elderly inpatients in state hospital (N=56)

Skill(s): Starting a conversation

Experimental design: Skillstreaming plus high versus moderate versus low overlearning by presence versus absence of material reinforcement

Results: Significant skill acquisition effect across Skillstreaming conditions; significant transfer enhancement effect for both overlearning and concrete reinforcement

Magaro, P., & West, A.N. (1983). Structured Learning Therapy: A study with chronic psychiatric patients and levels of pathology. *Behavior Modification, 7,* 29–40.

Trainees: Adult, chronic psychiatric patients (N=38)

Skill(s): A graded series of 20 Skillstreaming skills, from starting a conversation to self-control and decision making

Experimental design: Six-month course of Skillstreaming provided to eight patient groups. Grouping based on initial skill levels.

Results: Pre-post comparisons revealed general increase in skill competence across groups, with greatest gains among patients categorized with paranoid or disorganized features.

McGinnis, E. (1985). Skillstreaming: Teaching social skills to children with behavioral disorders. *Teaching Exceptional Children, 17,* 160–167.

A description of the procedures, curriculum, and modifications in the Skillstreaming approach as applied to behavior disordered elementary-age children.

McGinnis, E., & Goldstein, A.P. (1984). *Skillstreaming the elementary school child: A guide for teaching prosocial skills.* Champaign, IL: Research Press.

A practitioner-oriented trainer's manual presenting the background, procedures, materials, and measures necessary to successfully organize and effectively manage Skillstreaming groups for elementary-age children.

Contents: (1) Introduction; (2) Components of Structured Learning; (3) Assessment for Selection and Grouping; (4) Beginning a Structured Learning Group; (5) Conducting a Structured Learning Group; (6) Prosocial Skills; (7) Structured Learning in Use; (8) Suggestions for Use; (9) Managing Behavior Problems

McGinnis, E., & Goldstein, A.P. (1990). *Skillstreaming in early childhood: Teaching prosocial skills to the preschool and kindergarten child.* Champaign, IL: Reseach Press.

A presentation of procedures and materials needed to initiate and carry out successful Skillstreaming instruction with children ages 3 to 6.

Contents: (1) Introduction; (2) Components of Skillstreaming; (3) Identifying and Evaluating Children for Skillstreaming; (4) Planning and Beginning Skillstreaming Instruction; (5) Implementing Skillstreaming Instruction; (6) Prosocial Skills; (7) Managing Behavior Problems

Miller, M.C. (1992). Student and teacher perceptions related to behavior change after Skillstreaming training. *Behavior Disorders, 17,* 271–295.

Trainees: Behavior-disordered adolescents (N=70)

Skill(s): Several Skillstreaming skills

Experimental design: Pre-post comparisons of skill competence as perceived by trainees and by their teachers

Results: Substantial effects as a function of Skillstreaming as rated by the trainees' teachers; absence of such effects in trainee's own ratings

Miron, M., & Goldstein, A.P. (1978). *Hostage.* New York: Pergamon.

An applied presentation oriented toward law enforcement and criminal justice personnel concerned with hostage and terrorism situations.

Contents: (1) Introduction; (2) The Cotton Case; (3) The Kiritsis Case; (4) The Hanafi Muslim Case; (5) The Hearst Case; (6) The Media, "Shrinks," and Other Civilians; (7) Hostage Negotiation Procedures; (8) A Method for Effective Training: Skillstreaming; (9) Skillstreaming Manual for Police Trainers

Moses, J. (May, 1974). *Supervisory relationship training: A new approach to supervisory training, results of evaluation research.* New York: AT&T Human Resources Development Department.

Trainees: Supervisor trainees (N=183)

Skill(s): Effective management of an array of supervisor-supervisee relationship problems involving discrimination, absenteeism, and theft

Experimental design: Skillstreaming for supervisory relationship skills versus no training

Results: Trained supervisors significantly > untrained supervisors on all behavioral and questionnaire criteria

Muris, P., Heldens, H., & Schreurs, L. (1992). Goldstein training for children in special needs education. *Kind en Adolescent, 13,* 193–198.

A case study report of the impressionistically successful use of Skillstreaming with four mentally retarded Dutch adolescents.

O'Brien, D. (1977). *Trainer-trainee FIRO-B compatibility as a determinant of certain process events in Structured Learning Therapy.* Unpublished master's thesis, Syracuse University.

Trainees: Nurses and attendants at state mental hospital (N=60)

Skill(s): Structured Learning trainer group leadership behaviors vis à vis low affection (actor) trainees

Experimental design: Trainers with high versus low originator compatibility for FIRO-B control by compatible or incompatible trainees; also, trainers with high versus low originator compatibility for FIRO-B affection by compatible or incompatible trainees

Results: No significant between-trainer effects. No significant trainer by trainee effects. Trainers more competent but less warm with cold, versus neutral, trainees.

Orenstein, R. (1969). *The influence of self-esteem on modeling behavior in a psychotherapy analogue.* Unpublished master's thesis, Syracuse University.

Trainees: University undergraduates (all females; N=80)

Skill(s): Attraction to the psychotherapist

Experimental design: High versus low modeled attraction by high versus low subject self-esteem

Results: Significant modeling effect for attraction; no modeling effect for self-esteem. Subjects viewing a high attraction model were also significantly more willing to disclose, as were high self-esteem subjects. Low self-esteem subjects were significantly easier to persuade.

Orenstein, R. (1973). *Effect of training patients to focus on their feelings on level of experiencing in a subsequent interview.* Unpublished doctoral dissertation, Syracuse University.

Trainees: Psychiatric inpatients (all female; N=75)

Skill(s): Focusing (ability to be aware of one's own affective experiencing)

Experimental design: (1) Skillstreaming for focusing, (2) focusing manual, (3) brief instruction for focusing, (4) attention control, (5) no-treatment control

Results: No significant between-group differences in focusing ability

Perry, M.A. (1970). *Didactic instructions for and modeling of empathy.* Unpublished doctoral dissertation, Syracuse University.

Trainees: Clergy (all male; N=66)

Skill(s): Empathy

Experimental design: High empathy modeling versus low empathy modeling versus no modeling by presence versus absence of instructions to be empathic

Results: Significant modeling effect for empathy. No significant instructions or interaction effects for empathy.

Perry, M.A. (1976). *Structured Learning Therapy for skill training of mentally retarded children.* Unpublished manuscript, University of Washington, Seattle.

Trainees: Mildly and moderately retarded halfway house residents (N=36)

Skill(s): Social interaction skills

Experimental design: Skillstreaming for social interaction skills versus attention control versus no-treatment control

Results: Skillstreaming significantly > controls on mealtime social interaction skills

Raleigh, R. (1977). *Individual versus group Structured Learning Therapy for assertiveness training with senior and junior high school students.* Unpublished doctoral dissertation, Syracuse University.

Trainees: Senior and junior high school students (N=80)

Skill(s): Assertiveness

Experimental design: Individual versus group Skillstreaming by senior versus junior high school student trainees plus attention control and no-treatment control

Results: Skillstreaming in groups significantly > all other Skillstreaming and control conditions on assertiveness on both acquisition and transfer criteria

Reed, M.K. (1994). Social skills training to reduce depression in adolescents. *Adolescence, 29,* 293–302.

Trainees: Seriously depressed adolescents (N=10)

Skill(s): Social competency, self-evaluation, affective expression

Experimental design: Skillstreaming versus no-training control plus male or female

Results: Both immediate and sustained reduction in depression for male trainees, but not for females

Robertson, B. (1978). *The effects of Structured Learning trainers' need to control on their group leadership behavior with aggressive and withdrawn trainees.* Unpublished master's thesis, Syracuse University.

Trainees: Nurses and attendants at state mental hospital (N=60)

Skill(s): Skillstreaming trainer group leadership behaviors

Experimental design: Trainers high or low on need to control in interpersonal contexts versus controlling or cooperative actor trainees

Results: Trainers high on need to control significantly > competence with actively resistant trainees than trainers low on need to control. High need to control trainers significantly > attraction to actively resistive than to neutral trainees.

Robinson, R. (1973). *Evaluation of a Structured Learning empathy training program for lower socioeconomic status home-aide trainees.* Unpublished master's thesis, Syracuse University.

Trainees: Home-aide trainees (N=29)

Skill(s): Empathy

Experimental design: (1) Skillstreaming for empathy, (2) didactic training of empathy, (3) no-treatment control

Results: Skillstreaming > didactic training or no-treatment control on immediate posttest and generalization measures of empathy

Rosenthal, N. (1975). *Matching counselor trainees' conceptual level and training approaches: A study in the acquisition and enhancement of confrontation skills.* Unpublished doctoral dissertation, Syracuse University.

Trainees: Counselor trainees (N=60)

Skill(s): Confrontation (ability to point out to clients discrepancies in the verbal and/or nonverbal contents of their statements)

Experimental design: Skillstreaming for confrontation, training conducted by a trainer in "standard" Skillstreaming groups versus Skillstreaming for confrontation, self-instructional training format, by high versus low conceptual level trainees, plus attention control

Results: Significant interaction effects on confrontation skill for type of Skillstreaming (leader-led versus self-instructional) by conceptual level (high versus low). Skillstreaming (both types) > attention control on confrontation skill.

Sasso, G.M., Melloy, K.J., & Kavale, K. (1990). Generalization, maintenance, and behavioral covariation associated with social skills training through Structured Learning. *Behavioral Disorders, 16,* 9–22.

Three students with behavior disorders ranging in age from 8 to 13 years old participated in this study. All three were in a self-contained special education classroom (training setting) and were mainstreamed into at least one general education class (generalization setting). Before, during, and after an 8-week course of Skillstreaming, both they and three peers in the regular class were observed across target skill behaviors. All three trainees exhibited increases in three skill behaviors in the training setting during the program. Two of the three maintained these levels over a 10- to 20-week follow-up period in the training setting and in the mainstream setting. The third did so for only one of the trained skills. Despite these successful outcome data, the prosocial behavior of all three subjects remained significantly below that of their peers in the regular class.

Schneiman, R. (1972). *An evaluation of Structured Learning and didactic learning as methods of training behavior modification skills to lower and middle socioeconomic level teacher-aides.* Unpublished doctoral dissertation, Syracuse University.

Trainees: Teacher aides (30 middle class and 30 lower class; N=60)

Skill(s): Disciplining (appropriate use of rules, disapproval, and praise)

Experimental design: (1) Skillstreaming for disciplining, (2) didactic training for disciplining, (3) no-training control by middle class versus lower class aides

Results: Across social-class levels, Skillstreaming > didactic or no-training on immediate and generalization behavioral measures of disciplining

Shaw, L.W. (1978). *A study of empathy training effectiveness: Comparing computer assisted instruction, Structured Learning training and encounter training exercises.* Unpublished doctoral dissertation, Syracuse University.

Trainees: College undergraduates (N=93)

Skill(s): Empathy

Experimental design: Computer assisted instruction versus Skillstreaming versus encounter training versus no-training control for empathy

Results: Computer assisted instruction and Skillstreaming significantly > no-training control on level of empathy

Solomon, E.J. (1978). *Structured Learning Therapy with abusive parents: Training in self-control.* Unpublished doctoral dissertation, Syracuse University.

Trainees: Child-abusing parents (31 female and 9 male; N=40)

Skill(s): Self-control

Experimental design: Skillstreaming with and without structuring into helper role by Skillstreaming with and without mastery training plus brief instruction control

Results: All Skillstreaming groups significantly > controls on self-control on both acquisition and generalization criteria. Skillstreaming plus helper structuring plus mastery training significantly > all other Skillstreaming groups.

Sorcher, M., & Goldstein, A.P. (1973). A behavior modeling approach in training. *Personnel Administration, 35,* 35–41.

An overview of the nature and potential impact of Skill-streaming in an industrial context. Topics examined include the need for a concrete, behavioral training focus; the basis for the choice of modeling, role-playing, social reinforcement, and transfer training as the components of this behavioral approach; and a brief example of how these procedures are utilized.

Sprafkin, R.P., Gershaw, N.J., & Goldstein, A.P. (1978). Teaching interpersonal skills to psychiatric outpatients: Using Structured Learning Therapy in a community-based setting. *Journal of Rehabilitation, 44,* 26–29.

A presentation of the rationale, procedures, and materials of Structured Learning Therapy. Its potential rehabilitative usefulness in fostering effective and satisfying community functioning is stressed.

Sprafkin, R.P., Gershaw, N.J., & Goldstein, A.P. (1980). Skill training for the disruptive adolescent. *Directive Teacher, 13,* 14–19.

Skills training in general, and the Skillstreaming method in particular, is offered as a viable means for reducing the disruptive behaviors displayed by many adolescents in school and other settings.

Sprafkin, R.P., Gershaw, N.J., & Goldstein, A.P. (1981). Structured Learning Therapy: A skill training approach to social competence. In D.P. Rathjen & J. Foreyt (Eds.), *Social competence: Interventions for children and adults.* New York: Pergamon.

A presentation of the Skillstreaming approach to enhancing the social competence of both typical and atypical adolescents. The value of a psychoeducational strategy for this purpose is described, as are the Skillstreaming procedures and curriculum.

Sprafkin, R.P., Gershaw, N.J., & Goldstein, A.P. (1985). Structured Learning: Its cross cultural roots and implications. In P. Pedersen (Ed.), *Handbook of cross cultural counseling.* Fairfield, CT: Greenwood.

A description of the Skillstreaming method, curriculum, and evaluation research, with special emphasis on program relevance for and applicability to low-income trainee populations.

Sprafkin, R.P., Gershaw, N.J., & Goldstein, A.P. (1993). *Social skills for mental health: A Structured Learning approach.* Boston: Allyn & Bacon.

A description of the use of Skillstreaming with chronic adult mental patients, with emphasis on their preparation via this intervention for functional living in the community and in other noninstitutional settings.

Contents: (1) Introduction: The Skill-Deficient Client; (2) Structured Learning: Background and Development; (3) Structured Learning: Implementation Procedures; (4) Structured Learning Skills; (5) Managing Problematic Behaviors; (6) Structured Learning in Use

Sprafkin, R.P., & Goldstein, A.P. (1990). Behavior modeling. In S.S. Dubin (Ed.), *Models of professional updating.* San Francisco: Jossey-Bass.

Describes the Skillstreaming method and the wide range of trainees with whom it has been used. Emphasis in this chapter is on the program's utility in enhancing the competence and range of capabilities of various change agent trainees.

Stumphauzer, J.C. (1985). School programs: Staying in school and learning to learn. *Child and Youth Services, 8,* 137–146.

A review of delinquency prevention programs, including behavioral contracting, truancy control, parent training, vandalism reduction, school consultation, and Skillstreaming.

Sturm, D. (1980). *Therapist aggression tolerance and dependency tolerance under standardized client conditions of hostility and dependency.* Unpublished master's thesis, Syracuse University.

Trainees: Parent aides employed at child abuse agency (N=28)

Skill(s): Skillstreaming leadership skills

Experimental design: Two 2 × 2 factorial analyses: (1) high versus low hostile actor-clients by high versus low aggression tolerance aides, and (2) high versus low dependent actor-clients by high versus low dependency tolerance aides

Results: Significant hostile actor × aide tolerance effect; no dependency effects

Sutton, K. (1970). *Effects of modeled empathy and structured social class upon level of therapist displayed empathy.* Unpublished master's thesis, Syracuse University.

Trainees: Attendants (N=60)

Skill(s): Empathy

Experimental design: High versus low modeled empathy by high versus low structured social class

Results: Significant effect for modeled empathy on immediate but not generalization measurement. No significant social class structuring or interaction effects.

Sutton-Simon, K. (1974). *The effects of two types of modeling and rehearsal procedures upon schizophrenics' social skill behavior.* Unpublished doctoral dissertation, Syracuse University.

Trainees: Psychiatric inpatients (all male, all schizophrenic; N=83)

Skill(s): Social interaction behaviors

Experimental design: (1) Skillstreaming with behavioral and cognitive models, (2) Skillstreaming with behavioral models, (3) Skillstreaming with cognitive models, (4) attention control, (5) no-treatment control

Results: No significant between-condition differences

Swanstrom, C.R. (1978). *An examination of Structured Learning Therapy and the helper therapy principle in teaching a self-control strategy to school children with conduct problems.* Unpublished doctoral dissertation, Syracuse University.

Trainees: Elementary school children with acting-out problems (30 boys, 11 girls; N=41)

Skill(s): Self-control

Experimental design: Skillstreaming versus structured discussion by helper experience versus helper structuring versus no helper role plus brief instructions control

Results: Skillstreaming and structured discussion significantly > control on self-control acquisition. No significant transfer or helper role effects.

Trief, P. (1977). *The reduction of egocentrism in acting-out adolescents by Structured Learning Therapy.* Unpublished doctoral dissertation, Syracuse University.

Trainees: Adolescent boys with history of acting-out behaviors (N=58)

Skill(s): Perspective-taking, cooperation

Experimental design: Presence versus absence of Skillstreaming for affective perspective taking by presence versus absence of Skillstreaming for cognitive perspective taking plus no-treatment control

Results: All Skillstreaming groups significantly > controls on perspective-taking acquisition. Skillstreaming plus both affective and cognitive perspective-taking training significantly > controls on generalization criteria.

Walsh, W.G. (1971). *The effects of conformity pressure and modeling on the attraction of hospitalized patients toward an interviewer.* Unpublished doctoral dissertation, Syracuse University.

Trainees: Psychiatric inpatients (all female, mostly schizophrenic; N=60)

Skill(s): Attraction

Experimental design: Presence versus absence of high attraction modeling by presence versus absence of high attraction conformity pressure plus no-treatment control

Results: Significant main and interaction effects for modeling and conformity pressure on attraction. No significant generalization effect.

Wiken, J.P. (1988). Sheltered homes: A new field for clinical psychologists? *Psycholoog, 23,* 301–304.

Discusses the emerging role of clinical psychologists as diagnosticians and trainers for approaches such as Skill-streaming in sheltered homes, community placement locations increasingly being used for mental patients in the Netherlands.

Wood, M.A. (1977). *Acquisition and transfer of assertiveness in passive and aggressive adolescents through the use of Structured Learning Therapy.* Unpublished doctoral dissertation, Syracuse University.

Trainees: Ninth-grade students (N=74)

Skill(s): Assertiveness

Experimental design: Skillstreaming led by (1) teacher, (2) parent, or (3) student trainers by (1) passive or (2) aggressive trainees plus brief instructions control

Results: All Skillstreaming groups significantly > control on assertiveness criteria and on acquisition and transfer criteria. Skillstreaming-teacher trainer > Skillstreaming-student trainer > Skillstreaming-parent trainer on acquisition and minimal transfer criteria.

APPENDIX B

Skillstreaming Checklists and Grouping Chart

TEACHER/STAFF SKILLSTREAMING CHECKLIST

Student:_____ Class/age: _____

Teacher/staff: _____ Date: _____

INSTRUCTIONS: Listed below you will find a number of skills that children are more or less proficient in using. This checklist will help you evaluate how well each child uses the various skills. For each child, rate his/her use of each skill, based on your observations of his/her behavior in various situations.

Circle 1 if the child is *almost never* good at using the skill.

Circle 2 if the child is *seldom* good at using the skill.

Circle 3 if he child is *sometimes* good at using the skill.

Circle 4 if the child is *often* good at using the skill.

Circle 5 if the child is *almost always* good at using the skill.

Please rate the child on all skills listed. If you know of a situation in which the child has particular difficulty in using the skill well, please note it briefly in the space marked "Problem situation."

almost never seldom sometimes often almost always

1. **Listening:** Does the student appear to listen when someone is speaking and make an effort to understand what is said?   1   2   3   4   5

   Problem situation:

2. **Asking for Help:** Does the student decide when he/she needs assistance and ask for this help in a pleasant manner?   1   2   3   4   5

   Problem situation:

3. **Saying Thank You:** Does the student tell others he/she appreciates help given, favors, and so forth?

    1 2 3 4 5

Problem situation:

4. **Bringing Materials to Class:** Does the student remember the books and materials he/she needs for class?

    1 2 3 4 5

Problem situation:

5. **Following Instructions:** Does the student understand instructions and follow them?

    1 2 3 4 5

Problem situation:

6. **Completing Assignments:** Does the student complete assignments at his/her independent academic level?

    1 2 3 4 5

Problem situation:

7. **Contributing to Discussions:** Does the student participate in class discussions in accordance with classroom rules?

    1 2 3 4 5

Problem situation:

8. **Offering Help to an Adult:** Does the student offer to help you at appropriate times and in an appropriate manner?

   1 2 3 4 5

   Problem situation:

9. **Asking a Question:** Does the student know how and when to ask a question of another person?

   1 2 3 4 5

   Problem situation:

10. **Ignoring Distractions:** Does the student ignore classroom distractions?

    1 2 3 4 5

    Problem situation:

11. **Making Corrections:** Does the student make the necessary corrections on assignments without getting overly frustrated?

    1 2 3 4 5

    Problem situation:

12. **Deciding on Something to Do:** Does the student find something to do when he/she has free time?

    1 2 3 4 5

    Problem situation:

13. **Setting a Goal:** Does the student set realistic goals for himself/herself and take the necessary steps to meet these goals?

     1   2   3   4   5

Problem situation:

14. **Introducing Yourself:** Does the student introduce himself/herself in an appropriate way to people he/she doesn't know?

     1   2   3   4   5

Problem situation:

15. **Beginning a Conversation:** Does the student know how and when to begin a conversation with another person?

     1   2   3   4   5

Problem situation:

16. **Ending a Conversation:** Does the student end a conversation when it is necessary and in an appropriate manner?

     1   2   3   4   5

Problem situation:

17. **Joining In:** Does the student know and practice acceptable ways of joining an ongoing activity or group?

     1   2   3   4   5

Problem situation:

almost never	seldom	sometimes	often	almost always

18. **Playing a Game:** Does the student play games with classmates fairly?

    1   2   3   4   5

    Problem situation:

19. **Asking a Favor:** Does the student know how to ask a favor of another person?

    1   2   3   4   5

    Problem situation:

20. **Offering Help to a Classmate:** Can the student recognize when someone needs or wants assistance and offer this help?

    1   2   3   4   5

    Problem situation:

21. **Giving a Compliment:** Does the student tell others that he/she likes something about them or something they have done?

    1   2   3   4   5

    Problem situation:

22. **Accepting a Compliment:** Does the student accept these comments given by adults or his/her peers in a friendly way?

    1   2   3   4   5

    Problem situation:

23. **Suggesting an Activity:** Does the student suggest appropriate activities to others?

    1   2   3   4   5

    Problem situation:

273

24. **Sharing:** Is the student agreeable
    to sharing things with others and,
    if not, does he/she offer acceptable
    reasons for not sharing?

    Problem situation:

    1   2   3   4   5

25. **Apologizing:** Does the student tell
    others sincerely that he/she is
    sorry for doing something?

    Problem situation:

    1   2   3   4   5

26. **Knowing Your Feelings:** Does the
    student identify feelings he/she is
    experiencing?

    Problem situation:

    1   2   3   4   5

27. **Expressing Your Feelings:** Does
    the student express his/her
    feelings in acceptable ways?

    Problem situation:

    1   2   3   4   5

28. **Recognizing Another's Feelings:**
    Does the student try to figure out
    in acceptable ways how others are
    feeling?

    Problem situation:

    1   2   3   4   5

29. **Showing Understanding of Another's Feelings:** Does the student show understanding of others' feelings in acceptable ways?   1 2 3 4 5

Problem situation:

30. **Expressing Concern for Another:** Does the student express concern for others in acceptable ways?   1 2 3 4 5

Problem situation:

31. **Dealing with Your Anger:** Does the student use acceptable ways to express his/her anger?   1 2 3 4 5

Problem situation:

32. **Dealing with Another's Anger:** Does the student try to understand another's anger without getting angry himself/herself?   1 2 3 4 5

Problem situation:

33. **Expressing Affection:** Does the student let others know in acceptable ways that he/she cares about them?   1 2 3 4 5

Problem situation:

34. **Dealing with Fear:** Does the student know why he/she is afraid and practice strategies to reduce this fear?

     1   2   3   4   5

Problem situation:

35. **Rewarding Yourself:** Does the student say and do nice things for himself/herself when a reward is deserved?

     1   2   3   4   5

Problem situation:

36. **Using Self-Control:** Does the student know and practice strategies to control his/her temper or excitement?

     1   2   3   4   5

Problem situation:

37. **Asking Permission:** Does the student know when and how to ask whether he/she may do something?

     1   2   3   4   5

Problem situation:

38. **Responding to Teasing:** Does the student deal with being teased in ways that allow him/her to remain in control?

     1   2   3   4   5

Problem situation:

39. **Avoiding Trouble:** Does the student stay away from situations that may get him/her into trouble?

    1 2 3 4 5

Problem situation:

40. **Staying Out of Fights:** Does the student know of and practice socially appropriate ways of handling potential fights?

    1 2 3 4 5

Problem situation:

41. **Problem Solving:** When a problem occurs, does the student think of alternatives, choose an alternative, then evaluate how well this solved the problem?

    1 2 3 4 5

Problem situation:

42. **Accepting Consequences:** Does the student accept the consequences for his/her behavior without becoming defensive or upset?

    1 2 3 4 5

Problem situation:

43. **Dealing with an Accusation:** Does the student know of and practice ways to deal with being accused of something?

    1 2 3 4 5

Problem situation:

	almost never	seldom	sometimes	often	almost always

44. **Negotiating:** Is the student willing to give and take in order to reach a compromise?

    1   2   3   4   5

Problem situation:

45. **Dealing with Boredom:** Does the student select acceptable activities when he/she is bored?

    1   2   3   4   5

Problem situation:

46. **Deciding What Caused a Problem:** Does the student assess what caused a problem and accept responsibility if appropriate?

    1   2   3   4   5

Problem situation:

47. **Making a Complaint:** Does the student know how to express disagreement in acceptable ways?

    1   2   3   4   5

Problem situation:

48. **Answering a Complaint:** Is the student willing to arrive at a fair solution to someone's justified complaint?

    1   2   3   4   5

Problem situation:

49. **Dealing with Losing:** Does the student accept losing at a game or activity without becoming upset or angry?

       1   2   3   4   5

Problem situation:

50. **Being a Good Sport:** Does the student give a sincere compliment to others about how they played a game?

       1   2   3   4   5

Problem situation:

51. **Dealing with Being Left Out:** Does the student deal with being left out of an activity without losing control?

       1   2   3   4   5

Problem situation:

52. **Dealing with Embarrassment:** Does the student know of things to do that help him/her feel less embarrassed or self-conscious?

       1   2   3   4   5

Problem situation:

53. **Reacting to Failure:** Does the student figure out reason(s) for his/her failure and ways to be more successful the next time?

       1   2   3   4   5

Problem situation:

54. **Accepting No:** Does the student accept being told no without becoming unduly upset or angry?

    Problem situation:

    1   2   3   4   5

55. **Saying No:** Does the student say no in acceptable ways to things he/she doesn't want to do or to things that may get him/her into trouble?

    Problem situation:

    1   2   3   4   5

56. **Relaxing:** Is the student able to relax when tense or upset?

    Problem situation:

    1   2   3   4   5

57. **Dealing with Group Pressure:** Does the student decide what he/she wants to do when others pressure him/her to do something else?

    Problem situation:

    1   2   3   4   5

58. **Dealing with Wanting Something That Isn't Yours:** Does the student refrain from taking things that don't belong to him/her?

    Problem situation:

    1   2   3   4   5

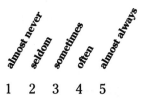

59. **Making a Decision:** Does the student make thoughtful choices?   1   2   3   4   5

Problem situation:

60. **Being Honest:** Is the student honest when confronted with a negative action?   1   2   3   4   5

Problem situation:

PARENT SKILLSTREAMING CHECKLIST

Name: _____ Date: _____

Child's name: _____ Birth date: _____

INSTRUCTIONS: Based on your observations in various situations, rate your child's use of the following skills.

Circle 1 if the child is *almost never* good at using the skill.

Circle 2 if the child is *seldom* good at using the skill.

Circle 3 if the child is *sometimes* good at using the skill.

Circle 4 if the child is *often* good at using the skill.

Circle 5 if the child is *almost always* good at using the skill.

	almost never	seldom	sometimes	often	almost always
1. **Listening:** Does your child listen when you or others talk to him/her? Comments:	1	2	3	4	5
2. **Asking for Help:** Does your child decide when he/she needs assistance and ask for this help in a pleasant manner? Comments:	1	2	3	4	5
3. **Saying Thank You:** Does your child tell others he/she appreciates help given, favors, and so forth? Comments:	1	2	3	4	5

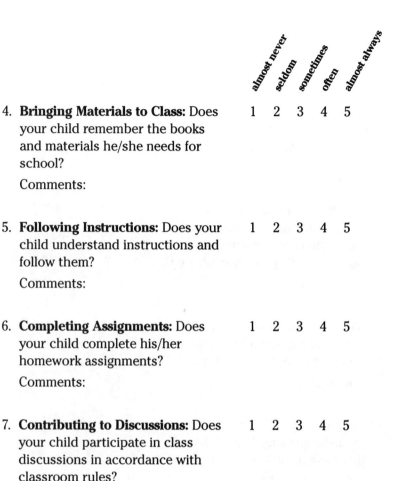

4. **Bringing Materials to Class:** Does your child remember the books and materials he/she needs for school?

    almost never seldom sometimes often almost always

1 2 3 4 5

Comments:

5. **Following Instructions:** Does your child understand instructions and follow them?

1 2 3 4 5

Comments:

6. **Completing Assignments:** Does your child complete his/her homework assignments?

1 2 3 4 5

Comments:

7. **Contributing to Discussions:** Does your child participate in class discussions in accordance with classroom rules?

1 2 3 4 5

Comments:

8. **Offering Help to an Adult:** Does your child offer to help you at appropriate times and in an appropriate manner?

1 2 3 4 5

Comments:

9. **Asking a Question:** Does your child know how and when to ask a question of another person?

1 2 3 4 5

Comments:

10. **Ignoring Distractions:** Does your child ignore distractions in order to get his/her work done?

    1   2   3   4   5

Comments:

11. **Making Corrections:** Does your child make the necessary corrections on assignments without getting overly frustrated?

    1   2   3   4   5

Comments:

12. **Deciding on Something to Do:** Does your child find something to do when he/she has free time?

    1   2   3   4   5

Comments:

13. **Setting a Goal:** Does your child set realistic goals for himself/herself and take the necessary steps to meet these goals?

    1   2   3   4   5

Comments:

14. **Introducing Yourself:** Does your child introduce himself/herself in an appropriate way to people he/she doesn't know?

    1   2   3   4   5

Comments:

15. **Beginning a Conversation:** Does your child know how and when to begin a conversation with another person?

    Comments:

    1   2   3   4   5

16. **Ending a Conversation:** Does your child end a conversation when it is necessary and in an appropriate manner?

    Comments:

    1   2   3   4   5

17. **Joining In:** Does your child know and practice acceptable ways of joining an ongoing activity or group?

    Comments:

    1   2   3   4   5

18. **Playing a Game:** Does your child play games with friends fairly?

    Comments:

    1   2   3   4   5

19. **Asking a Favor:** Does your child know how to ask a favor of another person in an appropriate way?

    Comments:

    1   2   3   4   5

20. **Offering Help to a Classmate:**   1   2   3   4   5
    Does your child recognize when
    someone needs or wants assis-
    tance and offer this help?

    Comments:

21. **Giving a Compliment:** Does your   1   2   3   4   5
    child tell others that he/she likes
    something about them or something
    they have done?

    Comments:

22. **Accepting a Compliment:** Does   1   2   3   4   5
    your child accept compliments
    given by adults or his/her peers
    in a friendly way?

    Comments:

23. **Suggesting an Activity:** Does your   1   2   3   4   5
    child suggest appropriate activities
    to others?

    Comments:

24. **Sharing:** Is your child agreeable to   1   2   3   4   5
    sharing things with others and, if
    not, does he/she offer acceptable
    reasons for not sharing?

    Comments:

25. **Apologizing:** Does your child tell others sincerely that he/she is sorry for doing something?

    1   2   3   4   5

Comments:

26. **Knowing Your Feelings:** Does your child identify feelings he/she is experiencing?

    1   2   3   4   5

Comments:

27. **Expressing Your Feelings:** Does your child express his/her feelings in acceptable ways?

    1   2   3   4   5

Comments:

28. **Recognizing Another's Feelings:** Does your child try to figure out in acceptable ways how others are feeling?

    1   2   3   4   5

Comments:

29. **Showing Understanding of Another's Feelings:** Does your child show understanding of others' feelings in acceptable ways?

    1   2   3   4   5

Comments:

30. **Expressing Concern for Another:** Does your child express concern for others in acceptable ways?

    1   2   3   4   5

Comments:

		almost never	seldom	sometimes	often	almost always

31. **Dealing with Your Anger:** Does your child use acceptable ways to express his/her anger?

       1   2   3   4   5

Comments:

32. **Dealing with Another's Anger:** Does your child try to understand another's anger without getting angry himself/herself?

       1   2   3   4   5

Comments:

33. **Expressing Affection:** Does your child let others know in acceptable ways that he/she cares about them?

       1   2   3   4   5

Comments:

34. **Dealing with Fear:** Does your child know why he/she is afraid and do positive things to reduce this fear?

       1   2   3   4   5

Comments:

35. **Rewarding Yourself:** Does your child say and do nice things for himself/herself when a reward is deserved?

       1   2   3   4   5

Comments:

36. **Using Self-Control:** Does your child know and use positive ways to control his/her temper or excitement?

       1   2   3   4   5

Comments:

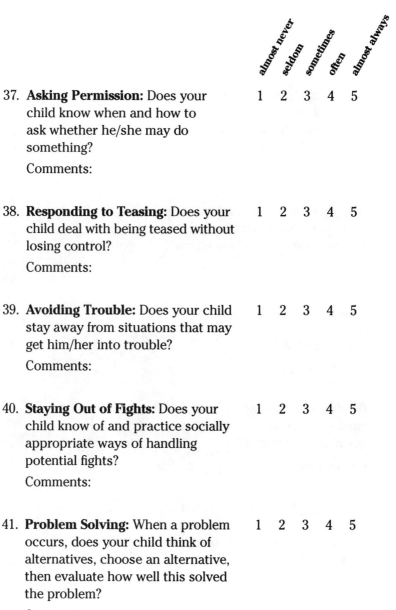

	almost never	seldom	sometimes	often	almost always

37. **Asking Permission:** Does your child know when and how to ask whether he/she may do something?

    Comments:

    1 2 3 4 5

38. **Responding to Teasing:** Does your child deal with being teased without losing control?

    Comments:

    1 2 3 4 5

39. **Avoiding Trouble:** Does your child stay away from situations that may get him/her into trouble?

    Comments:

    1 2 3 4 5

40. **Staying Out of Fights:** Does your child know of and practice socially appropriate ways of handling potential fights?

    Comments:

    1 2 3 4 5

41. **Problem Solving:** When a problem occurs, does your child think of alternatives, choose an alternative, then evaluate how well this solved the problem?

    Comments:

    1 2 3 4 5

almost never · seldom · sometimes · often · almost always

42. **Accepting Consequences:** Does your child accept the consequences for his/her behavior without becoming defensive or upset?

    1   2   3   4   5

Comments:

43. **Dealing with an Accusation:** Does your child deal in positive ways with being accused of something?

    1   2   3   4   5

Comments:

44. **Negotiating:** Is your child willing to give and take in order to reach a compromise?

    1   2   3   4   5

Comments:

45. **Dealing with Boredom:** Does your child select acceptable activities when he/she is bored?

    1   2   3   4   5

Comments:

46. **Deciding What Caused a Problem:** Does your child assess what caused a problem and accept responsibility if appropriate?

    1   2   3   4   5

Comments:

47. **Making a Complaint:** Does your child know how to express disagreement in acceptable ways?

    1   2   3   4   5

Comments:

48. **Answering a Complaint:** Is your child willing to arrive at a fair solution to someone's justified complaint?

Comments:

1   2   3   4   5

49. **Dealing with Losing:** Does your child accept losing at a game or activity without becoming upset or angry?

Comments:

1   2   3   4   5

50. **Being a Good Sport:** Does your child give a sincere compliment to others about how they played a game?

Comments:

1   2   3   4   5

51. **Dealing with Being Left Out:** Does your child deal with being left out of an activity without losing control?

Comments:

1   2   3   4   5

52. **Dealing with Embarrassment:** Does your child know of things to do that help him/her feel less embarrassed or self-conscious?

Comments:

1   2   3   4   5

53. **Reacting to Failure:** Does your child figure out the reason(s) for his/her failure and ways he/she can be more successful the next time?

    1   2   3   4   5

Comments:

54. **Accepting No:** Does your child accept being told no without becoming unduly upset or angry?

    1   2   3   4   5

Comments:

55. **Saying No:** Does your child say no in acceptable ways to things he/she doesn't want to do or to things that may get him/her into trouble?

    1   2   3   4   5

Comments:

56. **Relaxing:** Is your child able to relax when tense or upset?

    1   2   3   4   5

Comments:

57. **Dealing with Group Pressure:** Does your child decide what he/she wants to do when others pressure him/her to do something else?

    1   2   3   4   5

Comments:

58. **Dealing with Wanting Something That Isn't Yours:** Does your child refrain from taking things that don't belong to him/her?

    1   2   3   4   5

Comments:

59. **Making a Decision:** Does your child make thoughtful choices?

    1   2   3   4   5

Comments:

60. **Being Honest:** Is your child honest when confronted with a negative action?

    1   2   3   4   5

Comments:

STUDENT SKILLSTREAMING CHECKLIST

Name: _____ Date: _____

INSTRUCTIONS: Each of the questions will ask you about how well you do something. Next to each question is a number.

> Circle number 1 if you *almost never* do what the question asks.
>
> Circle number 2 if you *seldom* do it.
>
> Circle number 3 if you *sometimes* do it.
>
> Circle number 4 if you do it *often*.
>
> Circle number 5 if you *almost always* do it.

There are no right or wrong answers to these questions. Answer the way you really feel about each question.

	almost never	seldom	sometimes	often	almost always
1. Is it easy for me to listen to someone who is talking to me?	1	2	3	4	5
2. Do I ask for help in a friendly way when I need help?	1	2	3	4	5
3. Do I tell people thank you for something they have done for me?	1	2	3	4	5
4. Do I have the materials I need for my classes (like books, pencils, paper)?	1	2	3	4	5
5. Do I understand what to do when directions are given, and do I follow these directions?	1	2	3	4	5
6. Do I finish my schoolwork?	1	2	3	4	5
7. Do I join in on class talks or discussions?	1	2	3	4	5
8. Do I try to help an adult when I think he/she could use the help?	1	2	3	4	5

9. Do I decide what I don't understand about my schoolwork and ask my teacher questions in a friendly way?   1   2   3   4   5

10. Is it easy for me to keep doing my schoolwork when people are noisy?   1   2   3   4   5

11. Do I fix mistakes on my work without getting upset?   1   2   3   4   5

12. Do I choose something to do when I have free time?   1   2   3   4   5

13. Do I decide on something I want to work for and keep working until I get it?   1   2   3   4   5

14. Is it easy for me to take the first step to meet somebody I don't know?   1   2   3   4   5

15. Is it easy for me to start a conversation with someone?   1   2   3   4   5

16. When I have something else I have to do, do I end a conversation with someone in a nice way?   1   2   3   4   5

17. Do I ask to join in a game or activity in a friendly way?   1   2   3   4   5

18. Do I follow the rules when I play a game?   1   2   3   4   5

19. Is it easy for me to ask a favor of someone?   1   2   3   4   5

20. Do I notice when somebody needs help and try to help the person?   1   2   3   4   5

21. Do I tell others that I like something nice about them or something nice they have done for me or for somebody else?   1   2   3   4   5

	almost never	seldom	sometimes	often	almost always

22. When someone says something nice about me, do I accept what the person says?   1   2   3   4   5

23. Do I suggest things to do with my friends?   1   2   3   4   5

24. Am I willing to share my things with others?   1   2   3   4   5

25. Do I tell others I'm sorry after I do something wrong?   1   2   3   4   5

26. Do I know how I feel about different things that happen?   1   2   3   4   5

27. Do I let others know what I am feeling and do it in a good way?   1   2   3   4   5

28. Do I try to tell how other people are feeling?   1   2   3   4   5

29. Do I show others that I understand how they feel?   1   2   3   4   5

30. When someone has a problem, do I let the person know that I care?   1   2   3   4   5

31. When I am angry, do I deal with it in ways that won't hurt other people?   1   2   3   4   5

32. Do I try to understand other people's angry feelings?   1   2   3   4   5

33. Do I let others know I care about them?   1   2   3   4   5

34. Do I know what makes me afraid, and do I think of things to do so I don't stay afraid?   1   2   3   4   5

	almost never	seldom	sometimes	often	almost always

35. Do I say and do nice things for myself when I have earned it? 1 2 3 4 5

36. Do I keep my temper when I am upset? 1 2 3 4 5

37. Do I know when I have to ask to do something I want to do, and do I ask in a friendly way? 1 2 3 4 5

38. When somebody teases me, do I stay in control? 1 2 3 4 5

39. Do I try to stay away from things that may get me into trouble? 1 2 3 4 5

40. Do I think of ways other than fighting to take care of problems? 1 2 3 4 5

41. Do I think of ways to deal with a problem and what might happen if I use these ways? 1 2 3 4 5

42. When I do something I shouldn't have done, do I accept what happens then? 1 2 3 4 5

43. Do I decide what I have been accused of and why, then think of a good way to handle the situation? 1 2 3 4 5

44. When I don't agree with somebody, do I help think of a plan to make both of us happy? 1 2 3 4 5

45. When I feel bored, do I think of good things to do and then do them? 1 2 3 4 5

46. Do I know when a problem happened because of something I did? 1 2 3 4 5

47. Do I tell others without getting mad or yelling when they have caused a problem for me?   1   2   3   4   5

48. Do I help think of a fair way to take care of a complaint against me?   1   2   3   4   5

49. When I lose at a game, do I keep from getting upset?   1   2   3   4   5

50. Do I tell others something good about the way they played a game?   1   2   3   4   5

51. Do I decide if I have been left out, then do things in a good way to make me feel better?   1   2   3   4   5

52. Do I do things that will help me feel less embarrassed?   1   2   3   4   5

53. When I don't do well on something (on a test, doing my chores), do I decide ways I could do better next time?   1   2   3   4   5

54. When I am told no, can I keep from becoming upset?   1   2   3   4   5

55. Do I say no to things that might get me into trouble or that I don't want to do, and do I say it in a friendly way?   1   2   3   4   5

56. Can I keep my body from getting tight and tense when I am angry or upset?   1   2   3   4   5

57. When a group of kids wants me to do something that might get me into trouble or that is wrong, do I say no?   1   2   3   4   5

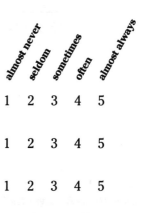

	almost never	seldom	sometimes	often	almost always
58. Do I keep from taking things that aren't mine?	1	2	3	4	5
59. Is it easy for me to decide what to do when I'm given a choice?	1	2	3	4	5
60. Do I tell the truth about what I have done, even if I might get into trouble?	1	2	3	4	5

SKILLSTREAMING GROUPING CHART

	student names								
GROUP I **Classroom Survival Skills**									
1. Listening									
2. Asking for Help									
3. Saying Thank You									
4. Bringing Materials to Class									
5. Following Instructions									
6. Completing Assignments									
7. Contributing to Discussions									
8. Offering Help to an Adult									
9. Asking a Question									
10. Ignoring Distractions									
11. Making Corrections									
12. Deciding on Something to Do									
13. Setting a Goal									

	student names							
GROUP II **Friendship-Making Skills**								
14. Introducing Yourself								
15. Beginning a Conversation								
16. Ending a Conversation								
17. Joining In								
18. Playing a Game								
19. Asking a Favor								
20. Offering Help to a Classmate								
21. Giving a Compliment								
22. Accepting a Compliment								
23. Suggesting an Activity								
24. Sharing								
25. Apologizing								

GROUP III **Skills for Dealing with Feelings**	student names									
26. Knowing Your Feelings										
27. Expressing Your Feelings										
28. Recognizing Another's Feelings										
29. Showing Understanding of Another's Feelings										
30. Expressing Concern for Another										
31. Dealing with Your Anger										
32. Dealing with Another's Anger										
33. Expressing Affection										
34. Dealing with Fear										
35. Rewarding Yourself										

GROUP IV **Skill Alternatives** **to Aggression**	student names									
36. Using Self-Control										
37. Asking Permission										
38. Responding to Teasing										
39. Avoiding Trouble										
40. Staying Out of Fights										
41. Problem Solving										
42. Accepting Consequences										
43. Dealing with an Accusation										
44. Negotiating										

**GROUP V
Skills for Dealing
with Stress**

	student names								
45. Dealing with Boredom									
46. Deciding What Caused a Problem									
47. Making a Complaint									
48. Answering a Complaint									
49. Dealing with Losing									
50. Being a Good Sport									
51. Dealing with Being Left Out									
52. Dealing with Embarrassment									
53. Reacting to Failure									
54. Accepting No									
55. Saying No									
56. Relaxing									

	student names								
57. Dealing with Group Pressure									
58. Dealing with Wanting Something That Isn't Yours									
59. Making a Decision									
60. Being Honest									

Supplementary Skillstreaming Components

All that is truly needed to implement a Skillstreaming program for elementary-age students is this program text. However, a number of other Skillstreaming materials, both print and video, will make the task easier. Supplementary Skillstreaming components for elementary-age students are described in this appendix. Skillstreaming materials for young children and adolescents are listed in Appendix D.

For current prices and ordering information,
write, call, or fax:

Research Press
2612 North Mattis Avenue
Champaign, Illinois 61821
Phone: 217-352-3273
Toll-Free: 1-800-519-2707
Fax: 217-352-1221

Print Components

Program Forms

Skillstreaming the Elementary School Child: New Strategies and Perspectives for Teaching Prosocial Skills—Program Forms (rev. ed.), by Dr. Ellen McGinnis and Dr. Arnold P. Goldstein, 1997 (papercover, 8 ½ × 11–inch format, 64 pages, ISBN 0–87822–374–6).

CONTENTS

- Teacher/Staff, Parent, and Student Skillstreaming Checklists
- Skillstreaming Grouping Chart
- Homework Reports
- Group Self-Report Chart
- School-Home Note
- Parent/Staff Skill Rating Form
- Skill Awards
- Skill Contracts
- Self-Recording Forms

Student Manual

Skillstreaming the Elementary School Child—Student Manual, by Dr. Ellen McGinnis and Dr. Arnold P. Goldstein, 1997 (papercover, 8 ½ × 11–inch format, 80 pages, ISBN 0–87822–373–8).

A clear, concise guide for students, designed to enhance active involvement in the Skillstreaming group. Serves as a reference and organizer.

CONTENTS

1: Introduction to Skillstreaming.   Provides an overview of Skillstreaming and its purposes. Having students read this section as a group and then complete the Student Skillstreaming Checklist included is a good orientation to the group.

2: Parts to Learning Skillstreaming. Briefly describes Skillstreaming's four instructional methods: modeling, role-playing, feedback, and transfer (homework). This overview prepares students for the next section, which applies these methods to specific skill learning.

3: Skillstreaming in Action. Gives step-by-step guidance through the modeling, role-playing, and feedback process for one skill, Responding to Teasing. Clarifies the roles of main actor, co-actor, and observers during the role-play.

4: Skill Homework. Gives detailed instructions for completing skill homework assignments. Includes sample homework reports filled out by a student learning the skill of Responding to Teasing.

5: Skillstreaming Skills. Lists the 60 Skillstreaming skills according to their five categories: Classroom Survival Skills, Friendship-Making Skills, Skills for Dealing with Feelings, Skill Alternatives to Aggression, and Skills for Dealing with Stress. Gives a brief rationale for skill learning in each category in order to help students identify which skills they would most like to learn.

6: Making It All Work. Offers suggestions to improve skill performance and success. Topics include nonverbal communication; what to do when a skill does not bring about a desired outcome; adjusting skills relative to people, places, and situations; and skill shifting and skill combinations.

Skill Cards

Skillstreaming the Elementary School Child—Skill Cards,
by Dr. Ellen McGinnis and Dr. Arnold P. Goldstein, 1997.

Convenient 3×5–inch cards designed for student use during Skillstreaming sessions and homework assignments. Cards list the behavioral steps for each of the 60 elementary Skillstreaming skills. Eight cards are provided for each skill (480 cards in all).

Video Components

People Skills: Doing 'em Right! (Elementary Level), by
Dr. Ellen McGinnis and Dr. Arnold P. Goldstein, 1997
(17 minutes).

Shows an elementary-level Skillstreaming group in progress to
help prospective group members learn what is expected in the group,
understand how skill learning can help them, and motivate them to
participate. Group leaders model the skill of Dealing with Group
Pressure; students role-play the skill, receive feedback from other
group members, then choose their real-life homework assignments.

*The Skillstreaming Video: How to Teach Students Prosocial
Skills,* by Dr. Arnold P. Goldstein and Dr. Ellen McGinnis,
1988 (26 minutes).

Designed for teachers and other staff, this videotape shows
Drs. Goldstein and McGinnis in actual training sessions with educators and small groups of adolescents and elementary-age children.
Clearly demonstrates the Skillstreaming teaching model and the
program's four main components—modeling, role-playing, performance feedback, and transfer training.

Skillstreaming Materials for Other Instructional Levels

Young Children

Program Text

Skillstreaming in Early Childhood: Teaching Prosocial Skills to the Preschool and Kindergarten Child, by Dr. Ellen McGinnis and Dr. Arnold P. Goldstein, 1990 (papercover, 200 pages, ISBN 0–87822–320–7).

Program Forms

Skillstreaming in Early Childhood: Teaching Prosocial Skills to the Preschool and Kindergarten Child—Program Forms, by Dr. Ellen McGinnis and Dr. Arnold P. Goldstein, 1990 (papercover, 8 ½ × 11–inch format, 80 pages, ISBN 0–87822–321–5).

Adolescents

Program Text

Skillstreaming the Adolescent: New Strategies and Perspectives for Teaching Prosocial Skills (rev. ed.), by Dr. Arnold P. Goldstein and Dr. Ellen McGinnis, 1997 (papercover, 352 pages, ISBN 0–87822–369–X).

Program Forms

Skillstreaming the Adolescent: New Strategies and Perspectives for Teaching Prosocial Skills—Program Forms, by Dr. Arnold P. Goldstein and Dr. Ellen McGinnis, 1997 (papercover, 8 ½ × 11–inch format, 48 pages, ISBN 0–87822–371–1).

Student Manual

Skillstreaming the Adolescent—Student Manual, by Dr. Arnold P. Goldstein and Dr. Ellen McGinnis, 1997 (papercover, 8 ½ × 11–inch format, 64 pages, ISBN 0–87822–370–3).

Student Video

People Skills: Doing 'em Right! (Adolescent Level), by Dr. Arnold P. Goldstein and Dr. Ellen McGinnis, 1997 (17 minutes).

Skill Cards

Skillstreaming the Adolescent—Skill Cards, by Dr. Arnold P. Goldstein and Dr. Ellen McGinnis, 1997.

Professional Training

The Skillstreaming Video: How to Teach Students Prosocial Skills, by Dr. Arnold P. Goldstein and Dr. Ellen McGinnis, 1988 (26 minutes).

REFERENCES

Alberto, P.A., & Troutman, A.C. (1982). *Applied behavior analysis for teachers: Influencing student performance.* Columbus, OH: Charles E. Merrill.

Argyle, M. (1981). The experimental study of the basic features of situations. In D. Magnusson (Ed.), *Toward a psychology of situations: An interactional perspective.* Hillsdale, NJ: Erlbaum.

Ascher, C. (1994). *Gaining control of violence in the schools: A view from the field* (ERIC Digest No. 100). New York: ERIC Clearinghouse on Urban Education.

Ayllon, T., & Azrin, N.H. (1968). *The token economy: A motivational system for therapy rehabilitation.* New York: Appleton-Century-Crofts.

Azrin, N.H., & Holz, W.C. (1966). Punishment. In W.K. Honig (Ed.), *Operant behavior: Areas of research and application.* New York: Appleton-Century-Crofts.

Backman, C. (1979). Epilogue: A new paradigm. In G. Ginsburg (Ed.), *Emerging strategies in social psychological research.* Chichester, England: Wiley.

Bandura, A. (1973). *Aggression: A social learning analysis.* Englewood Cliffs, NJ: Prentice Hall.

Bandura, A. (1977). *Social learning theory.* Englewood Cliffs, NJ: Prentice Hall.

Benson, P.L., & Roehlkepartain, E. (1992). Youth violence in middle America. *Source Newsletter, September,* pp. 1–3. (Available from Search Institute, 700 S. Third St., Suite 210, Minneapolis, MN 55415)

Bornstein, P.H., & Quevillon, R.P. (1976). The effects of a self-instructional package on overactive preschool boys. *Journal of Applied Behavior Analysis, 9,* 179–188.

Bourland, E. (1995). *RRFC Links 2*(3). (Available from Federal Resource Center for Special Education, Academy for Educational Development, 1875 Connecticut Ave., NW, Washington, DC 20009–1202)

Brown, P., & Fraser, C. (1979). Speech as a marker of situations. In K. Scherer & H. Giles (Eds.), *Social markers in speech.* Cambridge, England: Cambridge University Press.

Camp, B.W., & Bash, M.A.S. (1981). *Think aloud: Increasing social and cognitive skills—A problem-solving program for children* (Primary Level). Champaign, IL: Research Press.

Camp, B.W., & Bash, M.A.S. (1985). *Think aloud: Increasing social and cognitive skills—A problem-solving program for children* (Grades 1–2). Champaign, IL: Research Press.

Carr, E.G. (1981). Contingency management. In A.P. Goldstein, E.G. Carr, W. Davidson, & P. Wehr (Eds.), *In response to aggression.* New York: Pergamon.

Cartledge, G. (1996). *Cultural diversity and social skills instruction: Understanding ethnic and gender differences.* Champaign, IL: Research Press.

Cartledge, G., & Feng, H. (1996). The relationship of culture and social behavior. In G. Cartledge (Ed.), *Cultural diversity and social skills instruction: Understanding ethnic and gender differences.* Champaign, IL: Research Press.

Cartledge, G., & Johnson, C.T. (1997). School violence and cultural sensitivity. In A.P. Goldstein & J.C. Conoley (Eds.), *The school violence intervention handbook.* New York: Guilford.

Cartledge, G., & Milburn, J.F. (1980). *Teaching social skills to children.* New York: Pergamon.

Cartledge, G., & Milburn, J.F. (1996). A model for teaching social skills. In In G. Cartledge (Ed.), *Cultural diversity and social skills instruction: Understanding ethnic and gender differences.* Champaign, IL: Research Press.

Cautela, J.R., & Groden, J. (1978). *Relaxation: A comprehensive model for adults, children, and children with special needs.* Champaign, IL: Research Press.

Chapman, W.E. (1977). *Roots of character education.* Schenectedy, NY: Character Research Press.

Coben, J.H., Weiss, H.B., Mulvey, E.P., & Dearwater, S.R. (1994). A primer on school violence prevention. *Journal of School Health, 64*(8), 309–313.

Cox, R.D., & Gunn, W.B. (1980). Interpersonal skills in the schools: Assessment and curriculum development. In D.P. Rathjen & J.P. Foreyt (Eds.), *Social competence: Interventions for children and adults.* New York: Pergamon.

Csikszentmihalyi, M., & Larsen, R. (1978). *Intrinsic rewards in school crime.* Hackensack, NJ: National Council on Crime and Delinquency.

Dewey, J. (1938). *Experience and education.* New York: Collier.

Dil, N. (1972). *Sensitivity of emotionally disturbed and emotionally non-disturbed elementary school children to emotional meanings of facial expressions.* Unpublished doctoral dissertation, Indiana University.

Dreikurs, R., & Cassel, P. (1972). *Discipline without tears.* New York: Hawthorn.

Dreikurs, R., Grunwald, B., & Pepper, F. (1971). *Maintaining sanity in the classroom.* New York: Harper and Row.

Dryfoos, J.G. (1994). *Full-service schools.* San Francisco: Jossey-Bass.

Ellis, H. (1965). *The transfer of learning.* New York: Macmillan.

Emery, J.E. (1975). *Social perception processes in normal and learning disabled children.* Unpublished doctoral dissertation, New York University.

Epps, S., Thompson, B.J., & Lane, M.P. (1985). *Procedures for incorporating generalization programming into interventions for behaviorally disordered students.* Unpublished manuscript, Iowa State University, Ames.

Feindler, E.L. (1979). *Cognitive and behavioral approaches to anger control training in explosive adolescents.* Unpublished doctoral dissertation, West Virginia University, Morgantown.

Feindler, E.L., & Ecton, R.B. (1986). *Adolescent anger control: Cognitive-behavioral techniques.* New York: Pergamon.

Ferster, C.B., & Skinner, B.F. (1957). *Schedules of reinforcement.* New York: Plenum.

Feshbach, N.D. (1982). *Empathy training and the regulation of aggression in elementary school children.* In R.M. Kaplan, V.J. Konecni, & R. Novaco (Eds.), *Aggression in children and youth.* Alphen den Rijn, The Netherlands: Sijthoff/Noordhoff.

Feshbach, N.D., & Feshbach, S. (1969). The relationship between empathy and aggression in two age groups. *Developmental Psychology, 1,* 102–107.

Firestone, P. (1976). The effects and side effects of time out on an aggressive nursery school child. *Journal of Behavior Therapy and Experimental Psychiatry, 6,* 79–81.

Galassi, J.P., & Galassi, M.D. (1984). Promoting transfer and maintenance of counseling outcomes. In S.D. Brown & R.W. Lent (Eds.), *Handbook of counseling psychology.* New York: Wiley.

Gemelli, R.J. (1996). Understanding and helping children who do not talk in school. In N.J. Long & W.C. Morse (Eds.), *Conflict in the classroom: The education of at-risk and troubled students.* Austin, TX: PRO-ED.

Gibbs, J.C., Potter, G.B., & Goldstein, A.P. (1995). *The EQUIP program: Teaching youth to think and act responsibly through a peer-helping approach .* Champaign, IL: Research Press.

Glasser, W. (1995, September). *Quality schools.* Paper presented at the Marshalltown Community Schools, Marshalltown, Iowa.

Golarz, R.J., & Golarz, Marion J. (1995). *The power of participation: Improving schools in a democratic society.* Champaign, IL: Research Press.

Goldstein, A.P., Apter, S.J., & Harootunian, B. (1984). *School violence.* Englewood Cliffs, NJ: Prentice Hall.

Goldstein, A.P., & Glick, B. (1987). *Aggression Replacement Training: A comprehensive intervention for aggressive youth.* Champaign, IL: Research Press.

Goldstein, A.P., Glick, B., Carthan, W., & Blancero, D. (1994). *The prosocial gang.* Thousand Oaks, CA: Sage.

Goldstein, A.P., Glick, B., Irwin, M.J., Pask-McCartney, C., & Rubama, I. (1989). *Reducing delinquency: Intervention in the community.* New York: Pergamon.

Goldstein, A.P., Heller, K., & Sechrest, L.B. (1966). *Psychotherapy and the psychology of behavior change.* New York: Wiley.

Goldstein, A.P., & Kanfer, F.H. (1979). *Maximizing treatment gains.* New York: Academic.

Goldstein, A.P., & McGinnis, E. (1988). *The Skillstreaming video: How to teach students prosocial skills.* Champaign, IL: Research Press.

Goldstein, A.P., & Michaels, G.Y. (1985). *Empathy: Development, training and consequences.* Hillsdale, NJ: Erlbaum.

Goldstein, A.P., Palumbo, J., Striepling, S., & Voutsinas, A.M. (1995). *Break it up: A teacher's guide to managing student aggression.* Champaign, IL: Research Press.

Grayson, M.C., Kiraly, J., Jr., & McKinnon, A.J. (1996). Using time-out procedures with disruptive students. In N.J. Long & W.C. Morse (Eds.), *Conflict in the classroom: The education of at-risk and troubled students.* Austin, TX: PRO-ED.

Greenwood, C.R., Hops, H., Delquadri, J., & Guild, J. (1974). Group contingencies for group consequences in classroom management: A further analysis. *Journal of Applied Behavior Analysis, 7,* 413–425.

Guzzetta, R.A. (1974). *Acquisition and transfer of empathy by the parents of early adolescents through Structured Learning training.* Unpublished doctoral dissertation, Syracuse University.

Hartwig, E.P., & Ruesch, G.M. (1994). *Discipline in the school.* Horsham, PA: LRP Publications.

Homme, L., Csanyi, A.P., Gonzales, M.A., & Rechs, J.R. (1970). *How to use contingency contracting in the classroom.* Champaign, IL: Research Press.

Johns, B.H., Carr, V.G., & Hoots, C.W. (1995). *Reduction of school violence: Alternatives to suspension.* Horsham, PA: LRP Publications.

Kaplan, J.S., & Carter, J. (1995). *Beyond behavior modification: A cognitive behavioral approach to behavior management in the school* (3rd ed.). Austin, TX: PRO-ED.

Karoly, P. (1980). Operant methods. In F.H. Kanfer & A.P. Goldstein (Eds.), *Helping people change.* New York: Pergamon.

Karoly, P., & Steffen, J.J. (Eds.). (1980). *Improving the long term effects of psychotherapy.* New York: Gardner.

Kazdin, A.E. (1975). *Behavior modification in applied settings.* Homewood, IL: Dorsey.

Keeley, S.M., Shemberg, K.M., & Carbonell, J. (1976). Operant clinical intervention: Behavior management or beyond? Where are the data? *Behavior Therapy, 7,* 292–305.

Kendall, P.C., & Braswell, L. (1985). *Cognitive behavioral therapy for children.* New York: Guilford.

Knight, B.J., & West, D.J. (1975). Temporary and continuing delinquency. *British Journal of Criminology, 15,* 43–50.

Kohlberg, L. (Ed.). (1973). *Collected papers on moral development and moral education.* Cambridge, MA: Harvard University, Center for Moral Education.

Kohn, A. (1986). *No contest.* Boston: Houghton Mifflin.

Kounin, J. (1970). *Discipline and group management in classrooms.* New York: Holt, Rinehart and Winston.

Ladd, G.W., & Mize, J. (1983). A cognitive-social learning model of social skill training. *Psychological Review, 90,* 127–157.

Lantieri, L. (1995). Waging peace in our schools: Beginning with the children. *Phi Delta Kappan, 76*(5), 386–388.

Linquanti, R., & Berliner, B. (1994). *Rebuilding schools as safe havens: A topology for selecting and integrating violence prevention strategies.* Portland, OR: Western Regional Center for Drug-Free Schools and Communities.

Little, V.L., & Kendall, P.C. (1979). Cognitive-behavioral interventions with delinquents: Problem solving, role-taking, and self-control. In P.C. Kendall & S.D. Hollon (Eds.), *Cognitive-behavioral interventions.* Orlando, FL: Academic.

Loeber, R., & Dishion, T. (1983). Early predictors of male delinquency: A review. *Psychological Bulletin, 94,* 68–99.

Luria, A.R. (1961). *The role of speech in the regulation of normal and abnormal behavior.* New York: Liveright.

McGinnis, E., & Goldstein, A.P. (1984). *Skillstreaming the elementary school child: A guide for teaching prosocial skills.* Champaign, IL: Research Press.

Meichenbaum, D.H. (1977). *Cognitive-behavior modification: An integrative approach.* New York: Plenum.

Miller, J.P. (1976). *Humanizing the classroom.* New York: Praeger.

Modro, M. (1995). *Safekeeping: Adult responsibility, children's right.* Providence, RI: Behavioral Health Resource Press.

Morris, R.J. (1976). *Behavior modification with children.* Cambridge, MA: Winthrop.

Morrison, R.L., & Bellack, A.S. (1981). The role of social perception in social skills. *Behavior Therapy, 12,* 69–70.

Natale, J.A. (1994). Roots of violence. *The American School Board Journal, March,* 33–40.

National Association for the Education of Young Children. (1993). NAEYC position statement on violence in the lives of children. *Young Children, 48*(6), 80–84.

National Coalition on Television Violence. (1990). *NCTV News* (Vol. 2). Champaign, IL: Author.

National School Boards Association. (1994). *Violence in the schools: How America's school boards are safeguarding your children.* Alexandria, VA: Author.

Neilans, T.H., & Israel, A.C. (1981). Towards maintenance and generalization of behavior change: Teaching children self-regulation and self-instructional skills. *Cognitive Therapy and Research, 5,* 189–196.

Nelsen, J., Lott, L., & Glenn, H.S. (1993). *Positive discipline in the classroom: How to effectively use class meetings and other positive discipline strategies.* Rocklin, CA: Prima.

Osgood, C.E. (1953). *Method and theory in experimental psychology.* New York: Oxford University Press.

Patterson, G.R., Reid, J.B., Jones, R.R., & Conger, R.E. (1975). *A social learning approach to family intervention* (Vol. 1). Eugene, OR: Castalia.

Redl, F., & Wineman, D. (1957). *The aggressive child.* New York: Free Press.

Remboldt, C. (1994). *Violence in schools: The enabling factor.* Minneapolis: Johnson Institute.

Robins, L.N., West, P.A., & Herjanic, B.L. (1975). Arrests and delinquency in two generations: A study of black urban families and their children. *Journal of Child Psychology and Psychiatry, 16,* 125–140.

Rothenbert, B.B. (1970). Children's social sensitivity and the relationship to interpersonal competence, interpersonal comfort, and intellectual level. *Developmental Psychology, 2,* 335–350.

Sarason, I.G., Glaser, E.M., & Fargo, G.A. (1972). *Reinforcing productive classroom behavior.* New York: Behavioral Publications.

Sautter, R.C. (1995). Standing up to violence. *Phi Delta Kappan, 76*(5), K-1–K-12.

Simon, S.G., Howe, L.W., & Kirschenbaum, H. *Values clarification.* New York: Hart.

Skinner, B.F. (1938). *The behavior of organisms: An experimental analysis.* New York: Appleton-Century-Crofts.

Skinner, B.F (1953). *Science and human behavior.* New York: Free Press.

Slavin, R.E. (1980). *Using student team learning* (rev. ed.). Baltimore: Johns Hopkins University, Center for Social Organization of Schools.

Sloane, H.N. (1976). *Classroom management: Remediation and prevention.* New York: Wiley.

Stokes, T.F., & Baer, D.M. (1977). An implicit technology of generalization. *Journal of Applied Behavior Analysis, 10,* 349–367.

Sulzer-Azaroff, B., & Mayer, G.R. (1991). *Behavior analysis for lasting change.* San Francisco: Holt, Rinehart and Winston.

Tharp, R.G., & Wetzel, R.J. (1969). *Behavior modification in the natural environment.* New York: Academic.

Thorndike, E.L., & Woodworth, R.S. (1901). The influence of improvement in one mental function upon the efficiency of other functions. *Psychological Review, 8,* 247–261.

U.S. Department of Justice. (1993, May 19). *Bureau of Justice news release.* Washington, DC: Author.

Violence in the schools: A national, state, and local crisis. (January, 1994). Albany, NY: New York State Education Department, Office for Planning, Research, and Support Services.

Walker, D. (1995). *School violence prevention* (ERIC Digest No. 94). Eugene, OR: ERIC Clearinghouse on Educational Management.

Walker, H.M. (1979). *The acting-out child: Coping with classroom disruption.* Boston: Allyn & Bacon.

Werner, E.E., & Smith, R.S. (1982). *Vulnerable but invincible.* New York: McGraw-Hill.

White, G., Nielson, G., & Johnson, S. (1972). Time out duration and the suppression of deviant behavior in children. *Journal of Applied Behavior Analysis, 5*(2), 111–120.

Wilson, K.G., & Daviss, B. (1994). *Redesigning education.* New York: Henry Holt.

Name Index

SUBJECT INDEX

ABOUT THE AUTHORS

Ellen McGinnis earned her Ph.D. from the University of Iowa in 1986. She holds degrees in elementary education, special education, and school administration. She has taught elementary and secondary students in the public schools in Minnesota, Iowa, and Arizona. In addition, she has served as a special education consultant in both public and hospital schools and as assistant professor of special education at the University of Wisconsin–Eau Claire. For the past 5 years, Dr. McGinnis has served with the Des Moines Public Schools as the principal of the education program at Orchard Place, a residential and day treatment facility for children and adolescents with emotional/behavioral disorders. The author of numerous articles on identifying and teaching youth with emotional/behavioral disorders, Dr. McGinnis is coauthor with Dr. Arnold P. Goldstein of *Skillstreaming in Early Childhood* and the newly revised edition of *Skillstreaming the Adolescent.* She and her husband, Carl Smith, are the parents of Sara, age 14, and Alex, age 10.

Arnold P. Goldstein joined the clinical psychology section of Syracuse University's Psychology Department in 1963 and both taught there and directed its Psychotherapy Center until 1980. In 1981, he founded the Center for Research on Aggression, which he currently directs. He joined Syracuse University's Division of Special Education in 1985 and in 1990 helped organize and codirect the New York State Task Force on Juvenile Gangs. Dr. Goldstein has a career-long interest, as both researcher and practitioner, in difficult-to-reach clients. Since 1980, his main research and psychoeducational focus has been youth violence. He is the developer of psychoeducational programs and curricula designed to teach prosocial behaviors to chronically antisocial persons. Dr. Goldstein's many books include, among others, *Aggression Replacement Training: A Comprehensive Intervention for Aggressive Youth, The Prepare Curriculum: Teaching Prosocial Competencies, Delinquents on Delinquency, The Gang Intervention Handbook,* and *Break It Up: A Teacher's Guide to Managing Student Aggression.*

DATE DUE

JAN 3 0 2006			
AUG 0 7 2006			
jan 3, 2013			
GAYLORD			PRINTED IN U.S.A.